THE CRIMSON TIDE

A Story Of
Alabama Football

THE CRIMSON TIDE

A Story Of
Alabama Football

by Clyde Bolton

THE STRODE PUBLISHERS
Huntsville, Alabama 35802

"I'm just too full of Alabama."

—Tommy Lewis

To
My Wife
Sandra Jean Bolton

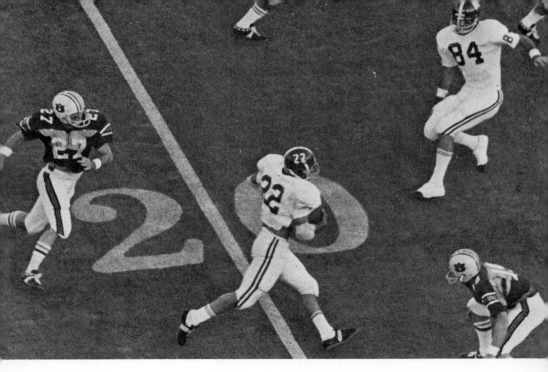

Contents

Foreword

President David Mathews and Coach Paul Bryant have contributed at length to the following pages. It is a privilege to add my thoughts to this history of Crimson Tide football.

Few Crimson Tide fans can open this book without finding themselves completely absorbed with the stories and history which have woven the web of the University of Alabama tradition. Everyone is aware of our great football tradition at the Capstone. Yet not until we find it in a book of this stature are we so completely overwhelmed by all that is Tide football. Yes, we have heard some of the names and seen some of the pictures. But have we been aware of so many names and such great achievements for such a long football tradition?

As the following pages show, the football Tide has changed much over the years as befits a history of more than three-quarters of a century. Yet throughout this football history there is a common flow of greatness, perseverance, dedication, and steadfastness that is the tradition of what can only be called a truly great Crimson Tide.

I have known the author, Clyde Bolton, as one of the most dedicated scribe followers of the Crimson Tide in the past decade. Particularly, I have been impressed by the high esteem in which he is held by fellow writers. No one can look at the following pages without being caught up with the author's delight in preserving for us the many stories which might otherwise never be generally known. Alabama football has a proud standard bearer with this book. Every single reader will enjoy the thrilling moments of the great and relentless tradition of the Crimson Tide.

Jefferson J. Coleman
Director of Alumni Affairs
The University of Alabama

Folklore

Summer's sun turned the pavement in front of the University of Alabama Athletic Department into a bed of coals that a Fiji Island firewalker (much less a barefoot co-ed) would not dare. The adjacent practice field was baking, and every player who happened by said a little prayer of thanks that he would not have to be out there for a couple more months.

The heat was most unfootballish, but inside, in the air-conditioned darkness, projectors were whirring. Projectors run the year 'round in football coaches' offices.

A quarterback takes the snap and steps to the left. That move, requiring a fraction of a second, lights up the screen a dozen times before the coach is satisfied that he has spotted whatever it was he was trying to spot.

A man could go blind. Football coaches stepping into the light squint like miners leaving the earth. And when they take a break from thinking about next season, likely as not they will talk about seasons past. On this day, during a break, someone asked Bill Oliver, the secondary coach, to tell his favorite Pat Trammell story again.

"Well, I came to Alabama as a quarterback," Oliver began. "We freshmen were going to have our first meeting with Coach Bryant.

"We were waiting for him to come in, and Pat stood up and asked how many other quarterbacks were there. He took out a knife and stuck it in the table and said, 'You'd better sleep light tonight. I might cut your throats.'

11

"I was a li'l ole country boy and it scared the heck out of me. Of course I found out later he was kidding—but he was determined to have that quarterback job."

Football is nourished by its stories, like a baby by rich milk. Its folklore is as important to its continuity as home-and-home scheduling is. Coach, player and fan feel what nearly amounts to an obligation to tell football tales.

Jay Morris, the Midfield police chief and one of the all-time Alabama fans, still shakes his head and marvels about the day in the 1940s when he was standing on the sidelines and Charley Compton, a tackle, left the game with two front teeth broken off. "He got the wire pliers and pulled them himself. Then he rinsed his mouth out with water and ice and went to Coach Thomas and said, 'Coachman, I'm ready to go back in.'"

Fred Sington winces when he tells about Hank Crisp, who lost his hand in a childhood accident, joining in scrimmages with his players, his swinging nub a weapon for all to avoid. An official really could not call it slugging, could he?

And a man has to feel warm when he hears the one about broken-legged Nick Terlizzi sitting on the bench late in the Rose Bowl game of January 1, 1946. "Nick, would you like to say you have played in the Rose Bowl?" Coach Frank Thomas asked.

"Yes sir, Coach!" Terlizzi brightened.

"Well, go out there, but don't get in any mixups and get hurt," Thomas instructed. "Stay out of the way of all plays."

Alabama men are sober when they recount homecoming, 1953, when Thomas, dying, leaned on the arm of his son Frank, Jr., and walked onto the field at Denny Stadium and received a replica of his Football Hall of Fame Award and told the crowd, "Friends, this is the happiest day of my life."

Sportswriters laugh about the time Paul Bryant was playing Captain Bligh in a fishing boat loaded with newsmen. "Somebody's doing a sorry job of steering this boat," Bryant said.

"What's that, Paul?" came a voice from the stern. It was Dr. Frank Rose, president of the University of Alabama, who could steer a college better than he could steer a boat. Bryant refrained from further comment on the good doctor's driving.

Nobody believes it really happened, but they do not let the story die about the afternoon tough Wallace Wade asked one of

12

*his injured players what was wrong. "I think my leg is broken,"
the boy said. "Well, you've got another one, haven't you?"
Wade is supposed to have replied.*

*No school has a richer football history than the University of
Alabama has. The Rose Bowl... national championships...
Wade... Thomas... Bryant... Gilmer... Howell...
Namath. All blending into a football monolith that charms its
supporters and confounds its opponents.*

Here, then, is the story of Crimson Tide football.

A Game Is Born

On Saturday, November 6, 1869, sometime after 3 p.m., an old Rutgers professor brought his bicycle to a stop beside a field in New Brunswick, New Jersey. Fifty men, 25 to a side, were crashing into each other and chasing a round rubber ball over the lot.

His frown grew more pronounced and after a few minutes he rode away shouting, "You men will come to no Christian end!"

The target of his anger was the United States' first intercollegiate football game. Captain William S. Gummere of Princeton had challenged Captain William Legett of Rutgers. The challenge had been accepted and the game was played on the Rutgers grounds. Rutgers won by six goals to four, immediately establishing what would become known as the home field advantage.

The old professor had disparaged a game that would mushroom into a national mania. The 100 spectators at Rutgers would become 100,000 in huge stadia across the land. Coaches would become more famous than governors and quarterbacks as adored as saints. Otherwise-sane folks would fight you about football.

College lads had played football as early as the 19th century, but always informally, as grammar school kids might play a game of choose-up at recess today. No one had ever thought of matching one school against another.

The Harvard faculty banned football on that campus in 1860, and town authorities at New Haven, Connecticut, told Yale

14

students they could not play on the public green in 1858.

But football continued to grow in popularity, and in 1867 the Princeton rules were drawn up, specifying 25 players to a side. The first intercollegiate game between Princeton and Rutgers was only a step away.

That first match, of course, did not involve what we call football today. The game was closer to soccer. A goal was scored when the round rubber ball was kicked under the cross-bar and between the uprights of a goal post defended by the opponents. The ball could be batted with the hands or kicked but not carried.

The Rutgers University newspaper, the *Targum*, saw the game thusly:

"To sum up. Princeton had the most muscle, but didn't kick very well and wanted organization. They evidently don't like to kick the ball on the ground. Our men, on the other hand, though comparatively weak, ran well and kicked well throughout. But their great point was their organization, for which great praise is due to the Captain, Legett, '72. The right men were always in the right place.

"After the match, the players had an amicable 'feed' together, and at 8 o'clock our guests went home, in high good spirits but thirsting to beat us next time, if they can."

They could. A week later at Princeton, New Jersey, Princeton whipped Rutgers 8-0.

Columbia fielded an intercollegiate team in 1870, losing to Rutgers. Yale became a participant in 1872, beating Columbia. Harvard's faculty lifted its ban in 1871, and the game reappeared on campus.

Harvard allowed carrying of the ball, though, and when Yale, Princeton, Columbia, and Rutgers met in 1873 in New York to adopt a uniform code of rules, Harvard did not attend.

That same year Yale played an English team that used 11 players. Yale quickly became an advocate of 11-man teams.

Harvard, insisting on running the ball, could not get games with United States teams, so in 1874 it scheduled two matches with McGill University in Montreal, Canada. The first would be played under Harvard's rules, the second under rugby rules. Canadian rugby rules allowed touchdowns (running with the ball across the goal line) as well as goals to count in the score.

Harvard was intrigued by the rugby rules and adopted them as its standards. Yale agreed in 1875 to a match with Harvard that was largely rugby. Harvard won the game, but Yale was won over to rugby rules.

Two Princeton players saw the Yale-Harvard game and invited Harvard, Yale, and Columbia to a convention. The Intercollegiate Football Association came out of that 1876 get-together. The round ball was replaced by the egg-shaped rugby ball and a slightly modified version of rugby chosen.

Yale was the first champion, though it considered itself a playing member only, not a full member, because it wanted 11-man sides rather than the 15 agreed upon.

In 1880 the sides were chopped to 11 men and the size of the field reduced from 140 by 70 yards to 110 by 53½ yards.

The first great rule change that splintered American football away from rugby came in 1880. The principle of continuous possession of the ball was established.

Before, the ball had merely been dropped between the opposing lines to start a play. A free-for-all ensued. Now, under rules proposed by Yale representative Walter Camp, the team holding the ball could put it in play by kicking it forward or kicking it backward to the quarterback. A team now could plan a play without having to battle for the ball in the line.

A flaw in the rule surfaced immediately. Yale and Princeton, each fearing the other, turned the 1880 and 1881 games into scoreless ties. The team receiving the kickoff simply retained the ball with no particular effort to advance it.

In 1882 Camp initiated a system of downs. It was to become the key to the modern game. A team must now either gain five yards or lose 10 yards in three downs or give up the ball. The striped football field made its appearance. Someone suggested it resembled a gridiron. That became its nickname.

Linemen had spread across the field, clasping hands, but in 1888 the rules insisted they keep their hands at their sides. Tackling, previously confined above the waist, was approved above the knee. So the linemen closed ranks and so did the backs, and the T formation was born. The open rugby game had ended. Football no longer was graceful. The attack now depended on power.

By then, football had spread to Michigan and Notre Dame, to

Trinity (later Duke) and North Carolina, to Virginia Military and Washington and Lee.

The game had such a grasp on the public fancy by 1889 that Caspar Whitney, assisted by Walter Camp, chose the first all-American team. It was published in his magazine, *The Week's Sport.*

The burgeoning game intrigued W. G. Little, a Livingston, Alabama, boy who was in prep school in Massachusetts. He had been sent to Phillips-Exeter Academy in Andover to prepare for Yale, but fate intervened.

A death in the family was to make Little the father of University of Alabama football, instead.

Pigskin, Probate, Pins, Plows

"You come on down to Selma and have dinner with us," Mrs. Royal Randolph Smith tells a telephoner from Birmingham. "We'll feed you some good country cooking."

The daughter of W. G. Little, the man who instigated football at the University of Alabama, is proud of her late father. She has his scrapbooks. She recalls that the University named a gymnasium for him, but she wishes more folks would refer to it by his name.

She remembers the later years in Livingston, after football had become big at the school, when her father would meet the trains carrying the Tide to the Rose Bowl games and present the boys with cakes his wife had baked.

"He was supposed to have gone to Yale," Mrs. Smith explains. "His oldest brother James Little had graduated from the University of Alabama.

"They had sent daddy to Phillips. But in the meantime Jimmy died. Daddy came home to be with his mother."

Little enrolled at the nearby University of Alabama. He brought his canvas football suit, his cleated shoes, and his pigskin ball with him. Other boys crowded around him to admire his trophies. Enthusiasm met his suggestion that they form a University of Alabama team.

Baseball already was a popular sport on campus. In 1891 an athletic field day, forerunner of today's A-Day, had been inaugurated. Hundreds watched fencing, wrestling, horizontal-bar, and other activities. It was such a success that in 1892 the faculty declared it an annual event, and by 1894 students from other colleges would be invited to take part. A Tulane boy, in fact, would win the medal as best athlete.

Little was named first football captain at Alabama. "Since he got up the team, they had to elect him captain," Mrs. Smith says with a chuckle.

Actually, he was a natural captain. He weighed 220 pounds and was the heaviest man on the squad. The lightest weighed 135. The team averaged only 162.

The University Athletic Association was born. Burr Ferguson was its first president and William M. Walker its first vice-president.

Every team needs a coach. A call for subscriptions was sounded, and money came in to hire Eugene Beaumont, who had attended the University of Pennsylvania, a football hotbed.

Members of Alabama's first team were Little, left guard; R. E. L. Cope, right guard; H. M. Pratt, center; F. M. Savage, right tackle; Eli Abbott, left tackle; D. A. Grayson, right end; Burr Ferguson, left end; W. M. Walker, quarterback; G. H. Kyser, right halfback; D. H. Smith, left halfback; W. B. Bankhead, fullback; and subs A. G. McCants, D. B. Johnson, T. Sydney Frazer, R. E. Boyle, C. C. Nesmith, M. P. Walker, Bibb Graves, and S. W. Henderson.

Remarkably, the roster included a future speaker of the House in the Congress of the United States, Bankhead, and a future two-term governor of Alabama, Graves.

As for Little, he would serve terms as tax assessor, tax collector, and probate judge in Livingston. He had farming interests and a country store where he sold, according to Mrs. Smith, "everything from pins to plows."

A turn of fate had resulted in Little coming to the University in the first place. Another turn would strike him later in life. "He signed the papers to buy a Ford business the night before the crash," Mrs. Smith remembers. "But later he was elected probate judge, so I guess that was a pretty good comeback."

Little attended Alabama's games in Birmingham and Tusca-loosa through the years. He often invited Alabama players to Livingston to hunt with him. Mrs. Smith remembers them searching for rabbits in the snow.

"He died when he was only 62," his daughter says. "But he

lived longer than any Little ever lived.

"Today, when I look at football on television, I think how much he would have loved that."

Alabama's First Football Squad—1892

Front row: Burr Ferguson, G. H. Kyser. Second row: D. A. Grayson, A. G. McCants, William M. Walker, T. Sydney Frazer. Third row: F. M. Savage, William B. Bankhead, Captain W. G. Little, S. W. Henderson. Back row: Eli Abbott, R. E. Boyle, F. T. Bush (manager), Henry M. Pratt, E. B. Beaumont (coach), R. E. L. Cope, Dan H. Smith.

20

Mom Said I Could Go
To Birmingham

A football team, to be a football team, must have games. And on November 11, 1892, the *Daily News* of Birmingham headlined:

GAME OF FOOTBALL

——————————————

THIS AFTERNOON AT 3
O'CLOCK SHARP

——————————

The University of Alabama
Team will play Prof.
Taylor's at the Base
Ball Park

——————

IT WILL BE A GREAT GAME

The story said Alabama's "famous" team would meet a "picked eleven from Professor Taylor's and the High School."

No one feared women libbers, for the reporter wrote, "There will be a large crowd of ladies, society belles and school girls to wear the colors of their favorites and to applaud the good work of their eleven. Of course they won't understand anything about the game, but that doesn't make any difference, for they will cheer and enjoy it just as much as if they were critical onlookers."

The ladies were not by themselves. Early football programs took care to explain the game in simple terms, for it was strange

21

to many who watched.

If women were different in 1892, so were students. Each Alabama player had to file with the president of the University written permission from parents or guardian to make the trip to Birmingham for Bama's first game ever.

The newspaper's advance story described football as "the great amateur game of America, which is played by gentlemen, and all lovers of a truly manly outdoor sport should lend their presence this afternoon, and witness a struggle where grit, endurance and skill will win the game without a suspicion of any jockeying."

Obviously, there was no jockeying in this game. Despite the presence of a ringer (Professor Taylor himself played center for the Birmingham team), it was a rout. Alabama won 56-0.

Whether the reporter leaned toward the home team or whether he was as puzzled as the paper said the ladies would be is lost in antiquity—but the newspaper's account of the game did not report the score.

"The school team was made up of a handsome crowd of boys," the *Daily News* story said, "but as soon as they came out on the grounds every one knew they were too light to cope with their heavy antagonists, and that no matter how quick their play, they must succumb to the cadets' strength."

Amid the advertisements for Bradfield's Female Regulator (cures all diseases and irregularities peculiar to women), the new Kentucky Livery Stable, and breakfast bacon at 12 cents a pound at Cooke's Cash Grocery, was the notice that on that afternoon, the day after the debacle against the high school boys, Alabama would face the Birmingham Athletic Club at Lakeview Park.

After all, you could not expect a team to make a trip to Birmingham for just one football game, could you?

Captain Little won the toss and chose the ball. Professor Taylor, captain of the Athletics (him again), took the south goal.

Alabama's record was about to be 1-1. The University scored a touchdown to a field goal for the Athletic Club—and lost 5-4 because in those days a touchdown counted four points and a field goal five.

Little scored on a guard-around for Alabama and Walker

missed the point-after (which would have counted two points) in the first half. But the play of the game was a field goal by J. P. Ross "which will make him famous wherever the game of football is known."

All Ross did was kick a 65-yarder just before the game ended. The crowd hoisted him to its shoulders and paraded him around the grounds.

It was a day of innocence in sports. Guess who the referee was? None other than Coach Beaumont of Alabama.

A month later Alabama returned to Lakeview Park and shellacked the Birmingham Athletic Club 14-0. Grayson scored a touchdown on a 65-yard end run, and it was his turn for a shoulder ride.

The fourth and final game of Alabama's first season would not be played until more than two months later. It was the inaugural of a series in which neither Bear Bryant nor Shug Jordan would ever be asked to referee.

To See The
Big Boys Fight

A match between the new football teams of Alabama and Auburn was as natural as paying 45 cents for a gallon of molasses. A game involving the state's largest schools was arranged for the 1892 season.

Or was it the 1893 season? The first Alabama-Auburn game actually was played February 22, 1893. Alabama's records consider it the final game of the 1892 season which began on November 11 against Professor Taylor's outmanned team. Auburn's records, on the other hand, list it as the first game of the 1893 season.

Auburn's first football team was born nearly a year earlier than Alabama's. Dr. George Petrie, who would serve the school as professor of history and as dean of the graduate school for 55 years, introduced the game on the Plain. He served as Auburn's first coach.

Auburn played its first game February 20, 1892. Dr. Petrie borrowed the money to pay the team's way to Atlanta where his boys, wearing cloth caps, rewarded his investment with a 10-0 victory over Georgia. The press described the game as the greatest athletic contest ever played in the South. A crowd of 3,000 gathered in Piedmont Park to watch.

Neither Dr. Petrie nor his assistant coach, a Professor Atkinson, was paid for coaching the team. The student body bought two gold-headed walking sticks for them, but President William Brown refused to allow professors to accept gifts from students.

Football, after four games, was a losing proposition at

Auburn, and the team was seeking a method to balance the budget. A post-season game with Alabama, played in Birmingham with its concentration of fans, was the answer.

Auburn sent its manager to Tuscaloosa to talk with Bill Bankhead, manager of the Alabama team. The game was scheduled for Washington's birthday.

Birmingham welcomed the game then as it does today. "The College Lads and Their Friends Have the Freedom of the City," the *Daily News* headlined on the day of the game.

The newspaper went on to exult that "Never before was there such enthusiasm over an athletic contest in the State."

A special train from "Tuskaloosa" arrived at 10 a.m. on game day, and 320 supporters, including 150 students, poured out the doors, eager for the first Alabama-Auburn game. The schoolboys were "as handsome a lot of young fellows as ever trod the depot platform," the *Daily News* reporter wrote.

A train from Auburn brought 226 fans, including 100 students who also "presented a handsome appearance." The reporter was playing this story straight down the line.

In fact, he was a master at keeping everyone happy, even the lady fans. "It is hard to decide which of the colleges has the prettiest young women to wear their colors. Both Universities brought a charming lot of young ladies with them," he cooed.

Alabama's fans set up headquarters in the Caldwell Hotel. They draped the front of the building, the rotunda, the dining room, and the parlors in red and white. Auburn chose the Florence Hotel and strung it in blue and orange.

An Auburn-Alabama game had not even been played yet, but already the embers of rivalry were being fanned, embers that in later years would become searing flames. Private homes were draped in school colors, and some families affected a compromise by displaying red and white and blue and orange. Merchants even chose sides and decorated their stores. Those who sold souvenirs wisely draped the colors of both colleges on their storefronts.

The *Daily News'* man was awestruck by every aspect of the day. "Every private vehicle, stable turn out and public hack was filled with people on the way to Lakeview Park," he reported the day after the game.

"The dummies and electric cars were crowded with lovers of

25

the manly sport of football.

"Men and women who heretofore have jeered at such exhibitions of brawn and muscle were eager to see the contest.

"Little children just beginning to toddle were anxious to see the big boys fight."

An estimated 5,000 persons gathered at Lakeview Park. Only one ticket booth had been set up, and emergency ticket men had to be hustled into action.

The gents who did not have ladies on their arms rushed to the sidelines of the playing field for choice standing room. They swarmed a dozen deep around the roped-in gridiron. Five policemen were unable to keep them from edging onto the field for a better view.

The east side of the field was reserved for carriages. The vehicles, like the houses and stores, were decorated with school colors.

The grandstands were packed and the bleachers were filled with "as jolly a lot of men as ever sat on hard planks, and from their faces and their merry talk it was evident that they had come out to make a happy afternoon of it." Perhaps the pregame cocktail party had just been invented!

Alabama's players took the field wearing white uniforms with "U of A" in red on their sweaters. Their stockings were red. Auburn's men were dressed in white pants, blue stockings, and blue sweaters with an orange "A."

The female fans recoiled at the rugged pregame practice. "As the boys would pile up on one another the ladies would get alarmed, fearing that they would have their bones broken, but their gentlemen friends would kindly assure the timid sympathetic women that the athletic youths could be dropped from the top of the grandstand to the ground without sustaining any injury," the *Daily News'* man wrote.

Despite his patronizing the lady fans, the *Daily News* reporter's knowledge of the game is suspect. Honey dripped from his accounts of the amazing deeds of individuals on both squads—but he never got around to telling his readers who scored and how.

Auburn won the game 32-22. Captain Daniel and his team gathered around Miss Delma Wilson who had been chosen to present a cup. "Gallant and victorious captain," she intoned, "in the name of the city of Birmingham I present you this cup. Drink from it and remember the victory that you have won this day. May you and your team live to see many more victories."

The Alabama-Auburn series had been born. It would lapse after 1907, be reborn in 1948, and become the crown jewel of sports in the state. There was one ticket booth when Alabama and Auburn played in 1893. Now there are none.

Paid In Full—30 Years Later

Alabama football in the Gay Nineties was haphazard, to say the least.

Coaches came and went with the changing winds, not only in the Nineties but for years afterward. Nine men coached the first 14 years, 13 men the first 26 years. The game was relatively new over the nation, and finding knowledgeable coaches was difficult. On the other side of the coin, facilities were poor and so were material and compensation.

E. B. Beaumont, the first coach, lasted only one season. "We were unfortunate in securing a coach," stated the school yearbook, the *Corolla*. "After keeping him for a short time, we found that his knowledge of the game was very limited. We therefore 'got rid' of him."

Eli Abbott, who had played tackle on the first Alabama team, coached the 1893-94-95 teams, but during his first and last years the club did not win a game.

Otto Wagonhurst succeeded Abbott and stayed one season. When the season ended, he was due some $550 of his $750 salary. In those days the senior class sponsored the football team. This one could not pay Wagonhurst in full. An athletic show the next spring raised only $50 which was mailed to him.

Some 30 years later, after Alabama had become a big name in football and had played in the Rose Bowl, the Athletic Association decided to pay the old debt. Wagonhurst was located in a rubber company in Akron, Ohio, and was shocked to receive the remainder of his salary for coaching the 1896 team.

Eligibility rules were loose. Walter Shafer had been a star fullback at Auburn for four years, but in the fall of 1896 he enrolled at Alabama to study law—and went out for the football team, much to the delight of Alabama supporters. Shafer, though, said he would not play in any game against Auburn. Auburn was not on the schedule that year, anyway.

Admission to games was 50 cents, but gatekeepers charged another 50 cents to bring a carriage in. When an Alabama lieutenant governor was told he owed an additional 50 cents for his carriage he said, "Damned if I'll pay that to see a football game!" and he turned around and left.

The 1893 team played the Birmingham Athletic Club twice but added a college opponent, Sewanee, to its four-game schedule that also included Auburn.

Games with Mississippi and Tulane replaced those against the Athletic Club in 1894. The 1895 team met Georgia, Tulane, LSU, and Auburn. Obviously, progress was being made in scheduling.

The *Corolla* was a fierce supporter of the team. It attributed a 6-0 loss of Mississippi to the Mississippians having had more practice and sniffed, "This is not the place to bring grievances against an umpire, so we desist."

The match, incidentally, was the first football game ever played in Jackson, a city that would become a regular stop for future Tides.

A crowd of 1,000 watched, but gate receipts amounted to only $180. Admission was 50 cents, so the press charged that some spectators had slipped in.

The 1894 Auburn game was controversial. Auburn protested Alabama's using two former University of North Carolina players, and they were declared ineligible. Auburn also charged two other Alabama men were paid salaries. Alabama denied it and they were allowed to play. Alabama won 18-0. The two schools frequently questioned eligibility of each other's men.

The *Corolla* could not resist rubbing it in: "The ease with which we defeated Auburn was surprising to many people, but not to us who knew what herculean efforts our boys had put forth in order to get in condition to play the great Thanksgiving game."

C. M. Pearce was a tackle on the 1895 Alabama team and

probably in later years was afflicted with as severe a case of mixed emotions as any man who ever lived. Not only did Pearce play for both Alabama and Auburn, he had a son who played at Auburn in the 1920's and another who played on Alabama's January 1, 1927 Rose Bowl team.

The beginning of football at the University of Alabama followed the first Deep South game by only two seasons. Vanderbilt beat the University of Nashville 46-0 on Thanksgiving Day, 1890.

The most powerful team of the Nineties in the South was the 1899 Sewanee squad, the first great team in Dixie. Sewanee went 12-0 and scored 322 points to 10 for the opponents. The Purple Tigers won five games in six days on a 3,000-mile swing through Texas, Louisiana, and Tennessee.

The Southern Intercollegiate Athletic Association was organized December 22, 1894, at the Kimball House in Atlanta. Charter members were Alabama, Auburn, Sewanee, Georgia, Georgia Tech, North Carolina, and Vanderbilt. Joining the next year were Cumberland, LSU, Ole Miss, Mississippi A&M (later Mississippi State), Tennessee, Tulane, and Texas. Object of the conference was "the development, regulation, and purification of college athletics in the South."

The SIAA became unwieldy and too far-flung, and its descendants are the Southern, Southeastern, and Atlantic Coast conferences.

Four games was the standard Alabama schedule in the Nineties. The 1894 team and the 1899 team had the best records of the era, 3-1, unless you prefer the 1897 club's 1-0 mark.

It was an irregular game, this football of the Gay Nineties, but students and fans adored it. They would be shocked numb in Tuscaloosa, though, because University of Alabama football was about to be wiped off the map.

Suspended Animation

Thomas Wert was an Alabama footballer in the late 1890s. Many years later he wrote how it was to have played during those days of brute power.

"We managed to get up a pretty good team, and we got a game with the University of Mississippi. We played at Jackson, Mississippi, in back of the old Capitol, and the odds were 5 to 1 against us. But we played like veterans and won 7 to 5 . . . In those days, football wasn't a lady's game. When one of the Mississippi players tried to move the ball after it was dead, I fell on his neck with my knee. I hadn't done so before the entire grandstand was empty and people came down on me with umbrellas, walking canes and the like, and if it hadn't have been for a bunch of policemen surrounding me, I'm afraid I would have been knocked out myself . . . The next day we left for New Orleans to play the Southern Athletic Team. They had prize-fighters, dockhands and everybody else on their team . . . They kicked me, trampled on me, and sometimes bit me all at the same time. In my experience I had never taken a minute out of the game until this one, but I took plenty out for this one . . . Frank White had been knocked out and I was left to do the kicking . . . I remember returning to the hotel on the street car. Cy Brown's nose was about as big as his fist. I had two black eyes, my nose was larger than Cy's, and I was also lame . . . We got beat that day, 22 to 0."

A passage from the *Corolla* of 1896 presaged what was about to happen: "Older people who forget that they were once boys,

31

not caring for little scratches, say that football is a brutal game, doing more harm than good, and that the foolish infatuation will soon die out."

As early as 1895, University of Alabama authorities began casting a critical eye at athletics, and not just because of the roughness of football. Obviously, there was a conflict between sports and academics.

The faculty ruled that players must be regular students who had enrolled within three weeks of the beginning of the fall term or within 10 days of the beginning of the winter or spring term. Time off for games must not exceed six days in the year and a player must not neglect his studies.

Under new safety rules, a player had to be examined and approved by the University surgeon before he could participate in athletics. Any student under 21 had to have special permission from his parents to play. Off-campus games must be restricted to collegiate opponents.

The faculty expressed the opinion that injuries in football were, "in nearly every case, the result of slugging and other forms of foul play," and suggested guilty players be kicked out of the game. The faculty asked the University surgeon to attend games.

In 1897 the University trustees got into the act with a ruling that led to football being dropped completely. They ruled that no more football games could be played off-campus.

Football's supporters screamed, students griped, and the *Corolla* wrote critical poems.

Obviously, athletics could not exist under such regulations. Students lost interest and few tried out for the team. The 1897 squad played only one game, beating the Tuscaloosa Athletic Club 6-0. The *Corolla* intoned, "In reviewing our past athletic season, we find very little to be proud of. Handicapped by the stringent law of the Trustees, which prevented our traveling, we were compelled to play our baseball and football games on the campus."

In 1898 Alabama did not even field a football team. "We have seen that it is useless to attempt to put out a football team so long as we are compelled to play all our games on the campus," the *Corolla* said.

The trustees had not expected this. Their attempts at regulation had resulted in them having nothing to regulate. They voted to return the rule of sports to the faculty.

The faculty could allow teams to travel but to not more than two games or series. The *Corolla* ran a drawing of a statue "Commemorating the Emancipation of Athletics—June, 1899."

Football resumed at Alabama in 1899 with two games on campus, one in Jackson and one in New Orleans. By 1902 the rule had been relaxed, and three games were played away from campus. Five of the seven 1903 matches were road games.

Football was under fire elsewhere. A grieving mother scotched a move that might have had reverberations throughout the South had it been successful.

Von Gammon was a 17-year-old star of Georgia's 1896 and 1897 teams. During the 1897 Virginia game in Atlanta, Gammon, a linebacker, was injured in one of the mass plays so common at the time.

"You're not going to give up, Von, are you?" Captain Billy Kent asked as Gammon left the field. "No, Bill, I've got too much Georgia grit for that," Gammon said.

They were the last words he ever spoke. Gammon became unconscious as he reached the bench and died that night in a hospital.

The Georgia Legislature was in session in Atlanta. Bills to abolish the brutal game were introduced in both houses. The vote was overwhelming against football. Only the signature of Governor W. Y. Atkinson was needed for the bills to become law.

Von Gammon's mother loved her son, but she also loved football because he loved it. She wrote letters to the legislature and to Governor Atkinson. She asked that her son's death not be used "to defeat the most cherished object of his life."

Governor Atkinson vetoed the bill, possibly heading off a wave of such laws throughout the Southland, or even the nation.

Alabama's concern with brutal football preceded the game's famous national crisis by 10 years. In 1905 18 deaths were reported on the nation's football fields.

Pennsylvania played Swarthmore that year. Swarthmore's club was built around Bob Maxwell, a 250-pound lineman. Penn concentrated its defense on Maxwell, and he resembled a

33

butchered hog when he left the field. President Teddy Roosevelt saw a photograph of Maxwell and issued his famed open-up-or-close-up edict to football.

A meeting was held on January 12, 1906, in New York, and what is today known as the NCAA football rules committee was born. The members created a neutral zone the length of the ball between opposing lines, required a minimum of six men on the line of scrimmage, increased first down yardage from five to ten yards and legalized the forward pass.

Three years later the rules were changed to require seven men on the offensive line. Pushing and pulling the ball carrier and interlocked interference were barred, crawling was prohibited, and the flying tackle was outlawed.

Football had been saved.

Turn On The Headlights

The young sport that resumed at Alabama still had its wacky moments. It would continue to be a loose-jointed endeavor for years.

Consider this *Birmingham News* report of the 1901 Alabama-Tennessee game that ended in a 6-6 tie in the Magic City:

"... A game that began with every prospect of a splendid struggle but ended in an unpleasant controversy, with an equal score and dissatisfaction. It was anything but an enjoyable game at times, play being entirely suspended at frequent intervals until the crowds could be persuaded to leave the gridiron to the players. After almost every down the spectators would rush across the side lines and form a compact ring around the struggling teams, preventing beyond a possibility any further play.

"The combined efforts of a squad of policemen, assisted by a number of citizens, were of little avail against the curiosity of the majority of the enthusiasts, who, forgetful of everything but that the game was in progress, rushed at will upon the gridiron, forcing the officials to call time until the players could secure more room. So much time was consumed in this way that even if the teams had not become involved in an argument concerning a decision in the last half, darkness would have prevented the game being completed.

"The controversy and cessation of play above referred to occurred in almost the first ten minutes of the second half, and was the result of Umpire Payne's granting the Tennessee team

Thomas Kelly coached '15, '16, '17 Tides.

ten yards on account of an alleged off side play of the Alabamians, the decision being contested by the Tuscaloosa boys. The ball at that time was within ten yards of Alabama's goal line, and the moment play was suspended the spectators surged over the field and crowded around the teams, yelling and gesticulating, demanding all manner of decisions of the officials.

"The Alabama team refused to continue the game if the decision was granted, and as Umpire Payne refused to change his decision, the affair was hopelessly tangled. The approach of darkness found the matter still in dispute and further operations were impossible.

"Many of the football fans who attended the game left the field sorely disappointed with the turn events had taken, and expressed themselves as being anything but pleased with the apparent mismanagement of the whole affair. It was the general opinion that a few strands of wire stretched around the field would have enabled the policemen to restrain the crowd, which, with nothing to mark the lines, naturally got as close to the teams as possible. From the first play it was evident that the game could only be played with great difficulty, and the final finish was not surprising.

"Almost every football game played in Birmingham in late years has been more or less marred by the inability of the managers to handle the crowd. Yesterday's game, however, was the worst of its kind ever seen here, and it is not surprising that it is looked upon as a failure from a standpoint of clean sport."

In 1904 Alabama won a forfeit game over Mississippi A&M at Columbus, Mississippi. Alabama had the ball on the A&M four-yard line in the second period and was about to run a play when the Mississippians' captain contended Bama already had had four downs. He and his team left the field, and a 10-5 game officially became 11-0.

In the 1906 game with Mississippi A&M at Starkville, spectators threw sticks and rocks at Alabama's players. Five times in the first half Alabama drove inside the opponent's five-yard line only to have the plays nullified by penalties.

Early in the second half Alabama gathered around an injured player. With the Crimsons tending to their wounded comrade, the ball was snapped and a field goal made. Alabama protested that it had called time out. The official said he had heard no time out called.

One printed version of the story says an official coaxed Mississippi A&M's players, "Kick a goal, kick a goal, quick," and that when Alabama's Auxford Burks returned a punt for a touchdown, the official told the A&M rooters, "That's a touchdown, boys. I'll have to let them have it." Somehow, Alabama won 16-4.

Alabama tried to cancel a game in 1906 because seven regulars were out with injuries. Vanderbilt refused—and won 78-0.

Bama whipped Tennessee 10-0 in Knoxville in 1909, and the umpire got whipped, too. Umpire Elgin called back a 40-yard Tennessee run and penalized the home team 15 yards for holding. The crowd followed him to his streetcar and beaned him with a rock.

In 1912 Georgia took the hideout play to extreme lengths. Its flanker was dressed in civilian clothes. He caught a pass for 35 yards on the first play of the game.

One report has it that Georgia's Coach Cunningham was conscience stricken and offered to forget the whole matter and start the game over. But the officials said there was nothing illegal. Justice won out because Georgia fumbled on the series and Alabama recovered. The rules committee, at its next meeting, outlawed such plays.

Spectators were a problem in the 1913 Tennessee game at

Corolla cartooned Coach D. V. Graves.

Tuscaloosa. Officials spent too much time clearing the field of fans, and there were so many time-outs because of injuries, the final few minutes of the game were played in darkness with only automobile headlights providing illumination.

Alabama beat a highly favored Tulane team 14-7 in New Orleans in 1921, and the game almost ended in a riot. Alabama players had removed their headgears and were leaving the field after the final whistle when Tulane snapped the ball and threw a 40-yard touchdown pass. Referee Finlay ruled the game over. Two dozen policemen finally hustled the crowd off the field and escorted Finlay to his hotel.

Travel could be difficult. The 1906 Howard game in Tuscaloosa did not get started until 4:30 because Howard's train was several hours late. The teams agreed to 15-minute halves, and Alabama won 14-0. The 1919 Georgia game kicked off an hour and a half late because a train wreck kept Alabama out of Atlanta until after 1 p.m.

The coaching situation remained unstable for years. The 1903 *Corolla* stated: "James O. Heyworth was a graduate of Yale in 1888 and came to Tuscaloosa as a member of a firm of contractors for the construction of locks and dams on the Warrior River. Mr. Sedgwick, the regular coach, had been called home for some cause and Mr. Heyworth volunteered his services as coach as did Eli Abbott, a former player and coach. Both refused to accept any compensation for their services. Mr. Heyworth not only did this because of his love for the game but he paid the expenses of the substitutes to the Georgia game in Birmingham."

In 1915 Coach Thomas Kelly was struck by—of all things— typhoid fever. Two days before the fourth game of the season he was taken to a hospital suffering with a fever. He was out for the year. Kelly, a 250-pounder, lost 100 of those pounds.

Athletic Director Lonnie Noojin took over the team with Farley Moody, captain of the 1912 club, as assistant. Kelly returned to coaching in 1916.

There was a minor disruption of the 1900 Auburn game when an Alabama supporter threw his hat into the air—and Auburn tackle H. M. Harvey kicked it for a mock field goal. Guess where Harvey was next season: he was head coach at Alabama.

39

Auxford Burks inspired poems.

1909 squad posed in sweaters.

Lonnie Noojin was an Athletic Director who was pressed into coaching duties.

40

Zipp Newman, now sports editor emeritus of the *Birmingham News*, popularized the nickname Crimson Tide after he came home from the army in 1919.

Alabama had been known as the Thin Red Line because of its small teams. Sometimes it was called Crimsons. Newman recalls using Crimson Tide in a big headline over an advance story. He said the name came to him after watching the tide pound a seashore. It suggested a force "that kept pounding at you."

Newman said the red elephant symbol was originally derogatory. An Atlanta writer who had been a Georgia Tech player used the term in a story because he considered Alabama's team big and dumb. "Coach Wallace Wade hated it," Newman recalls, "but I always thought an elephant was big and smart."

Alabama's adoption of crimson and white as its colors apparently dates back to prefootball days. One story has it that Mary Fearn, a New Orleans beauty, selected the colors for Alabama's Cadet Company E in 1885.

Miss Fearn was introduced to some of the officers at an exhibition drill in Mobile. "Miss Fearn asked us what were the University of Alabama's colors," John R. Vidmer told Zipp Newman years later. "We told her that Alabama didn't have any official colors. She then asked us the colors of our uniforms.

"I told her our caps were black, our coats grey and our trousers white. Miss Fearn said, 'Black is too funereal and gray is neutral.' She proposed crimson, white and gray." Somewhere along the way, the gray was abandoned.

There was an innocence among the students in the early days of Alabama football that seems quaint today. They recited a poem, "Farewell to Burks," in praise of the 1902-1906 half-back, one of the true stars of the primitive teams:

> Farewell to our hero, in triumph he leaves us,
> Honored and blessed be our champion and friend;
> Long may his fame, which with glory now wreathes
>   us,
> Lead on to success even unto the end.
> Heaven send him help anew,
> Earth lend him wisdom, too.

Or, if you preferred, there was this offering:

Greatly to prosper and proudly to grow,
While every hill and glen
Sends our shout back again,
B. Auxford Burks! Alabama! Ho! Ho!
Long shall old Auburn, with groans and with mad-
    ness,
Remember our half-back who played them so fast;
Long shall Sewanee, with wonder and sadness,
Remember our onslaught of November last.
Tho this season ends his fight,
Long shall the Auburnite
Think of Burk's tackling with fear and with woe,
Victory upon victory then,
Echoes his praise again,
B. Auxford Burks! Alabama! Ho! Ho!

Coach D. V. Graves wrote of Alabama spirit in the 1912 *Corolla:* "In September the squad looked light and of poor physical development. Everything was discouraging. I had not yet become familiar with the Alabama Spirit—that indescribable something which made the efforts of a light team bring seemingly impossible results."

Incidentally, you could not blame Graves for going by D. V. His name was Dorset Vandeventer.

Coach W. B. Blount's 1904 team became the first to play ten games. And the first to win seven. Jack Leavenworth's 1905 club played ten and won six with Auxford Burks returning a kickoff 95 yards in the opening game against Maryville to begin a brilliant season for himself. That team whipped Auburn, and the *Corolla* crowed: "After running over the records very carefully, I discover that we played a team by the name of Auburn on November the 18th. We scored 30 points, and if I remember correctly, they failed to score."

The schedule was trimmed to six games in 1906, though, with eight or nine becoming standard until the 1920 club played eleven.

Most of the teams of this era were winners, but two, three, and four losses dotted most schedules.

C. C. Countess, the 1908 center, made all-Southern. Bully Van de Graaff was an all-Southern tackle in 1914 and 1915 and Alabama's first all-American in 1915.

42

Dr. George H. (Mike) Denny, an ardent supporter of Alabama athletics, became president of the University in 1912 and would serve for 25 years, longest term of any University of Alabama president. During those years he was a regular sideline watcher at practice sessions. Dr. Denny died in 1955 at age 84.

He was a logical man whose circular theory was, "The better the team the larger the gate receipts the better the team." Four times his Tides would visit the Rose Bowl.

The *Montgomery Advertiser* once wrote of him: "It may be doubted if any single educator ever wielded the power in Alabama affairs that he did. Certainly no single educator possesses such power today. Where other school leaders have been inclined to rely upon the mass impact of men and women working for a great cause, Dr. Denny was a leader who got things done in Napoleonic fashion, through his own individual drive and powers of persuasion."

When Dr. Denny came to the Capstone in 1912, enrollment was 500, including 55 women. When he retired as president in 1937, it was 4,800 with 1,000 women.

Denny Chimes, a 115-foot carillon tower, is a campus landmark, and Denny Stadium is a memorial to Dr. Mike's interest in athletics.

The most tragic event of those early days was the cessation of athletic relations between Alabama and Auburn in 1908. Football fans would be deprived of Tide vs. Tiger until 1948.

Bickering was common in the series. Charges involving eligibility of players flew between the schools and tainted several games. Finally, after the 6-6 tie in 1907, there was trouble over the 1908 contract.

There were three points in question: Auburn wanted to bring more players than Alabama thought necessary; Auburn wanted more per-man, per-day expense money allocated than Alabama did; after the schools failed to select a Southern umpire, Auburn wanted an Easterner brought in.

Debates raged over the points. Finally, Alabama conceded the first two. Auburn then proposed the umpire be chosen by an impartial committee selected by the two institutions.

Alabama refused to submit selection of the ump to the committee.

Finally, Auburn wanted the matter of the umpire left in the

hands of the central board of officials of the general football rules committee of the United States. Alabama agreed.

But by then October had arrived and schedules were made. No common date could be arranged. Finally, Alabama said it would play anytime after the end of Thanksgiving weekend and before December 5. Auburn replied that its board of trustees provided years before that its season end on Thanksgiving Day.

What should have been this state's richest sports event lay dormant until 1948. There were periodic efforts made to revive the series, such as the Auburn senior class's petition to President Spright Dowell in 1922 that wisely pointed out that no student and few faculty members who were there in 1908 were still around.

Time Out: Derrill Pratt

Derrill Pratt saw his first football game in 1907. He saw it from up close. He was in the starting backfield for Alabama.

"I was a country boy, you know," Pratt said at his home in Galveston, Texas. "My brother Walker and I were going to the University and our train broke down out of Tuscaloosa. They had to send hacks to come and get us.

"We entered school on a Wednesday. Dr. Pollard was the coach and he didn't have any football players. We were two pretty good looking boys and he sent word he'd like to see us. We went down to the clubhouse, or gym. It was about the size of a good-size privy. We got our uniforms and went out to play football. I weighed about 150 and Walker about 160 or 165. He was a guard and I was an end on defense and a halfback. On Saturday I played in the first game I had ever seen, with three days' practice. I played the whole game."

Derrill Pratt is 84 years old. His mind is keen—"but I think old man arthritis is getting me down. But 84 years is a long time." Managing in the Texas League took him to Galveston. It was baseball that put his name in headlines and enshrined him in the state of Alabama's Sports Hall of Fame in 1972. He used to bat cleanup behind a young outfielder named George Ruth.

But Pratt was a part of those rollicking early football days at the University of Alabama, too. He captained the 1909 team under Dr. J. W. H. Pollard, and he likes to talk about how football was then.

"We played it because we loved it. We played it because it

45

Dr. John Pollard, inventor of
the "Pollard Two-Step."

was out there," Pratt stated a simple philosophy from a time when life was simpler. "Those were good days. We'd have 2,500 watching and think we had a million.

"I think I hold the world record for place kicks. I kicked one in 1909 58 yards against Georgia. I kicked one against the Haskell Indians in 1907 or maybe 1908 from the 47-yard line on a 45-degree angle. It was kicked from the sideline. In those days you kicked from where it was.

"Against Georgia, the ball went 20 yards into the grandstands and the grandstands were 20 yards from the end zone. I still have the ball that I kicked against Georgia about 60 years ago. It looks like a watermelon. It's about the shape of a watermelon. It's so big you couldn't hold it. You had to lay it on the palm of your hand and spin it off to pass it. It was quite an art.

"The headgear wasn't much more than a piece of leather with cotton under it. The big thing was the nose guard. That was about the only protection we wore and Dr. Pollard made most of them. He was quite clever. It was a leather pad that went over your nose and it had a piece on it that you could bite and hold in your mouth. If you had any shoulder pads you made them yourself and if you had any pads on your pants you put them on yourself.

"You took your life in your hands. When you got tackled

ALA-6 AUBURN-6

Tidesmen tied Auburn in 1907. Left to right: "Pap" Gresham, "Trig" Palmer, . . . , Henley Smith, Derrill Pratt, . . . , Darius Green. Others unidentified.

they held you down and didn't turn you loose until the ball was blown dead. You had to holler, 'Down!' sometimes when they'd pile on you.

"We had one play where they took the fullback by the seat of his pants and turned him a tumbleset over center. Dr. Pollard was tricky.

"You've heard of the Pollard two-step, haven't you? They finally kept us from using it because they said it was illegal. The line would come back and hold hands and we'd take a hop, skip and jump to the right or left and split. It was kinda tantalizing.

"I remember when we played Sewanee. They came down and played Auburn in Birmingham on Saturday, then played Alabama on Monday. We thought we were going to give them a good spanking but I think they beat us 54-4. I think they went on to LSU on the next Saturday. They won three games in eight days.

"Sewanee only had about 20 boys big enough to play football but they ran us to death. We played on the quad in those days with a canvas fence and a wire fence around it. The people came down in their buggies to watch.

"We were only allowed 18 men to dress out in those days. I noticed this year that when Bear Bryant opened practice he had 96 men. I don't understand that. We only had 350 students in 1907.

"I played pretty good football if I do have to say it myself. I didn't have enough sense to stay out of it.

"Dr. Pollard, I think, was the first real good coach at Alabama. He went up to Washington & Lee later and I went as his assistant. Later I was an assistant at Alabama."

But for Derrill Pratt, who rode that train from Pell City to Tuscaloosa to become a freshman, baseball was to be the foundation of his life.

"I sneaked off and went into baseball against my daddy's wishes. I was getting $12.50 a week selling shoes and somebody offered me $250 and I couldn't turn it down. But I don't think I made as much in 20 years as some players make in one year today."

His first baseball job was with Montgomery of the Southern Association, and soon he was with the St. Louis Browns in the American League. The Browns sold Pratt to the Yankees in 1918, and he was to hit cleanup in one of the most feared lineups in history.

Pratt was a member of Murderers' Row before Ruth arrived. Bob Ripley drew a cartoon of big bruisers swinging clubs and labeled them Roger Peckinpaugh, Wally Pipp, Frank Baker, Del Pratt, and Ping Brodie. He called it Murderers' Row, and a famous nickname was born. Six times second baseman Pratt hit over .300.

When Alabama inducted him into its Sports Hall of Fame, 24 members of his family attended the ceremony. "I don't believe I ever enjoyed anything in my life as much as I did that," Pratt said.

Time Out:
Bully Van de Graaff

A phone call found the old man at his home in Colorado Springs, Colorado. The operator asked for Mr. W. T. Van de Graaff. "Bully, telephone," his wife said.

"Pretty well for an ole timer," Van de Graaff answered an opening question. Did he have time to talk? "I've got more time than money."

He is an ole timer, but a spry one. Van de Graaff was the University of Alabama's first all-American football player. He was a massive man who captured the fancy of the fans of this relatively new game in 1912-15. He played tackle, but he could carry the ball, too—and did.

"I was down as a tackle but I ran with the ball, on the tackle-around, more than anybody else on the team," he reminisced.

Zipp Newman vividly remembers seeing Van de Graaff play. When Van de Graaff was inducted into the Alabama Sports Hall of Fame in 1970, Newman wrote in the program: "I have seen all the South's great tackles, but never one who contributed more to his team as a tackle, then a kicker and, lastly, a brutal runner, with high knee action that knocked out would be tacklers."

"It was fun," Van de Graaff said into the telephone, "just as much fun as it would be now. But it wasn't quite the same as playing at the University of Alabama would be now. We had a terrible time beating Sewanee back then.

"Sewanee was the big rival of Alabama at that time. We finally

49

Bully Van de Graaff was Alabama's first all-American.

Bully Van de Graaff kicks off in 1915 Sewanee game.

beat Sewanee, though. That was the greatest thing that happened while I was at the University of Alabama, winning a game against Sewanee."

Only one time, in 1894, had Bama whipped the Mountain Tigers. In 1914, Van de Graaff's junior year, Alabama had beaten Georgia Tech 13-0, and Tech had licked Sewanee 20-0. Bama supporters thought their team could not lose this Sewanee game. Perhaps that notion leaked into the locker room. Sewanee outplayed the Crimsons in every phase and won 18-0.

In 1915 Alabama's chances against the Tigers appeared dark. The Van de Graaff family—Bully and two brothers, Adrian and Hargrave—had tried for seven years to beat Sewanee but could not. Odds were they never would now.

Alabama Captain William Harsh ran 65 yards for a touchdown in the first period. Van de Graaff converted. He added three more points on a field goal. Alabama held Sewanee at the Crimson five, and Bully punted out. Bama led 10-0 at the half.

Four times in the third quarter Sewanee penetrated Alabama's 20, but the Crimsons would hold and Van de Graaff would kick out. Once he stood 5 yards inside his end zone and kicked to the Tiger 15.

Sewanee tied it at 10-all in the fourth quarter. The Crimsons were sinking. Would they never beat Sewanee?

The Tigers tried a pass play. Van de Graaff rushed the passer, knocked the ball out of his hand, caught it on the fly, and ran 65 yards for a touchdown. He added the PAT and later kicked two field goals. Alabama won 23-10, and Van de Graaff scored 17 of the 23 points.

Parke H. Davis, a member of the national rules committee, called Van de Graaff the best tackle in America.

"I was probably better at punting than anything else," Van de Graaff says today.

Van de Graaff went to West Point after his Alabama playing days, but a knee injury caused him to miss most of the one season he played there. He served as an assistant coach at Alabama under Xen Scott and Wallace Wade, later becoming head coach and athletic director at Colorado College. It is in that state that he will live out the rest of his life.

Van de Graaff never played high school football. That seems

incredible now, but it was not unusual at all then. "Things were a little different in those days. They hadn't played as much football as they do these days," he advises. "I went to a private school in Tuscaloosa and they didn't have a team."

How did he select the University of Alabama? "I was born in Tuscaloosa and raised in Tuscaloosa and the University of Alabama was in Tuscaloosa," he said with a touch of wit. "My people didn't have enough money to send me to Yale where my father wanted me to go. My freshman year, there were three of us brothers on the team."

I asked Bully Van de Graaff his age. "I'll have to figure it out," he said. "Just a minute. I'll ask my wife. I think I'm 76. I'm not sure."

It was a nice conversation on a lazy summer day.

A Writer Who Could Coach

The man who coached Alabama's first nationally important victory was equally at home behind a typewriter or walking the sidelines.

"He wrote horse racing for the Cleveland paper," Zipp Newman remembers of Xen Scott. "Coaches at Alabama did everything in those days to make a living. I doubt if they paid him $2,000. He would coach the team in the fall and go back to Ohio and cover the races in the summer."

Newman covered Alabama's famous 9-7 win over Pennsylvania in Philadephia on November 4, 1922. With that upset, Alabama gained more national prestige than it had in all its previous games combined.

Scott was a tiny man who had played football at Cleveland's Western Reserve University. Only 25 Alabama teams had ever lined up, but there had been 13 head coaches. Scott was the 14th.

The Scott era marked the appearance of Hank Crisp on the Alabama scene. He would become a fixture, as familiar as Denny Chimes.

Dr. Denny brought in Charles Bernier as athletic director, and Bernier wanted Crisp as line coach. Crisp had played for Bernier at Hampden-Sydney and Virginia Tech. Crisp had lost a hand in a childhood accident, but after he saw him play a game, General George Patton told Bernier, "I think I've seen the greatest player of the year. If you had 10 more men with a missing hand, you would have 11 all-American players."

Hank Crisp—"Always available."

When Bernier hired Crisp he said, "Crisp will always be available to do anything he is asked to do." How true: during his career of more than 40 years at the Capstone, Crisp coached the varsity line, the freshman team, the baseball, basketball and track squads, and served as athletic director. He died of a heart attack in 1970 on the night he was to be inducted into the Alabama Sports Hall of Fame. He was stricken at a reception just before the big event.

Crisp's son, Hank, Jr., received the plaque from Governor Albert Brewer that night. "Today was the happiest day of his life. It was the happiest I had ever seen him," his son said.

Bernier was a crack recruiter who combed the state for boys to play on Scott's teams.

Scott was an instant success. In fact, for some weeks it appeared Scott had discovered a magic method of keeping his goal line untouched. In its first five games the 1919 Tide was unscored upon. Riggs Stephenson, a back who in 1972 would be enshrined in the Alabama Sports Hall of Fame, was the offensive star. Alabama went 8-1, scored 280 points, and surrendered but 22.

Scott's 1920 team became the first Alabama club to win 10 games. But it was also the first one to play 11. Mully Lenoir scored five touchdowns in one game. That Tide also was the first to beat Vanderbilt. Bama and Vandy had played five times since 1903, and the Nashville team had won every one, including routs of 30-0, 34-0 and 78-0. Scott had no difficulty getting his club up for this one, and Alabama won 14-7.

The 1920 squad crushed Case College 40-0 in Cleveland. That was the first time an Alabama team ever played in the North. In fact, except for a 20-0 loss to Texas in 1915, it was the first time Alabama had ever played outside the South.

Georgia was the only team to whip that Alabama club. It cost the Tide the championship of the 30-member Southern Interscholastic Athletic Association. Georgia Tech was voted the championship.

Without Stephenson and Lenior, Scott's 1921 Alabama squad slipped to five wins, four losses, and two ties. Scott's 1922 team would not be famous for its 6-3-1 record, either, but it would never be forgotten as the club that screamed for, and got, the first national spotlight for Alabama.

Penn Gets Pinned

Grantland Rice tossed his felt hat (every newspaperman wore a felt hat in those days) on the desk and began typing: "Pennsylvania and Princeton, after their impressive achievements of a week ago, get a breathing spell, although Swarthmore is never to be taken too lightly."

Swarthmore was Princeton's opponent in 1922. John Heisman's Pennsylvania would host Alabama. Rice picked the Quakers 21-0. He had plenty of company—99.9 percent of the world, or at least of that part of the world that cared.

Pennsylvania writers generally adopted a sympathetic tone toward the Southerners. They noted that Georgia Tech beat Alabama 33-7, Navy beat Tech 13-0, and Penn beat Navy 13-7. If you knew simple arithmetic, you had to be aware a rout was about to occur. "They didn't give us any credit at all," Zipp Newman remembers.

Really, there was not much reason to. Alabama had a rugged first string, but its depth was suspect. The Tide had beaten Marion 110-0 and Oglethorpe 41-0, but those were warm-ups. Tech had blasted Alabama 33-7, Sewanee had tied 7-7, and Texas had won 19-10.

To add to the problems, Bama would have to travel 2,500 miles to Austin, Texas, back to Tuscaloosa, and to Philadelphia, playing two games in eight days. Long distance travel was a problem in those days. "It was something, with the cinders blowing through the train cars," Zipp Newman recalls. "But the food was good." Another newsman, Henry Vance, boarded the

56

train in Birmingham with two pieces of luggage and never saw them again.

Coach Scott had been sick most of the fall. He had lost 35 pounds before the trip to Austin, and his doctor told him not to make the Philadelphia journey, an order he ignored.

There were semi-bright spots in the loss to Texas. The Tide had outgained the Longhorns 76-31 in the air and 80-45 on the ground. Alabama should have won the game but lost five fumbles. And Auxford Burks, the old running star who was now living near Austin, cheered everyone up when he attended the game and pronounced the Tide wall "the greatest line I have ever seen at Alabama."

Scott was a thinker, one of the brainiest coaches in the South. He reasoned that his boys might be overawed by what they had heard of Eastern football. He arranged for the team to stop in Washington to watch the Navy-Penn State game in Griffith Stadium. Navy won 14-0 and the Crimsons came away with the impression that Easterners put their moleskins on one leg at a time, just like everyone else. It was a masterpiece of psychological strategy Scott had pulled.

Scott had coached at Penn State, and he had contacts in the East. Speedy Rush, a former Princeton coach, and Bob Folwell, who had coached Navy, gave Scott valuable information on the Quakers.

Scott even momentarily forgot his physical condition when two of his old 1908 teammates, George Beeman and Jay Wedor, came to sit on the bench with him.

A crowd of 25,000 gathered in Franklin Field. It was by far the largest audience an Alabama team had ever seen. No Pennsylvanian was worried. When the Tide's Bull Wesley kicked a field goal from the Penn 35 to make the score 3-0 early in the second period, the fans patronizingly applauded the Southerners for attempting offensive football instead of merely trying to hold the score down.

Alabama got off a short punt, and Penn had the ball on the Crimson 35. George Sullivan cut through the line for 20 yards, saw his path blocked, and reversed his field to a touchdown. The extra point made it 7-3 in the second period, and the fans smiled smugly and told each other the slaughter was about to begin.

57

Shorty Propst, lanky center.

Large crowd greeted Tide at Tuscaloosa station after Penn fell in 1922.

Al Clemens guarded the rounded football.

Xen Scott coached first big Tide victory.

If Alabama needed further motivation, it came in the third quarter when an all-American Penn tackle slugged Bill Baty, the smallest player on the field, and was thrown out of the game. Later, Baty ran 25 yards to the Penn four. Pooley Hubert dented the goal line but fumbled, and Shorty Propst recovered for a touchdown. Wesley missed the kick, but Bama led 9-7 in the third period and Penn's fans were not so sure of their team now.

That is the way it ended—and Bama almost got two more points on a safety but Penn's passer squeaked out of the end zone.

Southern football had been vindicated. The Eastern myth was for fairy tale anthologies. Congratulatory telegrams poured into Alabama's Philadelphia hotel. Perhaps the one the players appreciated most came from Bill Alexander, the Georgia Tech coach. He realized the national significance of the game. When the team arrived in Tuscaloosa, it received the most demonstrative welcome a Tide ever had.

Shortly, the laughing would stop. The *Birmingham News* broke a story that Scott had turned in his resignation October 6, a month before the Pennsylvania game. Prominent alumni persuaded him to remain in charge until the season ended.

Alabama followed the win over Penn with a 47-3 mashing of LSU, a 6-0 loss to Kentucky, a 10-6 decision over Georgia, and a 59-0 rout of Mississippi A&M.

The *Birmingham News* had written after the Penn game: "On the fevered forehead of Xen C. Scott should be placed the golden crown of glory. . ."

They were fitting words for an epitaph. Soon, Scott would be dead from cancer.

Time Out: Riggs Stephenson, Joe Sewell, Luke Sewell

The three old men sat down to supper in Tuscaloosa while it was still daylight. Daylight Savings Time in the summer plays tricks with night and day.

They had eaten together many times. Two of them, Riggs Stephenson, who was host on this night, and Joe Sewell, had waited on tables together at the University of Alabama. They and the third member of this get-together, Luke Sewell, had been teammates on the Cleveland Indians baseball club. All had played football and baseball at Alabama. Stephenson had been on football teams with both, but Joe and Luke did not play together.

"Luke was the manager one year and the next year he played quarterback," Stephenson explained. "He was so small that he made manager, but he got to where he could throw the ball well and became a quarterback. Luke always was smarter than the rest of us."

"I only played one year, 1920." said Luke Sewell, who lives in Akron, Ohio, and who was visiting with Joe and Riggs in Tuscaloosa. "I think they were short of players. I wasn't much of a football player. I could throw the ball but I couldn't kick it. But I didn't play enough to make a letter.

"When I was manager I learned to throw the football, that old balloon ball they had then. Xen Scott was trying to get some passing into his attack and he asked me if I thought I could throw the ball in a game. I told him I didn't see why not, so I played. They wanted me to come back here the next year but I went into baseball.

"You ran for manager in those days," Luke Sewell continued. "It was a political campaign. I ran and got elected. When I started to Alabama I was only 15 years old, five-foot, two inches tall and weighed 115 pounds. I wasn't much of a challenge to anybody. I didn't grow until I was 18 or 19 years old."

Stephenson was by far the best football player of the trio. He was all-Southern in 1920.

"I lived in Hale County. I was born and reared there," Stephenson said. "But my brother got a job in Guntersville and I went up there and played a couple of years in high school.

"We didn't have much training back when I entered the University. I think they had us report a week before school started. A lot of fellows had gone to war and we had a lot of young boys. I think the whole backfield was made up of freshmen, or maybe we had one man who had played. Thomas Kelly was the coach. We practiced a little in 1918 but we never did play because of the war.

"I had two years under Xen Scott. He had me back there throwing and running and kicking. He had a kind of spread formation and used me back there because I could throw and kick. I handled the ball on just about every play in the spread. He moved the ends out from the tackles about five yards and put a back behind each end. There was one short man in the backfield to keep them honest. But we had a closed formation, too, and Mully Lenoir, the other halfback, ran the ball in it.

"We had mighty bad uniforms. You can tell that from the cauliflower ears I have now. We only had a little piece of leather over our heads. Shoes were heavy and high-top and trousers were big and heavy with big old boards in the front.

"The longest regular trip we had was to New Orleans or Baton Rouge, but once we played Case College in Cleveland. Scott arranged it because he was from Cleveland and he knew the people at Case. I remember him saying we'd rather go up there and play somebody we could beat than to play Ohio State. They had Chick Harley then. Remember hearing of Chick Harley?

"I think a doctor scouted me for Alabama," Stephenson continued. "They gave me a job sweeping off the stoops of Garland Hall. We got good pay—about $5 a month and room.

The room didn't have anything in it but a light bulb.

"I wasn't such a good sweeper myself. I was supposed to sweep out some of the rooms in the dorm but the boys were pretty good to me because I played football. They'd say to just go on, the rooms didn't need sweeping, but I was supposed to sweep them every day.

"Most of the boys didn't have a job. It didn't cost much to go to school, though. Three or four hundred dollars was all it cost to go. We were pretty anxious in those days to go to school. It wasn't everybody who got to go.

"We had a training table back then and some of the players waited on the table. Joe Sewell and I waited on the table to get our meals. Scholarship? They might have had some but they didn't offer any to me. I didn't have much reputation, coming from a little school like Guntersville. But I don't think they had any scholarships at all."

Stephenson remembers Xen Scott as "a very nice fellow. I liked him. I don't know whether he knew too much about the line but he knew a good bit about the backfield. He put in one formation very much like the Heisman shift. Behind the center, he'd have the two guards, the fullback, the quarterback and the two halfbacks and they'd all shift out.

"Joe and Luke and I were playing baseball in Cleveland and Mrs. Scott called us and asked us to be pallbearers at his funeral. It was a very sad day for us all."

Luke Sewell said Scott was offensive-minded. "He didn't care about defense much. His theory was that if you could score more points you could win. If you'll look at his record you'll see he scored a lot of points. Oh, if you missed a tackle he'd bite you in the behind, but he spent most of his time setting up plays."

Although Luke was two years younger, he started college with Joe. "I finished in high school and just stayed in the same grade three years at Wetumpka," Joe explained. "See, my father had two girls and a boy already in college. He couldn't afford to send any more right then. That way, Luke caught up with me.

"I played halfback and safety, and we had to play the whole 60 minutes then. We didn't have many reserves. I think there were about 15 or 18 on the team. It was rough as a cob and the equipment wasn't nearly as good as it is now. But we played just as hard. We didn't have as many coaches as they do now. They've got more coaches at Alabama than they have football players. Nobody had any scholarships. I was a waiter in the mess hall—and I finally worked my way up to head waiter.

"We had some good players but not as many as now. But Riggs Stephenson was one of the finest players that ever came through Alabama. He'd be an all-American today, hand over fist."

The Sewells became one of baseball's most famous brother acts. Joe was a sure-handed shortstop who practically never struck out. Luke was a catcher.

Joe left Bama and went to New Orleans in the Southern League. When Ray Chapman was killed by a pitch, it was rookie Joe Sewell the Indians called up to play shortstop. In 10 of 14 seasons he hit .300 or better. His lifetime average was .312 with a high of .352 in 1923. His 1,107 consecutive games is the third best in baseball history.

No player who has batted more than 7,000 times can approach Joe Sewell's low of 114 strikeouts. No player can challenge his season low of four, either.

One of his fondest memories involves a day in 1931 after he had been traded to New York. Yankee Stadium was jammed with 78,000 fans who had come to see Babe Ruth hit homers. Ruth did not get a hit, but Joe Sewell went five-for-five. Later he became baseball coach at the University of Alabama.

Luke made the Cleveland team late in his rookie season, too, moving up from Columbus. He was a noted handler of pitchers, if not a terrifying hitter. He was an active catcher for 20 years and managed the St. Louis Browns and Cincinnati Reds. In 1944, his Browns won the American League pennant.

Stephenson, who played both infield and outfield, performed 14 years with Cleveland in the American League and Chicago in the National. His lifetime batting average was .336.

More than 10,000 players have appeared in the majors, but Stephenson rates No. 18 on the all-time batting average list. His greatest thrill was appearing in two World Series.

Dazzy Vance is his selection as the best pitcher he ever faced. He will take Ty Cobb as the best hitter he ever saw.

Time Out: Dr. W. C. Baty

Bill Baty was not the best football player Alabama ever had, but none has loved the game more. He played and played—and played.

He played for Alabama in 1920, 1921, 1922, and 1923. Then he played a season for the professional Providence Steamrollers. Then he played two more years for George Washington University under an assumed name.

Today, Dr. W. C. Baty serves as county health officer in Tuscaloosa, a post he has held since 1959. Recently he lost a leg, but he still attends football games. "I'll be there as long as I can crawl," Dr. Baty said.

Dr. Baty's career touched the tenure of two head coaches. He was under Xen Scott the first three years, Wallace Wade the fourth. Their personalities differed 180 degrees, Dr. Baty recalled.

"Scott was a real warmhearted person, a little guy, about as big as a minute. I don't know where he got his training because he was too little to be a big league player.

"As I remember, his resignation all happened very quickly. We were very much surprised when Scott left. We all loved him very much. He had Hank Crisp as his first assistant. Hank was the disciplinarian. He kept the players in line and Scott just coached. We loved Hank, though.

"Scott was not a disciplinarian like Wade was. Wade was a disciplinarian of the first order. He coached a lot through fear rather than through warmth and persuasion.

Bill Baty never wanted to stop playing.

"But I got along fine with Wade. I remember one time Wade called me into his office and read me up and down the back and said, 'I think you're loafing, and if you are you won't last long on this team. You either get going or you're finished. I think what's eating on you is that you thought you'd get elected captain and you weren't.'

"Wade was real smart. He figured I was loafing because I hadn't been elected captain, and he hit it right on the nail. He said get going or turn in your suit and I said I'd get going. Things like being captain mean a lot when you're a boy, but they don't mean anything now."

Football has been a lifelong passion with Bill Baty, who was Alabama's team physician from 1959 until 1971.

"I started playing when I was just a kid in Bessemer," he said. "I organized a team on Berkley Avenue and we called ourselves the Berkley Avenue Hillbillies. When I started to Bessemer High School, Coach Red Harris asked me why I didn't come out for the team. I said I was too little. 'Let me decide that,' he said.

'Come on out tomorrow and I'll give you a varsity sweater.' I did and I made all-state my junior and senior years and that got me started.

"Auburn and Georgia Tech and Alabama offered me a scholarship but I always wanted to go to Alabama. They gave me board and room but I had to get a job and earn my spending money."

Baty played in the famous 9-7 victory over Pennsylvania that focused national attention on Alabama football. His role in the game: that of punching bag. But he helped Alabama win.

"I was blocking back and they had a big tackle named Thurman," recalled Dr. Baty, who weighed 160 pounds in those days. "He started slugging me. I'd block him and he'd slug me. I told Shorty Cooper, our captain, to tell the referee to take a look at this guy Thurman, that he was beating me to death. I couldn't talk to the referee because I was just a player.

"About three plays later, the officials penalized Penn and threw Thurman out of the game. We won 9-7 and that was the turning point of the game.

"When the game was over, Thurman was on the sidelines waiting on the referee. He was going to beat him up. They had to pull him off the referee.

"After I finished at Alabama I went to Harvard Medical School and I saw Harvard play Yale. I thought I recognized the referee. He was the same one who had refereed our game with Penn. His name was O'Brien.

"I went down after the game and said, 'Mr. O'Brien, do you remember me? I'm Bill Baty.' He said, 'I'll never forget you. You almost got me killed. If it hadn't been for some of the other players Thurman would have murdered me.'"

Dr. Baty remembers that afternoon in Franklin Field as a key date in Alabama football history. "Alabama got the first publicity it had ever gotten after beating Penn," he said. "They started to sit up and take notice then.

"We weren't awed by Penn. Our coach, as I recall it, was trying to tell us this was just another game. He kept telling us not to be scared just because we were going to play a big Eastern school.

"We had played Texas in Austin the week before. I don't know how we ever passed any subjects at all, we were gone so

67

long. How did we practice? We didn't practice. We had to practice before we left, then play the game whenever we got there.

"It was the biggest crowd we'd ever seen, about 25,000. If we ever had 10,000 or 15,000 we thought that was a big crowd."

After he enrolled at Harvard, Baty began playing with the Providence professional team. "They paid me $75 a game, flat. I'd get paid off in 75 one-dollar bills. There was no league. We played the Philadelphia Yellow Jackets and other teams around the Eastern Seaboard."

When he switched to George Washington's medical school, he became a collegiate player again. "I used the name George Copeland. Copeland is my middle name," he explained. "They wanted me to play against Catholic, their big rival, on Thanksgiving Day. That was just like the Alabama-Auburn game to them. I told the coach, 'Suppose they find out I've already played at Alabama?' He said, 'They won't say anything. I know three or four boys they've got that aren't eligible.'"

Dr. Baty spent 30 years in the Navy and came out as a rear admiral. He became Tuscaloosa's county health officer and Tide team physician in 1959.

"The chances of getting hurt are about the same now as then," he said. "It's all about the same. But they do have a lot better protection now. They're better trained and better instructed, too."

I asked Dr. Baty who his favorite players were during his years as team physician. "Cotton Clark was one of my favorites. Pat Trammell was my No. 1 favorite. I loved Pat. He was a competitor first class. He'd knock your ears off and he was a wonderful person along with it. I was fond of Billy Neighbors, too. I hate to leave anybody out because there were so many."

I asked Dr. Baty if he counseled Trammell—who was a doctor when he died of cancer in the prime of his life—to enter medicine. "Pat used to talk to me about studying medicine and I would encourage him," Dr. Baty said. "But I didn't really have anything to do with him being a doctor. He wanted to be a doctor ever since he first came to Alabama."

Retirement is facing Dr. Baty. "I was supposed to retire last year," he said. "I hate to think about retiring in October. I'll be 71 this fall and I hope they'll keep me on another year. I feel real good. I lost a leg but I get around good on canes and crutches. I've got a real good peg leg but I'm going to get another one that's lighter."

Wade Wades In

A New Year's Day without football games would be as bland as a hamburger without mustard and catsup. Millions of Americans—many braving New Year's Eve hangovers—queue into cold stadia and flop onto sofas before television sets for the annual ritual of the bowls. Except for a few meaningless all-star games, the bowls are college football's last song of the season.

If your husband does not speak from midmorning until late night on New Year's Day, you can blame James Wagner, a young Easterner who moved to Pasadena, California, and became president of the Tournament of Roses around the turn of the century.

The Tournament of Roses had been floundering for a dozen years. It consisted of a parade with pretty girls tossing roses from carriages, speeches, foot races, races between horses and greyhounds, and an event known as the Tourney of the Rings in which mounted horsemen rode at various speeds and attempted to stick their lances through a ring of flowers hanging from a post.

Newspaper editors ho-hummed at the whole affair and searched for a good axe murder to fill a column. Wagner knew the Tournament of Roses needed an event with pizzazz, something the newspapers could not ignore. He decided a football game was just the thing.

Others harped that guaranteeing a couple of football teams a total of $3,500 would be the final, fatal stroke for the Tournament of Roses.

But Wagner was elected president, and he proceeded on the football course. He studied Michigan, winner of 10, loser of none, scorer of 501 points to zero for the opposition. Georgetown and the Carlisle Indians were Eastern prospects. California was unbeaten on the West Coast, and Stanford had suffered only a 2-0 loss to Cal. But even as late as December, 1901, there seemed no possibility of a 1902 game. The $3,500 guarantee was too large a roadblock.

But Fielding (Hurry Up) Yost, the Michigan coach, had a thirst for revenge. A year before, Stanford had fired him because of a new graduate-coach-only rule adopted by Western colleges. He believed the rule had been passed because other colleges were jealous of his success.

Yost issued a challenge to the University of California. He plainly wanted to bring his Michigan powerhouse back to the scene of the crime, the West Coast, and trounce a coast team. California backed off but Stanford rose to the bait.

Some 8,000 saw Michigan annihilate Stanford 49-0 on January 1, 1902, as the grandfather of the bowl games was born. The Tournament of Roses realized a profit of nearly $4,000 after the guarantee was paid.

But all was not rosy. The game itself had been such a rout that after 27 minutes of the second half Stanford had asked that it be stopped. Coast fans left the stadium with an acid taste in their mouths.

The second Rose Bowl game would not be played until 14 years later. During the interval the tournament ran Roman chariot races as its principal athletic event. Amateur drivers nearly killed each other. Professional drivers took over—and the cry of "fix" tainted the races. So the committee turned again to football, this time bringing Brown from the East to play Washington State in the 1916 game.

Washington State arrived a week early, and the players acted as extras in the filming of a football movie. They earned $100 each, pooled their resources, and bet they would whip favored Brown. They collected. The Cougars won 14-0 in a quagmire brought on by snow a couple of days before. There has been a Rose Bowl game ever since.

Playing for Brown at right guard was a Tennessee Scot named Wallace Wade. He would remember that trip to the Rose Bowl.

Wallace Wade was stern, no-nonsense coach.

Jack Langhorne pulverized opposing linemen.

He would return three times as head coach at Alabama and twice as head coach at Duke. His 1925 Bama team would be the first Southern club ever to play in the Rose Bowl.

Wade set out on a coaching career at Fitzgerald-Clarke, a prep school at Tullahoma, Tennessee, and his knack for winning attracted the attention of Dan McGugin at Vanderbilt. For two seasons he produced linemen for Vandy as the Commodores won 16 and lost 2.

Wade clearly was ready for a big-time head coaching job.

Alabama was faced with replacing popular Xen Scott. Alabama tried to get Dan McGugin. McGugin recommended Wade, and Wade accepted the job of head coach.

Wade was following a well-liked, easy-going little man who had given Alabama its greatest moment with the 1922 victory over Pennsylvania. But it was a different approach to football that Wallace Wade brought to Tuscaloosa. "Nobody ever got back-slapped into winning anything," he said. Wade's players feared him. Years later, after he left Alabama for Duke, he was driving some of his backs to a game. Wade stopped at an intersection, unaware that the car was on the edge of a ditch. The players tried to persuade each other to tell him, but none dared. When he attempted to drive away, the car turned over on its side and they had to hitchhike to the game.

Wade's iron discipline impressed players, fans and newsmen. "The spirit of Wallace Wade is already an institution around the Crimson stronghold," the *Birmingham News'* Howard Pill wrote before Wade's first team, the 1923 club, ever played a game.

"There has been a change in the football routine in Crimson town," the paper continued. "Xen Scott, fine little tutor that he was, was more or less of the easy going school. Long practices were not the rule under his regime. Firm, yes, but in the milder sense of the word. But Wade is different. And the warriors who were in harness under Scott were but one day finding this out.

"The writer strolled out to Denny Field in the early afternoon just to see if there were any changes since the last trip. 'Too early yet,' ran our thoughts, 'for the football boys.' It was not yet 2:30.

"But instead of just a football field and bleachers, he found almost the entire squad ready on the practice grounds. The coaches were not out yet and didn't show up for almost half an hour. But the Crimson jerseyed lads were hard at it, nevertheless."

Zipp Newman expected no miracles of Alabama's new coach. He wrote in a preseason prospectus article: "Alabama's football prospects for 1923 are only fair at the best way of looking at a situation brought on through the loss of ten letter men, including such outstanding stars as Stumpy Bartlett, Bull Wesley, Shorty Cooper, Jack Hovater and Tom Newton.

"Only two regular linemen will be in their places when the Crimson Tide starts meeting the stern competition ahead, leaving five positions to be filled. The chances are that this year's backfield will be better balanced than last, although there is no one to take the place of Stumpy Bartlett. Coach Wade's lot is a hard one. . ."

Alabama, he summed up, was large but inexperienced. The Tide would have to learn fundamentals.

But if Scott's 1922 team could beat Pennsylvania, anything could happen, Tide fans reasoned in 1923. They were optimistic. Perhaps it was not difficult to be optimistic in a time when Cruse-Crawford Manufacturing Company in Bessemer would sell you a car for $695, when Buster Keaton at the Bijou and Harold Lloyd at the Rialto made Birminghamians laugh, and when a fellow named Casey Stengel heroed the third game of the World Series with a home run that gave the Giants a 1-0 victory over the Yankees.

Alabama opened against little Union. The Tide was a two-touchdown favorite. Alabama scored twice in the final quarter and won 12-0. Pooley Hubert ran for one touchdown, and Ben Hudson caught a pass for another in the final 15 seconds. As expected, Alabama looked ragged, but Alabama won.

Six men who had never played in a varsity game were in the starting lineup. Only two Tiders who got in the game, Al Clemens and Jack Langhorne, had more than one year's experience.

Ole Miss was the first Southern Conference opponent. Alabama slaughtered the Rebels 55-0, and a sophomore named Johnny Mack Brown, who one day would go to the Rose Bowl and stay to make cowboy movies, scored his first Tide touchdown.

But patsy time was over. Syracuse, an Eastern power that had lost only 10 games in six years, was next up. The Tide, bolstered by memories of 1922's trip north to beat Penn, began the 1,800-mile trip to Syracuse by Southern and New York Central railways. A party of 30 made the trip, stopping off in Cincinnati so the team could practice on the University of Cincinnati field. Twenty Crimson blankets were packed to ward off the New York cold.

Harry Robertson, a Syracuse assistant who had scouted the

Tide-Ole Miss game, warned, "Those who figure the South hasn't got much are dead wrong. Those boys are loaded for Syracuse just as they were loaded for Pennsylvania last year and just as Centre College was loaded for Harvard the year before.

"Coach Wade, Brown University's player of the old days, is probably the most capable mentor in the South and one of the best in the country. He sticks pretty closely to the old-time plays. But he injects into them an effectiveness that is new—and dangerous."

There would be no Pennsylvania miracle here, though. Syracuse drubbed the young Tide 23-0. Wade often said he learned more football on that afternoon than on any other.

Alabama escaped with a 7-0 win over an underdog Sewanee team the next week. The Tide scored in the final two minutes after Johnny Mack Brown intercepted a pass. Pooley Hubert, the signal-calling fullback, led the 48-yard scoring drive.

The game marked a change in the Alabama-Sewanee series. The Mountain Tigers, scourge of the early days of Southern football, would never beat Alabama again. The Tide had won only five of 18 games against Sewanee until October 20, 1923. But now it would go on to win 12 in a row before they stopped playing for good in 1938, Alabama taking the road of a big-time power, Sewanee the path of de-emphasis.

Spring Hill was a 59-0 pushover, but Alabama and Georgia Tech played a weird scoreless tie in Atlanta the next week. In a driving rain, Tech made 18 first downs to none for Alabama. The Tide never got past its own 27-yard line.

Grant Gillis's punting saved Alabama. Five times he kicked from behind or near his goal. Each snap by center Shorty Propst was perfect, and Gillis averaged 40 yards on 16 punts. Five times Alabama stopped Tech inside its 20, once on the two. Clemens, Bill Baty, Pete Camp, and Bruce Jones led the Tide defense.

Homecoming was happy with a 16-8 victory over Kentucky, then LSU fell 30-3 with Ben Compton recovering a fumble and Tom Newton going 40 yards with an interception for Alabama's first two touchdowns. The Tide could do nothing wrong as Gillis and Propst led a 36-0 rout of Georgia.

Florida was the final opponent. Alabama supporters got the idea their team could not lose to the Gators. After all, while the

Tide had been working Georgia over, Florida had been getting itself tied by Mississippi A&M.

Champ Pickens, who later would found Montgomery's Blue-Gray Game, was Alabama's publicity man. He conceived an idea to create interest in the game. He would produce a composite picture of a real alligator being attacked by little Crimson Tide football players. The poster would draw fans to Rickwood Field.

"Where are you going to get an alligator?" Pickens' friends asked. "Oh, there are plenty of alligators around Birmingham," he supposed.

Pickens approached a photographer with the command, "Find an alligator and bring me a picture." The photographer had no idea where to find an alligator. Pickens handed him $20 and said, "See if this helps your memory. Surely you have seen an alligator somewhere in Birmingham."

The zoo had no alligator. There was no large picture of an alligator in the public library that could be copied. Pickens fed the photographer another 20 bucks, and he telephoned all of Birmingham's taxidermists. None had a gator.

Someone recalled a guy named Doc Bates owned some stuffed animals. Sure enough, he had an alligator. The photographer, being extra thorough, took snapshots, long time exposures, and flashlight exposures of the only alligator in Birmingham.

By now the game was only two days away. Pickens shelled out another $20, and the photographer brought in help to complete the complicated paste-up process. In 24 hours Pickens had his posters.

The picture appeared in the newspapers, tiny Crimsons swarming over the hapless alligator. Florida's coach gave each of his players a newspaper to ponder the picture.

The next day, while heavy rains melted his tacked-up posters, Champ Pickens, $60 poorer, watched Florida upset Alabama 16-6 in flooded Rickwood.

It was a disappointing finish, but the record had been seven wins, two losses, and a tie for the green-as-grass Tide. It served as a warning that Wallace Wade was bad news.

Except For Centre

Wallace Wade's 1924 club would not slip up on anyone. Everyone knew this would be a Tide to dread. The young, inexperienced men of 1923 were veterans in 1924, and they knew what winning was about.

The newspapers that had been unimpressed before the first kickoff of 1923 were hailing the 1924 Tide as a sure power. "Over in Tuscaloosa, students and alumni are feeling comfortable. They view prospects for the season through a rosy haze," International News Service's wires chattered.

"Nothing but an unbroken string of victories is expected by them and Alabama's chances of coming through the season undefeated never were better than this year. Tuscaloosa is all prepared to celebrate.

"There is an excellent excuse for the Capstone crowd to feel high-spirited. From that excellent eleven that Wallace Wade turned out in his first year at the Crimson stronghold, only two important cogs are gone. Those missing brothers are Al Clemens and Tom Newton, the two varsity ends."

But Alabama had to share wire time with this revolutionary development out of Baltimore:

"Something new in football this year—Johns Hopkins University has installed an up-to-date electric laundry. The players won't come breezing out of the dressing rooms each afternoon smelling like a passing stock train. They'll come out with freshly laundered moleskins and jersies.

"Hopkins always has had some sort of laundry but it was not

so up-to-date that daily washing could be had. The players had clean uniforms about once a week. Now they'll get 'em every day."

But clean or dirty, the Tide was being anticipated by its followers. None was more excited about the prospect than Dr. Mike Denny, the sports-loving president of the school. "You know, I would like to coach a football team or manage a baseball club when I finish as a university president," Dr. Denny remarked one afternoon while watching the 1924 team prepare for its opener. "Athletics have always appealed to me and I would just like to manage one baseball club."

Alabama scored six touchdowns in the first half and killed Union 55-0. Johnny Mack Brown made three, Dave Rosenfeld two, Grant Gillis, Pooley Hubert, and Andy Cohen one each in a display of backfield depth that the predictors had foreseen in their columns.

Furman fell 20-0, and Hubert scored three touchdowns in a 55-0 slaughter of Mississippi College. Sewanee was tougher but still lost 14-0 after Rosenfeld broke the ice with a 56-yard touchdown. Center Shorty Propst, guard William Buckler, and tackle Jack Langhorne led the line work that shut out the Mountain Tigers.

Georgia Tech was favored to trim the Tide in Atlanta, and a full house came to see it done. Bill Alexander had succeeded John Heisman as Tech's coach in 1920, and the Yellow Jackets had not lost to a Southern team since he had arrived.

Bama won 14-0. Gillis threw a 37-yard touchdown pass to Brown in the first period. Rosenfeld ran 44 yards to the Tech eight in the fourth, then scored three plays later. Tech's most serious threat came in the third period when the Jackets had fourth and one at the Tide six. Pete Camp stopped the run, and the ball went over. Brown gained 135 yards in 10 carries. Hubert starred as a blocker and linebacker, and Hulet Whitaker was tough at defensive end and offensive back.

Ole Miss was a 61-0 victim with Brown running 80 yards to score on the first play and Cohen going 75 for a TD in the fourth quarter.

The Tide was rolling. Kentucky fell victim 42-7 at homecoming in Tuscaloosa. Wade had spent much of the summer devising a passing attack, and it was evident on one drive.

Hubert threw 22 yards to Rosenfeld, then Gillis passed 10 to Hubert, and finally to Herschel Caldwell for a touchdown. But a pass backfired for Kentucky's only score, a Wildcat back returning a Gillis throw 95 yards. Rosenfeld brought Tide fans to their feet with a 76-yard touchdown, though.

Centre was the next opponent. The site was Birmingham, Alabama's "other home." Centre and Kentucky had tied. Alabama had beaten Kentucky 35 points. Years later, Paul Bryant would say it almost as a ritual: "Somewhere in the country, every week, somebody gets beat who can't lose."

It happened to Alabama this week, just as it would happen to a 1969 Bryant Tide that could not solve Vanderbilt.

The dream backfield was helpless against Centre. Hubert was dropped in his tracks. Brown and Rosenfeld were bottled up. Centre made 10 first downs to Alabama's one in the first half. The Colonels mixed passing and running and scored on a 70-yard drive in the second period. Brown lost 20 yards in two plays back to his seven in the third. After a punt, Centre kicked a field goal. The Colonels scored on a pass in the fourth. Alabama never moved the ball past Centre's 48-yard line, and the Colonels, who used only 12 men, won 17-0.

Centre may have altered history with that victory. Perhaps the 1924 Tide would have been the first Southern team to play in the Rose Bowl, instead of the 1925 Crimsons, if the Colonels had not been a perfect club that day.

Tide fans eyed the next game soberly. Georgia had won seven and lost only one, Yale slipping in by one point. The Bulldogs had given up only 14 points. Six of the victims had been shut out. With the embarrassing afternoon against Centre already in the books and another powerhouse upcoming, was Alabama's season about to crumble?

It was not. This time the lightning would strike the Bulldogs. Big Ben Compton boomed three-point placekicks of 33 and 35 yards in the first period, and the Tide went on to a 33-0 rout of the Athenians. Passing worked for Alabama and against Georgia. Hubert threw to Caldwell and to Ben Hudson for scores. Brown returned an interception 65 yards for seven points. Hubert intercepted a pass and set up a touchdown that he scored himself.

The season of 1924 was over. Alabama had won the

championship of the South. It was not a perfect season, but 1925 would be. Unless you are a stickler for technicalities and count the 1897 squad that went 1-0, Alabama was about to produce its first unbeaten team.

Undefeated, Untied

Southern football was growing up. No longer could the East, Midwest, and Pacific Coast smile patronizingly at teams from the South. The fact would be forcefully demonstrated on January 1, 1926, when the first Southern team to play in the Rose Bowl would beat the University of Washington 20-19. That Alabama club's coach, Wallace Wade, discussed the emergence of Rebel football in an article that appeared in the *Birmingham News* between the end of the regular season and the trip to Pasadena:

"Sectionalism in football is rapidly disappearing, due to the interchange of coaching ideas. Coaching schools are being held and attended by coaches in all parts of the country. Coaches are coming into the South from other sections; also coaches are carefully studying the football books put out by the leading coaches of the West and East.

"More men are devoting their entire time the year round to the study of football. This and many other conditions are putting the standard of football of the South on a plane with that in other sections. In spite of these conditions, Southern football continues to retain some distinctive characteristics. This fact must be recognized from the fact that few coaches who have come to Southern universities from the West or East have been successful until they have become familiar with conditions by a year or two of experience in this section.

"There is more sentiment in Southern football; the coaches appeal to the affections of the players. There is less driving and

Grant Gillis could boot 'em.

more loyal conscientious effort. The Southern coach holds a higher position in the hearts of his players and of the entire student body than does the coach of the North. Instead of being called by the affectionate term of 'Coach,' as the Southern coach is, the Northern coach is often called by his first name and is too often treated with very little respect. The Southern players are more easily 'keyed up' and also become stale more easily.

"Southern football has also retained certain technical characteristics. The forward pass has come to be used as a scoring weapon in the South while in the East, particularly, it is still largely used as a threat to make the running attack more effective. The North has come to use the long scoring pass and the dangerous pass into flat territory with deadly effect. Not so many years ago, passes were only employed when the running attack had failed. Now all good teams in this section are using the pass on first down and at times least to be expected. This change in tactics has become so effective that it is hard to complete a pass after the running attack has failed. Also, so few are completed and so many intercepted that coaches have concluded that they can only gamble with a pass which, if successful, will score or place one in a scoring position. This leads to the thought that the greatest improvement made in Southern football during the past few years has been in defense.

"Several years ago Southern teams were noted for their brilliant offenses. The Golden Tornado of Georgia Tech was a most striking example of this. During the past few years the defense has come into its own. One of the first outstanding defensive teams was the Vanderbilt team of 1922. This team held the powerful Michigan team scoreless and had only one touchdown scored on it by Southern teams. During the past two years Georgia Tech has been one of the hardest teams in the country to score on. Mike Donahue of Auburn and Louisiana State has always turned out teams strong on the defense.

"Increased interest in football throughout the South has helped to make it compare more favorably with that of other sections. Seating capacities are being increased and playing fields made better. Many times during the past season crowds ranging from 15,000 to 30,000 collected together. The newspapers are doing a great work to increase interest in football by giving much space to the accounts of games, written by trained experts and by reproducing important plays for their readers with action pictures."

Such was the status of Southern football by 1925, and its leading practitioner was Wallace Wade's Crimson Tide. Alabama could indeed pass and Alabama could indeed play defense. Only one team scored on the Tide during the regular season, and that one, Birmingham-Southern, got beat 50-7.

Alabama began practice in 1925 with enough fine backs to stock three teams. Johnny Mack Brown, Pooley Hubert, and Grant Gillis had made all-Southern Conference, Gillis in 1923 and Brown and Hubert in 1924.

"Alabama will have the greatest collection of smart running backs in the South. . .," Zipp Newman wrote. "Alabama will have the class of the Southern backfields with Mack Brown, brilliant broken field runner; 'Pooley' Hubert, one of the greatest all-around backs in America; Grant Gillis, a cool and steady punter; Red Barnes, punter and broken field runner; Jimmy Johnston, a line backer; and 'Red' Pepper, a 200-pound fullback; and 'Little Dave' Rosenfeld, Herschel Caldwell, and Red Brown, the flashy brother of Mack; and Harry Holder, Morrison, and Dick Hammer. Here is a collection of backs that do everything backs are supposed to do and do it well. Wade could shut his eyes and pick a good combination of backs from this collection."

Guard Bill Buckler had been an all-Southern Conference selection the year before. Guard Bruce Jones was elected captain. Tackle Pete Camp was expected to have his best year. End Ben Hudson had helped wreck Georgia in 1924. The biggest problem was replacing Shorty Propst as center. Propst, incidentally, had joined the staff as an assistant coach. Five good linemen were missing, but everyone knew Alabama had the potential to corral the undefeated record that barely escaped it the year before.

Alabama rolled over Union 53-0 and Birmingham-Southern 50-7 in its first two games. LSU was expected to provide strenuous opposition but fell 42-0. Hubert was an accurate passer in this game. His 23-yarder to Wu Winslett set up the first touchdown, and he completed several other important throws.

Sewanee, the old nemesis that was destined to never beat

another Tide, came to Birmingham. Alabama won 27-0. Winslett passed 28 yards to Emile (Red, Lovely) Barnes to set up the first touchdown. Barnes ran 29 to set up the second. Gillis's 35-yard pass to Caldwell got six points, and a 35-yarder from Hubert to Winslett carried to the two before Pooley scored. Alabama clearly was a team that could throw the forward pass.

Undefeated Alabama met undefeated Georgia Tech before 20,000 fans on a wet field in Atlanta. Alabama won 7-0, and the touchdown play was a marvel of team efficiency. Tech punted to Johnny Mack Brown on the Tide 45. Hubert was protecting Brown, and both Tech ends made for the cowboy star to be. Pooley cut them both down with one motion. Brown headed for the sidelines, and one by one Alabamians began blocking the Golden Tornadoes to the ground. Finally, only one man stood between Brown and a touchdown. Buckler put him on the turf, and Brown scored.

Alabama knocked down all 11 Georgia Tech defenders—and the referee—on the play.

Hubert's game was called the best of his career. He was hailed as the finest defensive back ever to show at Grant Field. Gordon (Sherlock) Holmes, who had capably replaced Propst at center, played 60 minutes though painfully injured in the opening moments.

Mississippi A&M was surprisingly tough in the rain the next week. Alabama won 6-0. Hubert passed to Winslett for the touchdown.

Kentucky fell 31-0 despite the heroic efforts of colorfully named Cave Man King, who spent the afternoon knocking down Tide inteference. Trouble was, Brown was busy running 79 yards and Barnes 75 yards for touchdowns, mentally thumbing their noses at Cave Man all the way.

Florida went down 34-0. Hubert threw touchdown passes to Brown and to Barnes.

Alabama finished an undefeated season with a 27-0 win over Georgia. Razzle dazzle scored the first touchdown with Hubert handing to Winslett who passed for a 50-yard touchdown to Gillis. Gillis later made 22 yards on a triple pass to Georgia's one, and Hubert scored.

Alabama and Tulane were the only undefeated squads in the

sprawling 22-team Southern Conference. The writers voted Alabama champion. Hubert was voted the conference's most valuable player, and International News Service hailed him as the best back in the South in 10 years.

The 1925 team was called Alabama's greatest ever. Newspapers ran pictures of the seniors, noting their playing days were over. The Rose Bowl (the only bowl) was 2,800 miles away, and no one believed the Tide would be going. The annual banquet honored "the seven members who have finished their careers at the Capstone institution."

On the same page of the *Birmingham News* with the story of the banquet, Zipp Newman mentioned in his column: "While a semi-official report says that Colgate will be invited to the Tournament of Roses as Washington's opponent on New Year's Day, it is a lead pipe cinch that the coast has heard of Alabama. All of the Coast papers from Seattle to San Diego have been full of copy about Alabama's great undefeated and untied eleven.

"The names of Hubert and Mack Brown are just as well-known on the coast as the names of Nevers and Wilson are known in Dixie. Alabama has received plenty of publicity throughout the nation and were she an Eastern eleven, would have been the first invited. However, being a Southern eleven she is handicapped as the Coast wants an Eastern team."

Meanwhile, Coach Andy Smith, whose California team had lost to Washington 7-0, was calling the Huskies "one of the greatest football aggregations that I have ever seen, and I believe they are as strong as any team in the country today." Only a tie with Nebraska marred Washington's record, and it was a natural choice to represent the Coast in the Rose Bowl game.

Things began to happen. A wire story reported: "For awhile it looked as though Colgate would go, but objections to making the trip appear to have developed among parties of influence among the alumni." The story said Dartmouth and Princeton were "approached" and declined to consider the transcontinental trip. "As the situation now stands, it would look as though the choice lies between Tulane and Alabama."

Wade said the Pasadena committee did not know its own mind, and that it was tentatively peddling the proposition among various institutions. Alabama said it would not be interested in any invitation.

Jack Benefield, the Tournament of Roses spokesman, evidently changed some Capstone minds. He issued an official invitation, and Alabama accepted. Benefield met with Tide brass in Birmingham.

"This is the first official invitation that has been offered by anyone," Benefield said. "I did take up the matter with Colgate authorities but their request for time to consider was out of the question. Tulane, nor any other college, has not been offered an invitation, as only feelers have been sent out.

"The inquiries were made only to find out if they would play in the classic should they be invited to do so."

Alabama was soothed, but the Rose Bowl's problems were not over. Only a small majority of Washington players voted to play in Pasadena. With such lukewarm interest among the participants, the school's board of control said Washington would not be there.

Finally, Tournament of Roses officials were relieved to read this newspaper story: "In light of an urgent request from the Pacific Coast Conference authorities, the Northwest Huskies agreed to reverse their decision and battle in the classic game of the year on January 1."

At last, the Rose Bowl had a game. And what a game it would turn out to be.

Rose Bowl Bound

If Alabama was eager to remove the cloak of inferiority that shrouded Southern football in the minds of many of the nation's fans, Washington was equally determined to demonstrate the superiority of the Western brand.

As Bama set to work preparing for the Huskies, a wire story reported that big George Wilson, Washington's all-American back, had turned down the incredible sum of $3,000 to turn professional.

"He passed up the handsome offer in order to test his line crashing power against the pride of the South," the story explained.

The first Alabamians to leave for the coast were two students in a flivver with an awning for a top. The car was loaded down with groceries and suitcases. Whether they ever made it is lost in antiquity.

The game was so late in being made that neither team knew much about the other. "Just plain old everyday football has been indulged in due to the utter ignorance of Washington's formations and plays. A jamb-up defense has been the main feature of development and more time has been spent on this department than any other," a *Birmingham News* story on Tuscaloosa practice sessions said.

Meanwhile, Wallace Wade signed a five-year contract, ending rumors that he would leave Alabama. His salary was not announced, but newspapers reported that one school had offered him $15,000 a year, another $10,000 a year, and that he could have gone to Oregon or to Washington State.

Round trip fare for the 2,800-mile train trip would be $250, it was announced. "This makes it a bit difficult for students, but the old grad element has fallen for the trip with fervor," the *Atlanta Georgian's* Ed Danforth reported.

Dr. Mike Denny suggested that the players take their books and devote off moments to study since mid-term exams were near.

The train left Tuscaloosa on December 19 and arrived in Pasadena December 24. Twenty-two players made the trip: Bruce Jones, Lovely Barnes, Herschel Caldwell, Pooley Hubert, William Buckler, Pete Camp, Claude Perry, Ben Enis, Fred Pickhard, Sherlock Holmes, Leslie Payne, James Bowdoin, James McDonald, H. S. Dismukes, Grant Gillis, Johnny Mack Brown, Tolbert Brown, James Johnston, Billy Morrison, Dave Rosenfeld, Ben Hudson, and Hoyt Winslett.

Dr. Denny waxed eloquent as the Tide departed: "Our team will strive to represent worthily our great commonwealth and our great section. We recognize the difficulties and the handicaps of a long trip to the distant region in which we shall be strangers both to the climate and to the people. We recognize we shall meet the champions of the Pacific Coast, one of the greatest teams of the country. . . The team as a whole is considered one of the most powerful America has produced in the history of football. Such is the collosal task to which our boys have set their hands. . .

"Win or lose, this trip means more widespread and sustained publicity for Alabama than any recent event in the history of the state."

The team rolled across the nation and marveled at eating six straight meals in six different states. But the Tiders did not let scenery shove the primary objective into corners of their minds. "There isn't a player on the train who can't tell you the name, weight, disposition and a few other little things about every player eligible on the Washington team," Zipp Newman reported in the *Birmingham News.*

The Tide saw the Grand Canyon and in Williams, Arizona, had its only workout of the trip. The players took off their coats and shirts, rolled up their trousers, and ran plays. A local high school coach arranged transportation to his gymnasium so they could shower. Champ Pickens, the publicity man, lost a game of marbles with two Mexican kids during the practice session.

Finally the journey ended on Christmas Eve. Pasadena citizens met the train, and Johnny Mack Brown and Pooley Hubert were the two players they wanted pointed out to them.

"Hubert and Mack Brown will have enough experience posing for the cameramen to enter the movies after their stay here," Zipp Newman wrote prophetically. Little did he know that Brown, indeed, would become one of the great heroes of the

Tide's 1925 Squad—First Southern Team In Rose Bowl.

Front row: Dave Rosenfeld, Wu Winslett, Grant Gillis, Capt. Bruce Jones, Emil Barnes, Ben Enis, Red Brown. Second row: James McDonald, Bill Morrison, Claude Perry, Freddie Pickhard, Bill Buckler, Ben Hudson, James Bowdoin. Third row: Pooley Hubert, Melvin Vines, Johnny Mack Brown, Leslie Payne, Raymond Pepper, Gordon Holmes, Pete Camp, Herschel Caldwell, Roy Dismukes.

"Saturday cowboy movie."

A special alumni train followed the players' choo-choo. Bob McDavid, president of the Birmingham alumni association, startled some of the Pullman passengers when he awoke from a dream hollering, "Hooray for Johnny Mack!"

Wade sent his troops onto the practice field Christmas Day while Washington took an off-day. The no-nonsense Tide coach wanted to make up for as much missed practice time as possible.

Tide players visited United and Warner studios, the beaches, and the Los Angeles district. They had their pictures made with Bebe Daniels who was starring in "Brewster's Millions." Zipp Newman reported that two months would be required to fill all the invitations the players had received.

Wade stopped the fun. "In order to get the right mental attitude, no more entertainment will be indulged in after Monday (December 28)," he said. The players were assigned a private dining room and were not allowed to spend much time in the hotel lobby.

"Coaches Wade and Bagshaw (Enoch, of Washington) met with the officials Thursday. Wade has been assured that Washington will not get away with any rough stuff as was alleged when the Huskies played California and Stanford," the *Birmingham News* reported.

The bookies made Washington a 2-1 favorite, or they would give Alabama and 10 points. But Stanford Coach Pop Warner watched the Tide work out and said Bama looked good to him and he was not at all sure Washington would win. By kickoff time the game was rated about even.

A Seattle writer still could not believe Southern football. "Washington figures to win from Alabama by two touchdowns...," he wrote. "... The Purple Tornado will have all its steam up to blow the Tide back across the continent as a pale pink stream."

Washington, he said, was coming to Pasadena to "uphold the belief of the West—that Pacific Coast football has no superior in America."

The big day began on a bizarre note when a grandstand fell, and 200 persons watching the Tournament of Roses parade were injured.

Shortly after the kickoff, Alabama appeared headed for a fall, too. The Tide drove to the Washington 15, but Wilson intercepted a Winslett pass and returned to the Bama 47 and the Huskies were away. They smashed downfield to the Tide three, and Patton scored. Guttormsen missed the PAT attempt.

In the second period Wilson carried 36 yards to the Bama 20, and the Crimsons were wishing Washington's great back had taken that $3,000 to turn pro a month before. Wilson passed to Cole for a 20-yard touchdown. Guttormsen's dropkick hit the crossbar, but Washington appeared comfortably ahead by 12-0. Some West Coast fans among the 45,000 present were politely applauding the Crimsons, feeling their brand of ball was safe against the Southerners.

Bama bounced back and got caught by the halftime whistle. Johnny Mack Brown returned a punt 39 yards, and Hubert passed to Brown who was tackled on the Washington 22 as the half ended with the Huskies owning a dozen points and the Tide none.

Johnny Mack Brown received national Football Hall of Fame recognition in 1957. Left to right: Bruce Jones, captain of 1926 Rose Bowl team; Brown; Tide All-American Hoyt Winslett; Brown's son Pat, then a cadet at Pensacola.

93

Bama was not done yet. The Crimsons appeared a different team after intermission. Washington punted, and on the first play Hubert exploded for 27 yards. He carried four more times in succession and scored from the one. Buckler converted, and Alabama was back in the game.

Alabama would score all of its 20 points in the third period. In fact, the Tide made its total in seven minutes. Washington fans would carefully point out that their stupendous back, George Wilson, was out of the game for 22 minutes with injuries and that it was during his inactivity that Bama scored.

Hubert, a brilliant field general on this day, spotted Washington's secondary playing tight and called for a pass. Gillis and Johnny Mack Brown teamed on a 63-yard touchdown throw. "All I had to do was sidestep one man and I was across," said Brown, who caught the ball at the 25. Buckler converted the score to Bama 14, Washington 12.

A few plays later Washington fumbled. Ben Enis recovered on the Huskies' 33. On first down Hubert told Johnny Mack Brown to run as fast as he could for the goal. "When I reached the three, I looked," Brown said. "Sure enough, the ball was coming down over my shoulder. I took it in stride, used my stiff arm on one man and went over carrying somebody. The place was really in an uproar." Buckler missed the PAT.

Bama got to the Washington 12 in the final period but lost the ball on downs. Washington drove it upfield, and Wilson passed to Guttormsen for a 30-yard touchdown. Cook drop-kicked the goal and it was 20-19.

After an exchange of interceptions the game ended with the Tide on Washington's 34.

Southern football, at last, had earned its place in the sun. The *Los Angeles Evening Herald* said it best: "Tuscaloosa, Alabama, which Western fans didn't know was on the map, is the abiding place of the Pacific Coast football championship today."

Time Out: Pooley Hubert

If the Southern Railway had run to Athens, Georgia, Pooley Hubert might never have played for the University of Alabama.

"I had a scholarship to Princeton, but I got up there too late," Hubert retraced the path that led him from Meridian, Mississippi, to Tuscaloosa. "I went to Princeton to summer school to get ready for the entrance exams, but I didn't have enough time.

"Then I decided I'd try to go South. I stopped off at Virginia for a couple of weeks but I didn't especially like it. I went to Georgia Tech and stayed around two or three days but I was too late and they didn't let freshmen play.

"Coach Alexander recommended I go to the University of Georgia. I asked him if the Southern Railway went to Athens and he said no. So I asked him what was the next school on the Southern and he said Alabama."

At 71, Allison Thomas Stanislaus Hubert lives in Waynesboro, Georgia. He runs a peach-packing shed and has a couple thousand peach trees. Incredibly, he finds time to coach a high school football team.

"I've coached Edmund Burke Academy, a little private school here in Waynesboro, the last couple of years," Hubert said. "They didn't have a regular coach and didn't have enough money to pay anybody so they asked me to coach and I said I would. We did all right last year against the smaller schools."

Hubert recalls Wallace Wade as most do. "He was a good disciplinarian and fundamentalist. I always got along with him

95

A pair of great backs: Johnny Mack Brown and Pooley Hubert.

fine. Coach Scott wasn't near the coach that Coach Wade was. He was offense-minded more than anything else and training didn't mean too much to him.

"He (Scott) suffered terribly his last season. We all knew something was wrong with his throat but we didn't know how serious it was."

Hubert remembers the 1925 team's long train trip to the Rose Bowl as "right pleasant. Country boys going to the Grand Canyon made quite an impression.

"It was quite a surprise that we even had the opportunity to go. We had had some indication that we might get to, but we were afraid to even hope.

"But coming back home, there were several places the train stopped and people came down to the station to see the team that had played in the Rose Bowl.

"Wade felt that we were representing a particular section in that game, the South. He told us it would mean great honor and prestige to conduct ourselves well.

"We had a lot of confidence in ourselves. We didn't even think about losing that game."

Alabama fell behind 12-0 at the half before beating Washington 20-19. "The reason for it was that Washington had two great linebackers and they had knocked Ernie Nevers out of the game twice when they played Stanford. Wade wanted me to be able to stay in there because I was the quarterback, so he told me not to run the ball in the first half.

"Well, we got behind and he said it didn't make any difference then if I ran it. I started running and it made a difference in the result of the game. I carried five straight times in our first touchdown drive."

Alabama used single wing, spread, and short punt formations. Wade moved his backs around like checkers. "I played fullback, blocking back and tailback," Hubert explained. "Gillis played wingback and tailback. Brown played wingback and tailback and Barnes played blocking back and fullback.

"Gillis could throw well. Brown couldn't pass at all. Brown was a good pass receiver and also a good running back. We'd use the spread and put Brown at tailback to run."

Hubert feels accurate reading of Washington's defenses eventually won the game for Alabama. "When they went to a six-man line, we'd run. When they went to a seven-man line, we'd throw. We had 'em all screwed up."

Hubert believes that under certain circumstances the teams of his day would battle today's squads evenly. "They are so much bigger and faster and stronger today, but if you could limit the number of people on the teams and you had to play both ways, there wouldn't be much difference.

"A lot of these big boys today wouldn't have the energy to play a full game. We had about 30 men on our squad ordinarily but only 12 or 15 ever played in a tough game. I always played 60 minutes. I weighed 191 which was pretty big for a linebacker then, but Washington weighed 212 and 225. They were the biggest we had ever played."

Hubert came to Alabama as a tackle. "Hank Crisp switched me. I asked him to. I had never played in the backfield but I thought I could. The first full game I ever played back there was in 1922 against Pennsylvania."

Hubert prided himself on his jarring tackles from the linebacker slot. "I might still hold the record at Georgia Tech," he said. "I read where I made 23 tackles over there. I guess my best game was either the Rose Bowl or that game against Tech. I had a good day against LSU one time. I think I scored five touchdowns."

Hubert turned pro after his college career ended with the Rose Bowl January 1, 1926. He played with Ironton, Ohio; Ashland, Kentucky; and the New York Yankees. The Yankees lined up with Red Grange at tailback and Hubert at fullback.

"I called the signals for him," Hubert said. "Grange was very sober and dedicated. His fame never went to his head. In fact, he was a little bit modest.

"We had some kind of regular league session but we also toured from Canada to California one year with George Wilson's Washington Wildcats. Wilson had played against Alabama in the Rose Bowl. We played in Toronto, Atlanta, Birmingham, Dallas, San Antonio and Los Angeles and won them all except one."

The best football players he has ever seen? Yankee teammates Grange and Eddie Tryon, George Wilson, and Johnny Mack Brown.

When his pro career ended, Hubert served as head coach at Mississippi Southern and Virginia Military Institute. Russ Cohen, who had been his coach at Alabama and an assistant on his staff at VMI, lived in Waynesboro. Hubert used to visit him, and they would hunt birds. Finally, Cohen talked Hubert into moving to Waynesboro to raise peaches. There he lives now with his wife, coaching his little high school squad, and occasionally attending a college game.

Wade and Crisp considered Hubert their "coach on the field." "He was the greatest player I ever helped coach in over 40 years," Crisp once said. "There never was a more fierce competitor. He was a born leader and at his very best when the going was tough. He was just as good on defense as offense."

Hubert was the school's second all-American. He is a member of the state Sports Hall of Fame.

Return To Pasadena

National major college football championships are purely mythical since no playoff system exists, but selection of the champion can set neighbor against neighbor.

The Helms Athletic Foundation of Los Angeles began naming a champion in 1889, three years before the University of Albama even had a team.

In 1924 an informal tribunal picked a national champ and awarded the Rissman Trophy. The name was changed to the Knute Rockne Memorial Trophy in 1931.

The Associated Press got into the act in 1936, and United Press followed in 1950. The Football Writers Association of America started giving its Grantland Rice Award in 1954, and the National Football Foundation and Hall of Fame inaugurated their General Douglas MacArthur Trophy in 1959.

Alabama's 1925 team, king of the Rose Bowl, was named winner of the Helms Award. Few thought the Tide had a chance to repeat in 1926. The Southern Conference champions were not even supposed to win that title again.

Graduation had been a great plague, especially in the backfield. Here is how Wallace Wade saw the team before the opener:

"The University of Alabama football team has been defeated by a Southern Conference team only once during the past three years. This record has been made through the good fortune of having a large part of the team remaining intact for three straight years. As a result of these men staying together a long while and a rather intensive spring practice campaign, the Alabama team developed unusual versatility and ability. The outstanding strength of the team lay in good blocking, excellent defensive line strength, accurate forward passing, good open field running and defensive generalship.

"The interesting question is how the 1926 team is going to compare with that of 1925. Through the loss by graduation of three all-Southern backs, Hubert, Brown and Gillis, the men who contributed the generalship, forward passing and open field running, it will become necessary to develop an almost entirely new offense.

"The outstanding defensive line strength was very largely the result of the fine charging and splendid tackling of the four linemen, Buckler, Jones, Camp and Hudson, who have also played their time.

"The men who must make up the offense of the Tide this fall are Barnes, Johnston, Caldwell, and Rosenfeld, all good backs, with the probable help of 'Red' Brown who played end last year. These men should be experienced, shifty and hard-running backs. They will lack weight and power as well as unusual forward passing ability. The linemen returning are Winslett, Pickhard, Perry and Holmes. . .

"Alabama has undoubtedly lost a large part of its football team and has no players as experienced and as skillful with which to replace the losses. The most encouraging aspect of the situation is the fact that a great deal of progress toward rebuilding was made during the Spring practice period.

"The players will . . . take their training seriously and will play the games with as much determination as any team. The indications are that the blocking, tackling, punting and running will be good. On the other hand, the team will be considerably lighter, both in the line and in the backfield. The team work will not be as good. The passing probably will be weaker and it will be most unusual if another field general of Hubert's ability can be developed. The schedule will be harder.

"The prospects are that Alabama will have a good team, probably almost as good as any other team in the South. But the prospects of winning another Southern Conference championship this fall are very slim."

Whereupon, Alabama promptly went out and won its third straight Southern Conference title and its second Helms

Babe Pearce blocked kick in 1927 Rose Bowl.

national crown in a row and returned to the Rose Bowl to tie favored Stanford 7-7.

Alabama ran over Millsaps 54-0 in the opener with Red Brown, Johnny's brother who had been moved from end to the backfield, scoring on runs of 92, 70, and 30 yards.

Wallace Wade met his old boss, Vanderbilt's Dan McGugin. Wade won 19-7. Brown had a 58-yard run that set up a touchdown pass from Hoyt Winslett to Herschel Caldwell. Lovely Barnes ran 21 for another, and Winslett threw a 36-yard scorer to Caldwell.

Mississippi A&M completed 15 passes against Alabama—but the Tide intercepted seven and won 26-7. Barnes ran one back 90 yards for a TD, and Melvin Vines also had an interception touchdown.

Georgia Tech was favored, but Alabama won 21-0. Winslett

ran more with the ball and led the victory. Scouts figured that when he dropped into the backfield from his regular end position, it meant a sure pass since they doubted his running ability. But he ran in this game. Still he completed touchdown passes to Vines and Archie Taylor. Barnes ran a TD.

Alabama edged the Mountain Tigers of Sewanee 2-0 on a blocked punt that rolled out of the end zone in the final minutes.

LSU was a 24-0 victim at homecoming in Tuscaloosa. Winslett and Ben Enis ran for touchdowns with blocked punts. Claude Perry and Fred Pickhard, the tackles, led the shutout.

Alabama held Kentucky to 35 yards rushing and won 14-0. Winslett scored on a couple of short runs.

Florida was a 49-0 victim with Brown scoring four touchdowns, including a 47-yarder.

Only Georgia stood between Alabama and an undefeated season. A close game was anticipated, but the Tide rolled 33-6 with Archie Taylor, Winslett, Barnes, and Jimmy Johnson in on the touchdowning.

Morgan Blake, the *Atlanta Journal* sports editor, poked gentle fun at his Birmingham colleague, Zipp Newman:

"In the past four battles between the football representatives of these two institutions of learning, we have seen Alabama score 129 points while the Bulldogs have scored but six. . . Alabama supporters actually seemed crushed in spirit over the Georgia score. Zipp Newman, Andy Jaffe and other gentlemen of the press box with Alabama leanings sobbed bitterly all the way back to the city as though Georgia had actually won the game.

"'Think of such a record,' sobbed Mr. Jaffe, Alabama alumnus who is a combination sport scribe, football coach and jeweler. 'If Georgia had not scored do you know it would have been four straight years that Alabama had held Tech, Georgia and Sewanee scoreless?'

"The Atlanta sports scribes tried their best to comfort the Alabama boys. We patted Mr. Jaffe on the back and told him that 'Never mind, Alabama will do better next year.' But he refused to be consoled."

Winslett, the passing end, was everybody's all-American in 1926. On the same page announcing Winslett's selection to the

102

Ben Enis' 1926 model helmet offered little protection.

International News Service all-American team was a two-paragraph story that a fellow named Frank Thomas had signed a renewed five-year contract as head coach of the University of Chattanooga.

"This year's Alabama team is probably stronger in the line than last year's, but not quite so strong in the backfield," Wade said at the end of the year. "The 1926 team has been fortunate in having unusual team work.

"The Alabama football team was not in mid-season form when Vanderbilt was met on the second of October. This year's team individually and collectively has improved as much as any other team I have ever coached.

"This improvement has been particularly marked in the play of the line both on offense and defense. The improvement of our backs has not been so apparent on account of the backfield being disorganized because of injuries."

Wade discussed a coach's role in the mental aspect of football: "It is impossible for any coach absolutely to control the mental condition of his entire football squad. All that a coach is to do is to study carefully the reaction of individual members and undertake to mold the morale. It often becomes necessary to replace certain members of the team on account of their mental attitude."

There was no confusion surrounding selection of teams for the 1927 Rose Bowl as there had been a year before. The Tournament of Roses had asked Wade after the Washington game if he would be interested in returning if he had a good team. He said yes. Before the sixth game of the 1926 season, Alabama was invited to the Rose Bowl. Wade pointed out that his team might lose two more games. But before the Georgia game, Alabama agreed to return to Pasadena, subject to Southern Conference approval.

Stanford Coach Pop Warner scouted the Tide against the Bulldogs, and Alabama assistant Shorty Propst saw Stanford beat California. Impressed with Alabama's speed, Warner ordered silk pants for his team, pants that weighed just a pound and a half.

Alabama, the nation's scoring leader for the five-year period just ended, left Tuscaloosa December 21 and arrived in Pasadena Christmas Day. The train carried 135, including 24 players.

The team reached Pasadena in better mental and physical condition than the 1925 squad did, Wade said. "This year the members of the squad were much more careful not to overeat," he said. "Undoubtedly as a result of a shorter time on the train, with less eating and more exercise, the team is nearer playing form." With many of them having been there before, the players felt "free and easier," he said. Wade had scheduled two practice stops to melt off more fat on this trip.

Alabama's great showing of the previous New Year's made the return game most attractive. Tickets were being scalped for $50 a pair, and the Rose Bowl added 4,000 seats. The game would be played before a packed house of 57,417, and gross receipts would be a record $218,047.

Still, the West Coast was having difficulty accepting Southern

football. Ernie Nevers, the former Stanford star, said two touchdowns would be the least possible winning margin for the
Indians. One writer said Stanford "has no parallel in coast
history." Another said the home team "has made a lot of us
believe that no team that ever played could beat it."

"They are trying to scare us all to death before the game,"
Morgan Blake of the *Atlanta Journal* wrote. Blake said he had
never before "run across such an atmosphere of brag and boast.

"Quite a contrast to this attitude is that of Coach Wade and
his men, nothing cocky about Alabama. Plenty of confidence,
but no boasting. Coach Wade, to tell the truth, is delighted that
his team has been such an underdog.

"The Alabama chief is doing everything in his power to lead
the enemy to overconfidence. He is writing articles for local
papers indicating, although not expressly at it, that Alabama is
only working on the defense and will only attempt to hold
down the score. As a matter of fact, Alabama has done nothing
but scrimmage on the offense since the trip started."

Alabama's players grew more determined with each boastful
article. Pickhard watched the Indians practice in their new red
silk pants and said, "I'm going to get me a pair of those pants
for a souvenir."

Stanford's Captain Swan called on Wade to pay his respects
but refused to meet Alabama's players. "Swan will have plenty
of time to get acquainted with us on New Year's Day," Lovely
Barnes muttered.

One who did not share the general Coast feeling of Stanford
superiority was Pop Warner, who must have winced everytime
he read a paper. "The game is a toss up. If I were a betting man
I'd place 10 smackers on Stanford and another 10 on Alabama," he said. Warner, it turned out, had doped the game
correctly.

But Coast fans' smugness appeared justified in the opening
moments of the game. Stanford's George Bogue threw a 36-yard
pass to Alabama's 30 on the first play. The Indians took it to
the 12 but missed a field goal attempt.

Bogue threw a 20-yard touchdown pass to Ed Walker as the
first period ended. It was Walker's first reception of the season.
Bogue converted.

Stanford drove to the Tide 10 in the third period but Bogue

missed a field goal try. Alabama got another break in the quarter when a Stanford receiver, with a clear field ahead, dropped a pass.

Only four minutes remained in the game when Stanford lined up in punt formation. Babe Pearce clawed his way through the line and blocked the kick. Stanford recovered but the ball went over on the Indians' 14.

Jimmy Johnson, who had missed much of the season with a dislocated shoulder, entered the game at halfback for Alabama. Winslett gained three and Johnson seven. Winslett carried to the one. Johnson charged over right guard and into the end zone.

Stanford's players probably still kick themselves for what happened next. Alabama lined up to tie or lose the Rose Bowl game on the extra point. Captain Barnes barked signals. Suddenly, he shouted, "Signals off!"

Stanford's line stood at ease in anticipation of another signal sequence. At the precise moment the Indians relaxed, Sherlock Holmes snapped the ball to Winslett who touched it down. With all the time in the world on his side, Caldwell kicked a perfect point.

Perhaps, as the Coast writer had said, no team that ever played could beat the Indians—but Alabama had just tied them.

Time Out: Wu Winslett

Football players, like women, should never be taken for granted.

"Dadeville was War Eagle country in 1922," Wu Winslett recalled. "They took it for granted I was going to Auburn and didn't do much. Later, when I decided to go to Alabama, I got a nasty letter from Mike Donahue, the Auburn coach."

Winslett's junior class at Tallapoosa High in Dadeville was the first to play football. They played two games and lost both. His senior year, with Winslett passing, Tallapoosa played a full schedule and won them all.

Alabama leaped into War Eagle country and recruited Winslett. Raymond Sturdivant, who had played at Alabama in the early days, loaded Winslett onto a train and off they roared to Tuscaloosa. Hugo Friedman, the graduate manager of athletics, met them in a Cadillac and showed Winslett the sights. One of the sights was pretty girls at the country club.

"I didn't see the country club again until I joined it in 1932," Winslett remembers today with a chuckle.

Winslett was both fish and fowl at Alabama. He was an end who threw passes.

"I used to just go back in the backfield to pass, especially against Vanderbilt," he said. He threw two touchdown passes in a 19-7 victory over the Commodores in 1926.

"But that let the other team know what we were going to do. That's what Georgia Tech thought when we played them, but I ran a lot that day and I ran a lot after that game. We didn't have

Wu Winslett kicks, Red Barnes holds, Herschel Caldwell watches.

Alabama's 1926 Team That Played In The Rose Bowl—Sitting: Douglass, Holder, Ellis, Rosenfeld, Barnes, Hamner, Brown, Caldwell, Dismukes. Kneeling: Enis, Morrison, Smith, Skidmore, Vines, McDonald, Black, Winslett, Hagler. Standing: Johnson, Bowdoin, Pepper, Holmes, Pickhard, Pearce, Hurt, Payne, Perry, Taylor.

anybody on that 1926 team who could throw a pass except me."

When the 1926 season ended, Winslett was an all-American, at end. But his offensive backfield work no doubt was a major factor in the selection.

Today he lives in Tuscaloosa. He is retired from the insurance business and is an expert fisherman. "We got back from the Rose Bowl on January 5, 1927, and I went to work for Protective Life January 18. That was the only job I ever had."

Winslett began passing from his end slot in 1925. "I'd do a lot of reverse passing," he said. "Pooley Hubert would hand off to me and I'd either run or pass, usually pass."

He was graduated by the 1926 season, but he still had a season of football eligibility remaining. "I started not to come back in 1926, but they talked me into it. It was a good thing I did. I don't know where I would be. Wallace Wade wrote to me. He was very nice. He said he thought we could have a good team, but he emphasized he needed passing, which he didn't have."

Winslett suspects the 1925 Alabama team was better than the 1926 squad, though both played in the Rose Bowl. "We had more great football players in 1925," he said.

Winslett was the holder on the famous "signals off" extra point play that tied Stanford 7-7 in the 1927 Rose Bowl.

"Herschel Caldwell was the kicker and he was cool as a cucumber, the great underrated player at Alabama. As we lined up, I said, 'Well, old boy, right through the middle.'

"I think Coach Wade had thought up the play. That was the only time we ever used it. When Barnes said, 'Signals off,' the Stanford guys just kinda leaned back on their haunches to get ready for the real play. They had lined up determined to block that kick, but that caught them unawares."

Winslett still chuckles about the trip to the West Coast. "I came from Horseshoe Bend over on the Tallapoosa River. You can imagine what an old country boy thought about it out there."

Winslett remembers Wade as "very thorough, very tough. He didn't take any foolishness. He knew football and he planned it well. He was cool and calm under all conditions. The one game he wanted most to win was against Vanderbilt in 1926. He had coached there."

Pooley Hubert and Johnny Mack Brown were the best players he every played with. Wildcat Wilson, the Washington back, was the best he ever played against.

Hoyt Winslett's nickname of Wu may not be the most unusual in sports, but it will do until something better comes along.

"Pooley started it," he said. "He called me Chink or Chinaman. He said I had slant eyes and looked like a Chinaman. One time a stage play came to Tuscaloosa and it was named 'Mr. Wu.' Pooley started calling me that and the papers took it up.

"Nobody ever calls me Hoyt now except two or three people over in Dadeville."

Wade Resigns

Wallace Wade lost only 13 games at Alabama. He was to lose 10 of them in the next three years. The 1927 team went 5-4-1, the 1928 squad 6-3, and the 1929 club 6-3.

How many football teams would be proud of those records! But Alabama could not be, and neither could Wade. One of the burdens of a big winner is the standard he sets for himself. The fans respond to high standards. How 'ya gonna keep 'em down on the farm when they've seen Paree?

Georgia Tech beat the 1927 club 13-0 on October 15 in Atlanta. It was the first time an Alabama team had lost since Centre pulled its famous upset on November 15, 1924. Still, with victories over Millsaps, Southern Presbyterian, Sewanee, Mississippi A&M, and Kentucky, and a scoreless tie with LSU in an ocean of mud, Alabama was able to carry a 5-1-1 mark into the final three games. But Florida, Georgia, and Vanderbilt beat the Crimsons. The Georgia game was Alabama's first appearance in Birmingham's Legion Field, which had been dedicated by Howard and Birmingham-Southern the week before.

Ole Miss and Mississippi A&M were easy for the 1928 team, and Alabama was favored over Tennessee, but the Vols won by two points as the Tide killed itself with penalties and fumbles. Immortal Gene McEver ran the opening kickoff back 98 yards for Tennessee.

Sewanee fell, but Wisconsin won in Madison against the school that had made such a name for itself by winning in faraway places. Alabama won three of its final four games, beating Kentucky, Georgia, and LSU, but lost to Georgia Tech.

The 1929 squad opened with wins over Mississippi College, Ole Miss, and Chattanooga, but McEver led Tennessee to a 6-0 decision. Bama beat Sewanee, Kentucky, and Tech and lost to Vanderbilt and Georgia. Back Tony Holm made all-American.

The Ole Miss game on October 5, 1929, was the dedicatory contest for Denny Stadium. Previously, the Tide had played on Denny Field which was located behind what is now referred to as "the old athletic department." Denny Field "had maybe 8,000 seats in wooden bleachers and one of my jobs as a freshman was to see that nobody slipped in," Fred Sington recalls today.

On April 1, 1930, the *Birmingham News* front page headlined a story that shocked most readers. A few were not surprised, though. The story said Wallace Wade had resigned as head coach at the University of Alabama for a similar job at Duke University.

"Coach Wade gave no reason for leaving the university, after being offered a five-year contract at Alabama. The Alabama coach informed the writer last fall that he would coach only one more year at the Capstone," Zipp Newman wrote.

Jeff Coleman was athletic business manager in those days. He is now director of alumni affairs. He said Wade was a sensitive person who was riled by criticism directed at him by fans.

"He talked to me in 1930 about his situation," recalls Hoyt Winslett, who played end for Wade on the back-to-back Rose Bowl teams. "They were criticizing him and he couldn't take criticism. And they had offered him a good deal at Duke."

Zipp Newman recalls Wade showing him a letter in which Duke asked him to help the school secure a coach. But, reading between the lines, one could tell it was Wade himself that Duke wanted, Newman said.

Wade still had one more year on his contract at Alabama. He would coach the 1930 squad—and thus sing one of the greatest swan songs in sports history. That team went undefeated and beat Washington State 24-0 in the Rose Bowl.

The 1930 team generally was not picked in the top five in the Southern Conference in preseason writings. Zipp Newman had a special vision for that Tide, though: "For a team not picked to go anywhere in particular, the Crimson Tide will be a most feared opponent. A team dreaded worse than the plague. And why? Because Wade will have another bone crushing line and a squad that will outfight its weight in wildcats."

"Alabama will be exceedingly hard to score upon," Wade said, "but Alabama opponents are going to be just as hard for Alabama to score upon, if not harder. We have despaired of uncovering a triple threat, even a great passer. Given a Pooley Hubert or Bobby Dodd, I would rate Alabama's chances with Tennessee, Georgia, and Vanderbilt."

Fred Sington made all-American tackle in 1930, a season that opened with Howard falling 43-0 as John Henry Suther recorded runs of 96 and 55 yards and Monk Campbell a 53-yarder.

Reserves played most of the way in a 64-0 smashing of Ole Miss with Suther running 58, Campbell 42, and Joe Causey 64 yards.

Sewanee, the once-feared lair of the Mountain Tiger, had become a breather. Alabama won 25-0 with Wade and his assistant Jess Neely in Knoxville scouting Tennessee and backs Suther and John Cain watching from the sidelines.

The first big game of the 1930 season caught Tennessee without Gene McEver, who had a knee injury. Both Vol first-team ends were out, too. Alabama won 18-6. Bama scored on runs of 14 yards by Cain and 31 by Suther in the second period. Campbell got a short TD in the third to make it 18-0.

Soph Cain quarterbacked a first team of 10 seniors to a 12-7 decision over Vanderbilt with Suther and Campbell scoring to give Bama a 12-0 lead.

The Tide beat Kentucky 19-0 with the big play a 44-yard pass from Jimmy Moore to Suther.

After spoiling the Wildcats' homecoming, Bama did the same trick for Florida, whipping the Gators 20-0. Campbell got things going with a 21-yard TD.

Louisiana State was a 33-0 victim with Campbell returning the second half kickoff for a score.

Georgia was the only obstacle between Alabama and an undefeated season. The Rose Bowl announced that the winner would be invited to play Washington State in Pasadena on New Year's Day. Georgia had lost to Tulane, but the Bulldogs had impressive intersectional wins over New York University and Yale.

"We have had a great year and a loss to Georgia will not change my opinion, as we have done much better than we ever dared hope we could do before the season started," Wade said.

Cain led Bama to a 13-0 victory. His high punts, accompanied by a downfield rush of Sington, Albert Elmore, Jess Eberdt, and John Miller, handcuffed the Bulldogs. Cain made a 24-yard run to set up a Campbell touchdown in the third period. Campbell returned a punt 58 yards to set up a Cain TD in the fourth.

Washington State line coach Buck Bailey scouted the Georgia game and pronounced Alabama one of the most powerful football teams he had ever seen.

The Rose Bowl game was loaded with meaning for Wade. In addition to wanting to close his Alabama career with a victory, he recalled the second Tournament of Roses game ever played, the 1916 match in which Washington State beat Brown 14-0. Brown had a young guard named Wallace Wade. Alabama's leader could become the first coach to win two Rose Bowl games. Southern Cal was the only team with two victories, but they were accomplished under different coaches.

"I have never seen two elevens more alike than the Washington University team we played in the Rose Bowl in 1926 and this Washington State team," Wade said. He called State's defense one of the greatest he had ever seen. Wade's own defense had led the nation by surrendering only 13 points.

Washington State was known as the "wonder team." The Cougars had been expected to be a mediocre club in 1930, but they had compiled a 9-0 record. Wade rated State back Elmer Schwartz on a par with Wildcat Wilson, the great back of the 1925 Washington club that lost by one point to Bama. On the other hand, Notre Dame's Knute Rockne said Alabama tackle Fred Sington probably was the nation's best lineman.

The 1930 Tide was drawing its share of praise. W. G. Little, captain of Alabama's first football team, the 1892 outfit, said he had never seen a Bama club to equal this one. Ed Danforth, the respected sports editor of the *Atlanta Georgian,* called 1930 Alabama's best ever. "Were there any way to reassemble those two older teams (1925 and 1926) and play them against this 1930 team on succeeding Saturdays, I'd take the new genera-

Jeff Coleman, Alumni Affairs Director.

tion to win," Danforth wrote.

H. C. Byrd, the Maryland coach, wrote in the *Washington Evening Star* that Alabama was the best team in the United States.

Governor Bibb Graves honored the team with a curious speech: "We have been hampered industrially by an unfair picture the world seems to have of Alabama as a state of undersized, weak people living in swamp lands full of malaria and tuberculosis. None who have seen Wade's Tide in action, or who read of the account of the game for the next day will continue to embrace this idea."

West Coasters were not predicting a rout for their side as they had in Alabama's other Rose Bowl years. Tide victories, plus a recent visit by Notre Dame to the oceanside, had mellowed them. Rockne's Irish had smashed a favored Stanford club 27-0. An Alabama victory over Washington State, they said, would mean the Coast "must pull in her ears and await better days for that highly touted national recognition they crave in this section."

The Southern Conference champions took 35 players on a train that carried 170 in all. Pooley Hubert was among 100 well-wishers who greeted the Tide during a stopover in Meridian.

116

John Henry Suther became somewhat of a hero at one Mississippi stopover. The dining car conductor stepped off to get some change and the train left without him. Suther jerked the emergency cord, halting the train.

The train made a special stop in Picayune, Mississippi, so that the mother of Frank Howard, who later would become Clemson's famous coach, could ride to New Orleans with her son.

"The Crimsons not only play good football, but dress smartly," Zipp Newman told readers of the *Birmingham News* in a trackside dispatch. "They are wearing the latest creations in two-tone sweaters, last minute styles in plus-fours and what the collegians use for headwear."

Wade originally announced the team would not have an en route practice, but decided on a San Antonio workout. "The ride takes a lot out of the players and too many stopovers for practices are more harmful than good," said the man who should know.

The Southern Conference champions, who had left December 19, arrived in Pasadena December 23. Captain Foots Clement was surprised to find Alabama favored over the Cougars. "I don't see why we should be given the edge after traveling clear across the country, but we'll sure put out everything we have. You all can bank on that," said the man who no doubt had heard stories of the psychological advantage underdog Tides had brought to Pasadena in earlier years.

Washington State Coach Babe Hollingberry greeted Wade and his men. "Gosh, they're big," he muttered. Alabama had boarded a black donkey mascot in Phoenix. The animal, named Poison, was more weary than the team and was taken to the hotel on the truck with the team baggage. Johnny Mack Brown, now a movie star, welcomed the boys from his old school.

Wade lived up to his reputation as a tough coach. The team was on the practice field at 9:15 a.m. Christmas Day, and Newman called the practice "one of the most strenuous workouts an Alabama team has ever gone through on California soil."

But there was the usual round of sightseeing. Tiders saw Johnny Mack and Wallace Beery acting in a gangster movie at MGM. Brown's role was to assist a fair lady through a door, and

Alabama's players laughed that anyone got paid for such.

This team would not win the Helms national championship (Notre Dame did), but it won the Rose Bowl game convincingly and as far as Tide fans were concerned that meant the national championship. A crowd of 60,000 was shocked by Wade's strategy of starting his second team. He felt the Tide was two touchdowns better.

Washington State had an edge over the subs, but did not come close to scoring. Late in the first period, Wade sent in his regulars and they initiated the rout.

After 13 straight ground plays, left end Jimmy Moore circled into his own backfield. He took the ball from signal-calling soph fullback John Cain and threw a long pass. Suther caught it on the 22 and ran it in. The touchdown play covered 39 yards. Campbell converted.

After Eberdt intercepted a Cougar pass, Moore threw a 40-yard pass to Ben Smith who outjumped two State defenders. Campbell ran a yard to score on the next play. Campbell kicked again.

Next time Bama got the ball, Campbell sped 43 yards for another touchdown. His PAT made it 21-0. The Tide had scored all those points in six minutes of the second period.

The second team was playing in the third quarter when J. B. (Ears) Whitworth, who later would become head coach at the Capstone, kicked a 30-yard field goal.

Every Alabama player who made the trip got into the game. The Tidesmen carried Wade off the field on their shoulders, and the first great era of Alabama football had ended.

Time Out: Fred Sington

Fred Sington, all-American tackle of Alabama's 1930 team, operates a sporting goods store on the block with the old Tutwiler Hotel in Birmingham. Sometimes he sits in his office and remembers a 1927 afternoon in the Tutwiler lobby.

"I was in the Alabama band when I was a freshman," Sington explained. "It was purely economic with me. I got to make all the trips and got two tickets for the games. I didn't have a nickel.

"But I also was on the freshman football team. The freshmen always ran the other team's plays against the varsity. Ten days prior to the varsity game with Georgia in Birmingham, we played the Georgia freshmen in Rome, Georgia. We were tied 7-7 at the half and I told Coach Shorty Propst that our trouble was that we were trying to run Alabama plays when we knew Georgia plays better. We started running our Georgia plays the second half and won by three touchdowns.

"Anyway, you wore canvas pants with steel staves in those days. The canvas got torn in one of the Georgia men's pants and the steel stave hit me in the face. It was like a knife and it peeled off half my face.

"Well, a few days later we're having a big pep rally in the lobby of the Tutwiler for the varsity game with Georgia. I'm in the band now, standing there with my white pants and red cloak and saxophone—with my face half ripped off.

"And I hear some guy behind me whisper to somebody, 'Hey, look at that big guy. He ought to be playing football.'"

Sington did not kill his critic, but he half-killed a lot of men on the field. He was generally recognized as the nation's best lineman of 1930.

A set of numbers sticks in Sington's mind. They indicate the difficulty of playing for Wallace Wade. "We had 128 freshmen report for the team. Included were 29 boys who were all-Southern or all-American or captain of their teams in high school. My last year, there were only 10 seniors."

Recruiting was no problem for the Capstone team. "Alabama had gone to two straight Rose Bowls. This was the first glamor period of Southern football and Alabama was the first glamor school. Scholarships were small and the monetary value was nil, but the glamor angle of the team that went to California was a drawing card.

"A kid would go to Alabama expecting to go to the Rose Bowl, but by the time he got his tail knocked off he would have decided, as the fellow says, that 'you've quit talking and started meddling.' Some of them were from New York and Illinois, and it never occurred to them that this kind of work went on."

Sington, who came from Phillips High in Birmingham, recalls long, arduous practices. "We'd go out for practice at 1:30 and stop when we got through. Five-hour practices were not uncommon.

"I remember one day we were having a real ragged session, and Wade got disgusted. He told the starting fullback to go sit in the stands, that maybe he could be a spectator because he didn't want to play.

"Finally, he divided us into three sections and told the coaches he wanted us to run plays until he told us to stop. We started that at 4:30 and about 5:55 Wade had a long distance call. He left the field and when he got through with the call he dressed and went home.

"Finally, it got pitch dark. You couldn't see your hand in front of your face, much less the ball, but we were still running plays. At about 7 o'clock somebody called his home and said, 'The boys are still running signals. Do you want them to stay out there?'

"He said, 'Naw, let 'em go home.' I guess if they hadn't called, we'd still be out there.

"If Wade found you having a date, going with a co-ed, he'd

120

Fred Sington was nation's top lineman.

Frank Howard sang "Football Freddie."

make your life unbearable. He had a big Chrysler and he would cruise around. If you were walking down the street and a girl was anywhere near, even if you didn't know her, you'd cross over to the other side because you didn't want him to see you and mistakenly think you were dating her.

"He wanted you to think of nothing but football. I punted a little and if I was free from 9 to 10, say, I'd go to the gym and practice dropping the ball to my foot. A punter today wouldn't do that.

"You never went to see Wade. It was like they tell you in the Navy: don't volunteer. Finally you'd get up the courage to see the old man, and here you'd be, 6-2 or 6-3 and 210, walking into his office with a trembling heart. You'd get up courage to speak and you'd say, 'Coach Wade, I'd like to do so and so.' He'd always say, 'How's that?!!!'

"Most of the time, you wouldn't even repeat it.

"We had very tough drills. Hank Crisp had a drill where he would draw a circle and put the tackles inside it. The guards ran

121

one at a time at you and if you got knocked out of the circle you got chewed out and you ran around the field.

"I learned that if you stood up and tried to fight them off you'd get knocked out of the ring everytime. So I got down with my elbows near my knees and instead of waiting for them I'd move into them.

"Jess Neely, who was the end coach, had a high, shrill voice and one day he saw some of the guards limping after I had been in the circle and he said, 'Hank, you could have used a shotgun if you wanted that effect.'

"We did a lot of live tackling instead of using dummies. When 220-pound linemen tackle each other it's like two blocks of stone hitting. Nobody knew how to fall. Backs instinctively know how, but linemen's heads bounce off the ground.

"The way I met Frank Howard, Coach Crisp didn't like the way I blocked so he made me run around the field. I met Howard running around the other way and that was the beginning of a long friendship.

"Rudy Vallee wrote a song, 'Football Freddie,' and dedicated it to me. Howard heard it on the radio and that was all he needed. In the Rose Bowl game, everytime we'd get down in the line, he'd start singing: 'Football Freddie, rugged and tan; Football Freddie, collegiate man.' "

Sington compares Wade and General Bob Neyland of Tennessee. "Both were military men and they used similar drills. Emotionally, they were cold and calculating. But there were times, particularly after we beat Georgia and clinched the bid to the Rose Bowl, that Wade showed emotion.

"We had a fellow named Bell from Berkeley, California. He didn't make the traveling squad to the Coast, so he hitch-hiked out. That meant he had to leave several days before our train did.

"He came to the Rose Bowl and there were no tickets to be had. So Wade gave him a uniform and told him he could sit on the bench.

"In the fourth period a couple of guys got hurt and Wade sent Bell into the game. He played three minutes and got a gold football with an American Beauty rose carved on it. This was a guy who had never made a trip or won a letter. So Wade wasn't inhuman."

When Wade left Alabama for Duke, he took Sington with him as an assistant coach, a position Sington would hold for four seasons.

Duke money lured Wade, but criticism of Alabama fans played a part in the switch, Sington said.

"You win three conference championships and go to the Rose Bowl twice when nobody has ever even been to Florida, then you lose a couple or three games and people start to ask what's wrong with the old coach. Not just the alumni, but people in general," Sington said.

Sington coached Duke and played professional baseball in the off-season. He put in six years in the big leagues with Washington and Brooklyn.

On June 21, 1955, he was elected to the National Football Hall of Fame. Elected on the same day was Wallace Wade.

Sington recalls another moment they shared. "I'll never forget the first skull practice after we went to Duke. A boy from Philadelphia held his hand up. We expected him to ask about some play he didn't understand.

"He said, 'Coach, I just wondered. They're having a dance Friday night before the game. Will it be all right if we go?'

"I nearly fell out of my chair. If we had been in a room full of gasoline and someone had struck a match I couldn't have been more apprehensive.

"But Coach Wade realized he was in a new world. All he said was, 'No.' "

Time Out: Wallace Wade

Wallace Wade says he lives on a small farm. Then he tells you it consists of 130 acres. Is that small?

"Well, it depends on what you compare it with," the ex-Alabama coach says, logically.

Wade, who took the Tide to Rose Bowls in 1926, 1927, and 1931, is 80 years old and living his twilight years raising 25-30 head of cattle near Durham, North Carolina. He retired to this farm after a football career that saw him coach eight years at Alabama and sixteen at Duke and serve as commissioner of both the Southern Conference and Atlantic Coast Conference. He lives with his second wife. The first died in 1947.

"I'm getting along pretty well," Wade told a caller. "I do some of the work around here but not as much as I used to." He was not a stranger to the rural life. He grew up on a farm in Tennessee.

"Yes, I got to a college game occasionally, but not often. Sometime I go to see Duke play."

Modern coaching has become bureaucratic, Wade feels, and that is a curious use of the world that has become rather ominous in present-day conversation. "They have such large staffs and are so highly organized. In my day, Hank Crisp and Russ Cohen and I did most of the coaching at Alabama. It was more personal."

"But the coaches today have a lot of problems we didn't have. The players are more independent."

I asked Wade if the course many young people take today

124

disturbs him. "Yes, it does. I'm afraid our young people are being misled by some misguided people." Was there more dedication to football when he coached? "Not only that, but more dedication to the worthwhile things in life."

Wade succeeded Xen Scott at Alabama. He never knew Scott, "but he apparently was an attractive man." Did Wade encounter any problems as successor to a popular, successful coach who was forced out by poor health? "If so, I didn't recognize them," he said.

"I had been an assistant at Vanderbilt two years and Alabama was looking for a coach," Wade explained. "Mr. Borden Burr, an old Birmingham alumnus, got in touch with me. I had had contact with several other institutions at the time so apparently somebody thought I was ready to be a head coach. I thought Alabama offered quite an opportunity for a very strong football program. They had a lot of good material and players who wanted to play.

"I didn't follow Scott's system of football very closely. We started out with the double-wing and then went to the single-wing. We always used the punt formation a lot, too."

Wade's 1925 team went 9-0, then whipped the University of Washington 20-19 in the Rose Bowl. It was the first big breakthrough for Southern football.

"We had an undefeated season and quite an outstanding football team. They selected an outstanding team from the rest of the country to play a West Coast team in those days. Now they take the Big Ten champion. But I still think the Rose Bowl has the most prestige of all the bowls. On the other hand, a game like last year's Alabama-Nebraska game in the Orange Bowl has a lot of prestige, too. I'd like to see all teams have a chance at the Rose Bowl, but I think the reason they tied up with the Big Ten years ago was that it had a lot of prestige at that time and they felt certain they would be assured of a good team.

"No, we weren't awed by the trip West. It took quite a bit to awe boys like Johnny Mack Brown and Bruce Jones and Grant Gillis.

"We didn't know very much about the University of Washington. We hadn't scouted them. The game was arranged after the season was well over, and all we knew about them was what we

*Russ Cohen, Wallace Wade's
assistant.*

read in the paper. Of course, we knew they had a good team,
but we also knew that we had a good team.

"The next year the Rose Bowl invited us in October, but I
told them I didn't think I had a good enough team to play in
the Rose Bowl, we had lost so many of our good first-string
players from the season before. They said they would hold it
open and wait and see what happened.

"Well, we went undefeated, and we accepted the Rose Bowl
again. We didn't have perhaps as versatile an offense as the year
before, but we had a strong defense. We played a very strong
Stanford team and tied them 7-7, so we were able to hold our
own."

The 1930 club was Wade's other Rose Bowl team. "That was
a real good team, but I don't know that we had as much
individual talent as in 1925," he said. "But in 1930 we had a
deep squad.

"We were so deep that we started the second team in every
game, including the Rose Bowl. They always played the first
quarter. There were several reasons we did that. One was
psychological. You see, that second team was able to hold
everybody scoreless the whole year. We knew it would help us
for an opponent to play the second team and not score and
then know we were sending in the first string."

126

Wade would not name his best Alabama player. "I've never undertaken to say that. There were a number of great players but three of them are in the National Football Hall of Fame, Fred Sington, Johnny Mack Brown, and Pooley Hubert."

Neither would he select his best team. "I've never been able to decide that. Each team plays under different conditions. But I would have to count the three Rose Bowl teams among the best, although 1924 was good, too."

Wade left Alabama for Duke after the 1930 team went 10-0. He had resigned before that season, though. He is vague on his reasons for leaving.

"I liked the situation at Duke and wanted to come up here. I don't know exactly why I left. It's been a long time ago and I don't know that I could pinpoint any particular reason."

He resigned early because that is when Duke offered him the job, he said. "But I had a contract at Alabama and in those days we lived up to contracts."

Wade is not worried about the future of college football, though there has been wringing of hands by some because of the popularity of the professionals. "It seems to me college football is about as attractive as it has ever been. When they have good games and good teams they have sellouts. Don't they have sellouts in Birmingham?"

He occasionally sees some of his old Alabama players. "Pooley Hubert drops by to see me and I see Johnny Mack Brown sometimes." Wade remembers Brown as "a particularly outstanding open field runner and pass receiver" and Hubert as "one of the outstanding leaders who ever played football."

If Wade ever tires of counting his cattle, he can count his sports halls of fame. He belongs to Alabama's, Tennessee's, North Carolina's, Brown University's, Helms', and the National Football Hall of Fame.

Wade won 61, lost 13, and tied 3 in 8 years at Alabama. His Duke record was 110-36-7 for 15 years. At Fitzgerald-Clarke, Vandy, Bama, and Duke he went 202-52-12.

His military career was as distinguished as his coaching record. He was a captain in the cavalry in World War I. When he walked off the field after the 1942 Rose Bowl, he was leaving coaching for four years. The United States had just entered World War II, and Wade immediately offered his services. He was commissioned a major and promoted to lieutenant colonel in the army field artillery battalion which he took overseas in 1944.

Wade participated in the Battle of Normandy, the Siegfried Line breakthrough, the Battle of the Bulge, the crossing of the Rhine, and the Ninth Army drive through Germany. He received the Bronze Star from the United States and the Croix De Guerre with Palm from the French.

Wade was a marvelous football coach, but he has an excellent sense of priority. He says he received more satisfaction from serving his country than from all his great teams.

Dr. Denny Hires His Winner

The train that returned to Tuscaloosa from Pasadena after the 1931 Rose Bowl not only carried the author of the first great era of Alabama football, Wallace Wade, but the man who would be the architect of the second great era, Frank Thomas.

Wade had invited Thomas to make the trip as a guest of the University of Alabama so that he could become more familiar with the players he would coach the next season. Thomas' brain must have pounded during that trip. Not only was he succeeding the great Wade, but his wife gave birth to Frank Thomas, Jr., back home in Athens, Georgia, on December 31, 1930.

"There is a young backfield coach at Georgia who should become one of the greatest coaches in the country," Wade had told Dr. Mike Denny when he resigned. "He played football under Rockne at Notre Dame. Rock called him one of the smartest players he ever coached. He is Frank Thomas, and I don't believe you could pick a better man."

Dr. Denny asked Wade to call Thomas for him. Wade told Thomas he wished to discuss an important matter with him and asked Thomas to meet him in Birmingham. No questions asked, Thomas said he would be there.

They met at a track meet at Legion Field. To escape the rain they stood under the west stands. Wade told Thomas he had resigned to coach Duke and had recommended Thomas as his successor. "You'll hear from Alabama soon," Wade said. Borden Burr, a powerful Alabama alumnus, had recommended Thomas,

Dr. George H. Denny with a "Cotton Bowl."

too. So did Ed Camp, an Atlanta newsman who had followed Thomas' success at the University of Georgia.

Dr. Denny called Thomas in Athens and asked to meet him in Borden Burr's office in Birmingham on July 15. Burr, Thomas, Dr. Denny, and Camp gathered in Burr's office, and after a brief discussion the job was Thomas'.

After the contract was signed, Dr. Denny, devout supporter of winning football, informed Thomas he had best produce those winning teams.

"Mr. Thomas," he said, "now that you have accepted our proposition, I will give you the benefit of my views, based on many years of observation. It is my conviction that material is 90 per cent, coaching ability 10 per cent. I desire further to say that you will be provided with the 90 per cent and that you will be held to strict accounting for delivering the remaining 10 per cent."

Thomas was stunned as he and Camp left the meeting. "Those were the hardest and coldest words I ever heard," Thomas said. "Do you reckon his figures are right?"

"I think the proportion was considerably off," Camp answered, "but there is no doubt the good doctor means what he said."

Dr. Denny would have his winners. Frank Thomas would coach Alabama 15 seasons before illness would force him out in his prime at age 46. He would take three Tides back to Pasadena as well as put teams in the Cotton, Orange, and Sugar bowls. His record would be 115 victories, 24 losses, and 7 ties.

Frank William Thomas was the son of James and Elizabeth Thomas, who came to the United States from Wales in 1882. He was the youngest of six children and the fourth to be born in America.

His father was an iron worker, and the family settled in East Chicago. He was an eighth grader when athletics began to fascinate him. Though a small fellow, Thomas was one of the better players on the elementary school basketball team.

Thomas was the star running back of Washington High School's state championship football team his junior year. He became the first Washington High athlete to win letters in football, basketball, baseball, and track.

But iron workers in the area were laid off during Thomas'

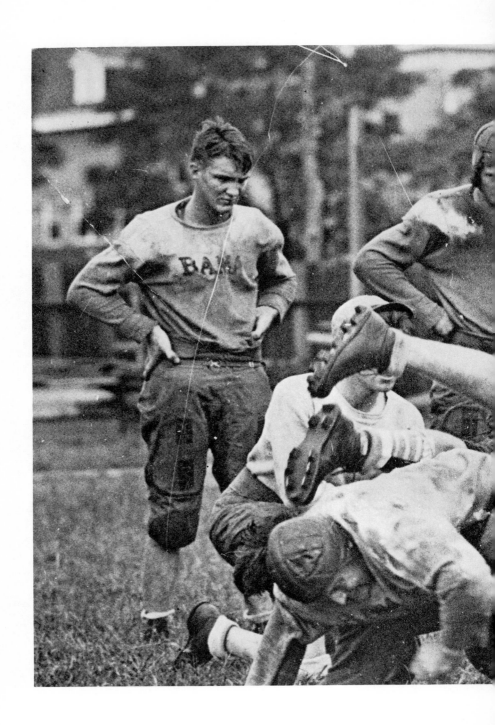

An early practice at Capstone.

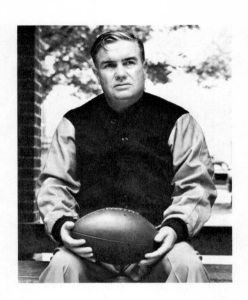

Frank Thomas took Bama to three Rose Bowl games.

senior year. His father was one of them. The boy thought he should quit school to help. But his coach, Floyd Murray, talked him out of it. "He made me want an education, something my father didn't have," Thomas said in later years. "He inspired me to become a coach, to follow in his footsteps. He built in me the determination to succeed even against handicaps."

An opportunity to continue his education came. Kalamazoo College called the young whiz, explained it had both high school and college courses, and asked him to enroll.

Thomas arrived at Kalamazoo with $7.50 and one change of clothes. He was given a job tending the school grounds. He ran errands at night to add to his meager billfold.

Frank Thomas, 17 years old, weighing 135 pounds, arrived at Kalamazoo on a Monday and played in a college football game—against the University of Michigan—on Saturday. Remember, he was still just a high school senior.

Thomas warmed the bench just three minutes before Kalamazoo's right halfback was injured. The coach motioned him onto the field. "I was scared stiff," he recalled later.

Thomas played 57 minutes and made an 85-yard run that set up the tying touchdown. Michigan won 17-14 on a field goal two minutes before the end of the game.

He scored a touchdown the next week as Kalamazoo beat

Michigan State 14-0. When football season ended, Thomas played on the college baseball team and the high school basketball team.

He returned to Kalamazoo the next fall and—as a freshman—was elected captain of the football team. He was a star, and his fame spread.

Thomas spent the next summer working with a guy named Clipper Smith, who had played at Notre Dame. Smith introduced Thomas to Knute Rockne, and in the autumn of 1919 Thomas enrolled at Notre Dame. He played quarterback on the freshman team and spent most of the fall trying to tackle the varsity's George Gipp in practice. Thomas always said Gipp was the best football player he ever saw.

Notre Dame was not Kalamazoo. Thomas was a third-string quarterback his first varsity season. But he was fortunate to room with Gipp, from whom he learned plenty of football.

After midseason of his junior year, Thomas became the first-team quarterback, but it was a sad season. Gipp, his friend, became ill early in the season and died.

Thomas was a star as a senior, and Rockne made a prophetic statement: "It's amazing the amount of football sense that Thomas kid has. He can't miss becoming a great coach some day."

The University of Georgia agreed and hired Thomas as an assistant. After one season, head coach George Woodruff asked him to install the Notre Dame offense.

In January, 1925, Chattanooga hired Thomas as head coach. Two men who would become famous in their own right, Red Drew and Scrappy Moore, later served as his assistants.

Georgia enticed Thomas to return as backfield coach for 1929. Drew was named Chattanooga's head coach.

Married now and the father of a child, Thomas was teaching Georgians how to run the Notre Dame offense when the phone rang and a voice said, "Frank, this is Wallace Wade. . ."

A Kid Named Dixie

As Frank Thomas arrived at Tuscaloosa, 10 starters off the 1930 team departed. Johnny Cain, a fine punter and Wade's signal caller, was the only first-stringer with eligibility remaining.

Thomas took over on January 10, 1931. One of the assistants he hired was Red Drew, who later would become head coach at the Capstone. Thomas installed the Notre Dame formation, junking Wade's single wing.

Thomas' Tide opened with a 42-6 rout of Howard as Leon Long scored three touchdowns. Thomas immediately caused some raised eyebrows among Tide fans when he relieved Cain of his signal calling duties after the Howard game and gave them to left half Hillman Holley. Cain was simply too modest and would not call his own signal enough.

Cain scored three touchdowns in a 55-6 thrashing of Ole Miss the next week. Mississippi State went under 53-0. But Thomas and his green team knew these were just preliminaries. The main event would be the next week in Knoxville. Thomas was nervous. He was aware of the rivalry that had existed between Wade and Tennessee's Bob Neyland.

Gene McEver, who had missed the 1930 season with injuries, led the Vols to a 25-0 blasting of Bama.

The Tide did not lose another one, though, beating Sewanee 33-0, Kentucky 9-7, Florida 41-0, Clemson 74-7, Vanderbilt 14-6, and Chattanooga 49-0. Cain made all-American.

Dr. Denny puffed on his smelly old pipe and smiled. One 9-1

season does not a career make, but he believed he had brought a winner to the Capstone.

The 1932 team won eight and lost two, beating Southwestern 45-6, Mississippi State 53-0, George Washington 28-6, Ole Miss 24-13, Kentucky 12-7, Virginia Tech 9-6, Vanderbilt 20-0, and St. Mary's 6-0, and losing to Tennessee 7-3 and Georgia Tech 6-0. J. B. Whitworth had joined on as an assistant coach. With Drew also on the staff, Thomas now was bossing two men who would later be head coaches at Tuscaloosa.

The Tennessee game of 1932 was one of the most famous matches in Tide history. It was the Johnny Cain-Beattie Feathers kicking duel.

A crowd of 20,000 shivered in a downpour in Birmingham's Legion Field. Cain punted 19 times for an average of 48 yards, though one of his kicks only went 12 yards. Feathers punted 21 times for an average of 43 yards, with an 18-yarder pulling

Alabama's All-Time First Team
Hometown • Hartford, Ala.
ALL SEC '33-'34
ROSE BOWL STAR 1934
ALABAMA 34 STANFORD 13

'BAMA ASSISTANT COACH

1934 Record
RUSHING · 114 TRIES · 668 YDS.
PASSING · 35 out of 61 · 489 YDS.
TOTAL YARDS 1157 YDS.

Pro·Baseball
DETROIT TIGERS

MILLARD "DIXIE" HOWELL
BACK WT. 160
ALL·AMERICAN 1934

Johnny Cain later coached at Ole Miss.

down the total. Both teams frequently punted on first and second down, neither wanting to handle the muddy ball.

Alabama scored in the second period. The Tide drove to the Tennessee six but the Vols held and Holley kicked a field goal. The Orange made the game's only touchdown in the third quarter. Feathers kicked dead on the Tide one. Cain dropped back to punt, but the snap from center was bad. Cain's kick went only a dozen yards. Feathers scored on the third play.

Highlight of the season was the intersectional win over favored St. Mary's at San Francisco. Cain was injured, but he closed his career with the only touchdown.

Thomas had won 17 and lost 3 in two seasons—but he heard rumblings. The big game of the year was against Tennessee, and Thomas had lost both years. Thomas told his wife Frances the "wolves are beginning to howl. They're demanding we beat Tennessee this year." He pointed out that with three children (Rita and Hugh had joined Frank, Jr.) now to feed, he had better beat Neyland in 1933. Thomas thought of fans who had criticized Wade.

The first job that faced Thomas was finding someone to fill Cain's shoes. After one game, a 34-0 rout of Oglethorpe, Thomas told his coaches, "I think we have our replacement for Cain." A kid named Dixie Howell had caught Thomas' eye.

Howell convinced Thomas the next week. Ole Miss tied Bama 0-0, but Howell gained 133 yards and probably would have scored twice except for poor downfield blocking.

Thomas installed some new plays built around Howell. Mississippi State tumbled 18-0, and Tennessee was next. "I think we can beat them this time," Thomas told his wife one night after practice.

Tension ran high that afternoon in Knoxville. Thomas inadvertently broke the tension for players when they saw him nervously stick the lighted end of his cigar in his mouth. They broke into laughter.

Feathers continued to be a nemesis by scoring first for Tennessee, and the Vols led 6-0 at halftime. Thomas ranted at his players and begged them to win.

In the third period Howell handed off to Erskine Walker. Howell's fake was so well executed that most of the Vols ganged him, and Walker was practically untouched, running for a touchdown. Howell scored in the final quarter, and Alabama won 12-6. Thomas told his wife Frances he supposed he had a job for another year.

Alabama lost to Fordham 2-0 before 60,000 in the Polo Grounds. Two Howell passes grazed the fingertips of an unheralded end named Don Hutson. Either would have scored a touchdown. Another young end on that squad was Paul Bryant, who was called Bear because he had once wrestled a bruin. The loss to the Rams was no disgrace, for they were one of America's better teams.

Alabama closed out by beating Kentucky 20-0, Virginia Tech 27-0, Georgia Tech 12-9, and Vanderbilt 7-0. Guard Tom Hupke was all-American.

The old Southern Conference had been so unwieldy that some of the teams had splintered off into a new league called the Southeastern Conference. Alabama was its first champion in 1933, and Howell and Hupke made the first all-SEC team ever selected.

The hoorahs of a 7-1-1 1933 team had hardly died before Thomas began anticipating the 1934 season. He knew he would have a strong team, and he believed the Howell-Hutson passing combination was a promising one.

139

Don Hutson, Late Bloomer

Don Hutson was a late bloomer. Back home in Pine Bluff, Arkansas, he had been a skinny kid who had not made his high school football team until his senior year.

He came to Alabama as a baseball player and drew no attention when he turned out for football. There was no market for 160-pound ends. After a few practice sessions, though, end coach Red Drew began to note his deceptive stride ("shuffling along," as Coach Thomas would later term it). Hutson was not particularly impressive as a freshman or sophomore and did not become a starter until midway of his junior year.

But if Hutson had developed slowly in high school and college, he was an instant success as a professional. On his first pro play, he caught an 87-yard touchdown pass from Arnie Herber that heralded one of the all-time National Football League careers.

The Green Bay immortal went on to lead the NFL in scoring five times, in touchdown passes eight seasons, and in receptions eleven times.

When the 1934 Tide opened practice, Thomas built his offense around the passing of Dixie Howell and the catching of Don Hutson, though he did not anticipate the greatness that was in store for them.

Joe Demyanovich scored a couple of touchdowns in an unimpressive 24-0 victory over Howard. Howell made a 61-yard touchdown run in a 35-6 rout of Sewanee. Young Boozer went 80 and 76 yards for TDs as the Tide killed Mississippi State

Don Hutson (right) was honored in 1970 as a member of college football's all-time team. He's pictured with Governor Warren Knowles of Wisconsin.

41-0.

Tennessee was next and Bama won 13-6, giving Thomas two in a row over Neyland. A Howell-to-Hutson pass set up the first touchdown, and Hutson, a 9.8 sprinter, scored the second on an end-around. "You've beaten Tennessee. You can go all the way," Thomas told his team.

Howell carried 15 times for 152 yards in a 26-6 blasting of Georgia. Howell sat out the second half because he was not needed.

Howell and Joe Riley completed six of nine passes for 170 yards and Kentucky fell 24-14. Clemson was a 40-0 victim. Howell-to-Hutson passes highlighted both victories.

The Crimsons slaughtered Georgia Tech 40-0 with a passing attack, and rumors began to fly that the Rose Bowl was considering Bama and Minnesota to play Stanford in the January 1, 1935, game.

"I want you to go out there and give your greatest show today," Thomas told his men before the Vanderbilt game, last of the regular season. "You have so much at stake, you can't afford to blow it. I believe we have a fine chance of getting the Rose Bowl bid and I know you fellows want it. Well, it's up to you."

Howell played his finest game as Vandy drowned 34-0. He punted for a 40-yard average, gained 124 yards on punt returns, and rushed for 162 yards. As James Angelich broke into the open on a 70-yard interception return for a TD, Alabama's band struck up "California, Here I Come!"

Minnesota had beaten Wisconsin 34-0—same score as the Tide-Vandy game—on the same afternoon to remain undefeated. Bama players gathered around Thomas and asked if he had heard from the Rose Bowl. Thomas, frowning, said he had heard nothing. He told his assistants the Tidesmen would be sick if they did not get the bid.

Thomas and his men arrived at their Birmingham hotel. As he walked through the lobby the desk clerk said, "Hey, Coach, Los Angeles has been trying to get you."

Thomas fretted as he returned the phone call. Perhaps the Rose Bowl was only politely informing him that Minnesota had been chosen.

His fears were unfounded. Thomas was told the Rose Bowl wanted all-winning Alabama. Thomas gathered his players around him in his room and broke the news.

Thousands of supporters greeted the team in Tuscaloosa. Thomas had to have police assistance to escape the frenzy.

Historically, Alabama had had to prove to some folks it deserved to be in the Rose Bowl. The situation would be no different this time. Midwestern and Eastern writers immediately cranked up their typewriters, charging that Minnesota would have been a better selection to play Stanford.

Bama's men did a slow burn. Later, Thomas would say that he never had a team before or afterward that worked as hard preparing for a game. "Those kids were determined to win and make their critics look bad. At times we had to slow their pace for fear they would grow stale before the game."

142

Shipwreck Kelly, the old Kentucky star who now owned the Brooklyn professional team, watched Alabama work out and pronounced the Tide the finest college team he had ever seen.

"If any of the Alabama seniors want to play professional football, they can get with Kelly's Brooklyn club and sign contracts immediately," Zipp Newman wrote. "He would take the Alabama squad as it is and be satisfied they could give the tough pros a big afternoon."

Alabama departed on December 21. The train stopped at New Orleans where sportswriters were guests at a dinner at the St. Charles Hotel. New Orleans papers were not sending anyone to the Rose Bowl. Their writers would be busy covering a brand new venture in football. Tulane and Temple were going to play in something called the Sugar Bowl game.

Stanford had only a tie with powerful Santa Clara to smudge its record, so Alabama's players chuckled as they passed around a *San Francisco Chronicle* article on the train. "On the day that Stanford played Washington, the Cardinals could have licked any team in the United States, including Minnesota and Alabama, etc. It was a glorious team. But the glory is all gone. Stanford has suffered a disastrous letdown. Ten to one that Alabama will lick the stuffin' out of Tiny Thornhill's boys," the story said. But the Tidesmen were not about to be lulled into feeling comfortable. They were still angry about other articles, those that said Minnesota should be headed west.

The train stopped in New Mexico, and Johnny Mack Brown got on. The old Tide star brought charts and diagrams. He had scouted Stanford. Another stop, in Texas, was an emergency. Substitute center Bill Young's appendix was removed. The Crimsons did not need more motivation, but all of a sudden they had it. They vowed to win the Rose Bowl for Young.

Alabama arrived to find some Californians openly jeering. They, too, wanted Minnesota. Thomas smiled when he saw his players become even more determined. "That's the way I like to hear 'em talk," he said to an assistant.

On December 23 the Rose Bowl closed its ticket office and announced an 84,474 sellout. On Christmas Day the *Birmingham News* sprouted a seven-column headline that read, "Scalpers ask $25 each for Rose Bowl tickets." Officials were able to erect 1,000 temporary seats before game time.

A column by Braven Dyer, an old Alabama friend, in the *Los Angeles Times,* set the stage for the game: "Alabama is the most impressive football squad I have ever seen come from east of the Rockies and Alabama is going to play the best Stanford team in history, a team as great as Southern Cal in 1931. If Alabama can beat Stanford, the Pacific Coast will give Alabama full credit for the greatest team ever to play in the Rose Bowl."

More than anything else, Dixie Howell wanted to beat Stanford. Secondmost on his list of wishes was half a dozen hot tamales. Four months of eating Thomas-prescribed food was getting to him.

"I want six hot tamales, win, lose or draw," Howell said. "I've been thinking about them so much out here that I've got to dreaming about them. I dreamed about hot tamales last night. That is, I dreamed about one hot tamale. It was as big as Bill Lee. I mean, it was too big for a football player and not big enough for a hippopotamus. The coach won't let us eat tamales now, but as soon as that game is over—well, you watch."

On December 26 Thomas abruptly announced there would be no more scrimmages. "The sudden soreness in leg muscles has me worried," he said.

The Crimsons took in the usual sights and were given almost free rein at Warner Bros. where they watched the shooting of *The Florentine Dagger, King of the Ritz, Go Into Your Dance, Gold Diggers of 1935,* and *Mid-Summer Night's Dream* and met Joe E. Brown, Al Jolson, Dick Powell, Pat O'Brien, Warren Williams, Donald Woods, Maxine Doyle, Grace Ford, Anita Louise, and Winifred Shaw.

Ty Cobb watched both Alabama and Stanford work out and picked Bama to win. He met Borden Burr, the prominent Alabama alumnus, for the first time in 29 years. They had played baseball against each other when Cobb was a minor leaguer at Anniston in 1905.

Stanford Coach Tiny Thornhill was asked for a comment and said, "I think the game is a toss-up, an even-money bet. The team getting the breaks will win the game."

"I think our team has an even chance to win," Thomas said. "No better or no worse."

Dixie Howell did not look well at breakfast on game day, and Thomas fretted. He told his players they were about to face the best team they had ever played. They would have to stop Bobby Grayson, Stanford's star fullback.

But Howell was well. The Howell-to-Hutson combo was about to beat Stanford 29-13.

The game began frightfully for Alabama. Demyanovich fumbled in the first period, and Stanford recovered. Grayson scored from the one-foot line.

The score was 7-0 in the second period when Howell returned a punt 25 yards to the Stanford 45. He passed to Hutson for 17 and to Angelich for 12. Bryant lost four on an end-around before taking a pass from Howell for 16 to Stanford's four. Howell scored, but Smith missed the PAT and Bama was still behind 7-6.

Howell passes of 26 yards to Hutson and 18 to Bryant set up a 30-yard Smith field goal in the second quarter. Moments later Howell ran 67 yards for a touchdown, and Smith converted. Now Bama led 16-7. Eight seconds before the half ended, Joe Riley threw a 54-yard touchdown pass to Hutson. The Tide went to intermission leading 22-7.

Before Riley passed the TD to Hutson, Thomas had sent in sub quarterback Happy Campbell with orders to keep the ball on the ground and kill the clock. But Riley Smith already had called the pass play before Campbell took his place.

A similar beneficial mix-up occurred in the fourth period. Stanford had scored, and the count was now 22-13 when Thomas dispatched Hutson into the lineup with orders to halt the passing. But before Hutson could deliver the message Howell was throwing him a 59-yard touchdown pass.

"No team in the history of football, anywhere, anytime has passed the ball as Alabama passed it today," wrote Bill McGill of the *Atlanta Constitution.* "And no man ever passed as did Dixie Howell, the swift sword of the Crimson attack."

Alabama was champion of the Rose Bowl, king of the Southeastern Conference, and had three all-Americans: tackle Bill Lee and Hutson and Howell. But the Helms and Knute Rockne national championship trophies had eluded the Crimsons. Minnesota won both.

A light controversy flared after the game. Some Coast newspapers claimed Howell thumbed his nose at the last Stanford defender on his 67-yard touchdown run. They called it an unsportsmanlike gesture.

Ten years later, when Alabama was returning for another Rose Bowl game, Vincent X. Flaherty recalled the incident in his *Los Angeles Times* column:

"Upon meeting Dixie the other night in Baron Long's Baltimore Hotel, I asked the old Tuscaloosa terror what provoked the five-fingered salute. You know what? I think Dixie lied to me. He said he didn't thumb his nose at all. He said it only looked that way.

" 'Nobody who saw that movie believes me,' said Dixie with great piety. And he wore an expression of such spotless innocence I almost thought I heard the rustle of little angel's wings.

" 'I saw that movie, too,' spake the outraged hero, 'and I'll be darned if it didn't look like I thumbed my nose. It must have been the angle of the camera. This is all I did.'

"With that, Dixie demonstrated. He looked back across his shoulder, ran his right arm and hand across his chest and went through the motions of the most sanctified hand-waving you ever saw.

" 'That's just what I did,' he said. 'I waved to Buck Van Dellen, who was the last Stanford man to miss me.'

"Just for good measure, Dixie gave me another demonstration. And although I felt like saying, 'Dixie, do you mean to stand there and tell me you didn't thumb your nose?' such magnificent prevarication deserves some premium. In fact, you can nourish naught but tremendous admiration for any man who can stick to his story after almost 11 years."

146

Time Out: Paul Bryant

Before he coached winning teams, Paul Bryant played on winning teams. He says he was not much of a player, but the records show he made second-team all-Southeastern Conference end in 1934.

The 1934 squad traveled to Pasadena to beat Stanford in the Rose Bowl. Here, Bryant tells the story of that trip:

"Vanderbilt was our final game of the 1934 season and we had an idea that we might get to go to the Rose Bowl if we won.

"I recall very well that after warming up in Legion Field, Coach Thomas told everybody to go back out except the starting team. Back then you played both ways and played most of the game if you were lucky.

"Coach Thomas read us a telegram from Masters, who was the graduate manager at Stanford, which is the same as athletic director now. The telegram said that if we won decisively we would get a call that night. I don't know about the rest of them, but cold chills went up and down my back and they still do when I think about it.

"Dixie Howell and Don Hutson played a great game, as they always did, and I remember I played most of the game until the latter part of the fourth quarter when Coach Thomas took me out. It just so happened that our band was playing 'California Here I Come', and that really excited me.

"I remember we went at practice for the bowl game real well. I think what really won the game was preparation and some-

147

thing Coach Thomas did that might have had more to do with it than anything that happened the day before we were leaving.

"We went over to Denny Stadium and played a game, first team against the second team. We just wallowed around and didn't get anything done. All of a sudden Coach Thomas called time out and started head-on tackling. It seemed like we did that for a couple of hours. But anyway, finally, we survived.

"We traveled by train in those days and lots of us hadn't been on a train many times, at least I hadn't. The train was supposed to leave at 11 the next morning from down at the station in Tuscaloosa, but when Coach Thomas came up after practice he really ate us up, as he should have.

"He said, 'Okay, see you out in full gear in the morning at 8 o'clock.'

"We were out there on the practice field and there wasn't any foolishness then, and I think that might have won the football game.

"I loved every minute of the trip by train. I really loved the food. Of course, it was free.

"Something I'll always remember is that I worked that summer in Houston in the oil fields. I worked for a roughneck driller, a guy named Big Boy Williams. He was supposed to be the toughest guy in the oil fields. Well, I worked hard and Big Boy kinda liked me, I guess. Hutson and I were playing baseball on the side for extra money, but I got fired from my baseball job. I was trying to con my way through but I just couldn't play. It was during the Depression, and Hutson, who was a fine baseball player, had gotten me the job.

"Big Boy kept me on the oil field job, though, and I remember telling him that I wasn't much of a baseball player, but we were going to the Rose Bowl that year and I would see him then.

"Sure enough, we stopped in Houston about 7 o'clock in the morning, and it was a big thrill for me when I stepped off the train and there was old Big Boy and some of my oil field buddies.

"We had our second practice in Tucson, Arizona. I remember that we ran a lot of signals in those days, just getting off the count and running down the field. We must have run for an hour, and in that altitude we were all about to die, at least I

Bill Lee, one of three 1934 all-Americans.

was.

"When we arrived in Los Angeles there were a lot of Alabama people and dignitaries there to meet us. I didn't get close to many of them, but being in the group I saw them. That was a thrill for me.

"We were staying at the Huntington Hotel in Pasadena, and that was a very big thing then. Every day there would be some stars and celebrities around, usually with Johnny Mack and Connie. People like Gail Patrick from Birmingham and Peggy Waters, who later became Dixie Howell's wife.

"I remember comedian Jack Oakie, Loretta Young and Mary Brown. I remember her because she was a good looking gal. Some of them I can't remember but I can picture them in my mind. The names just escape me.

"We made a trip to Warner Bros. studio and met Mickey Rooney and Dick Powell. Powell was from Arkansas and he had his picture made with all of our Arkansas boys, so I got in that picture. We saw a lot of things and a lot of people and I was in hog's heaven.

"We practiced out at Occidental College. Freddie Pickhard was assistant coach then. He had been a standout player at Alabama earlier. Some great writers were there, too, like Granny Rice, Braven Dyer and Henry McLemore and a little cub reporter for some radio stations and small papers named

Ronald Reagan, now the governor of California. He was out there every day at practice, talking with Coach Thomas.

"Coach Thomas apparently didn't have practice closed because people were everywhere, even a lot of them were right out on the field, and that burned Coach Hank (Crisp) up.

"We were running pass patterns and I recall he came back in the huddle and told us, 'Anybody who runs over somebody gets $2.'

"Howell called a pass and my pattern was to go deep. He threw it down to me and I ran right over somebody, so Coach Hank gave me $2.

"The next day Howell wanted his dollar and I learned a lesson right there. I said, 'Why, heck, Howell, I'm the one who ran over him.' He said, 'Why, I threw the ball down there.' I told him I just didn't know about that. I didn't give him his dollar.

"Well, he didn't throw me another pass during practice, so I went back and gave him the dollar.

"One day Hutson, the Walker boys, Joe Dildy, Kay Francis, and I broke training and went down to the ice cream store. Coach Thomas, Coach Burnam and Coach Drew all walked in and caught us eating the ice cream.

"I thought Dildy was going to faint. It scared all of us. But they just left and didn't say a word.

"We were all worried, but Dildy was really worried if they were going to send him home or something. A couple days later, though, he came in and said it must have been stupid.

"He said he had it figured out that if they sent all of us home, they wouldn't have but one end and one center left, so he shouldn't have worried so much.

"Howell, Hutson and Bill Lee were our all-Americans and were in great demand to make appearances and speak. They were invited along with Stanford's all-Americans to some kind of luncheon, and Stanford had a big tackle named Reynolds who was an all-American and I was dreaming about him and having nightmares.

"Hutson came back and said, 'Aw, that Reynolds looks like Ichabod Crane. I wish he were playing in front of me.'

"Well, he was playing in front of me and Hutson's remarks gave me a little courage and I could sleep a little better.

150

"Of course, when I saw Reynolds he didn't look like any Ichabod Crane. He was about 6-5, weighed 250 pounds and had big ole arms and hands.

"During the game there were several things I remember well. Stanford had long yardage and was about on our 40-yard line. We had the game won by then, I think. When they were back in the huddle, I looked down and there was a bunch of money. I mean it was to me. There was a silver dollar, two or three half dollars and some quarters.

"There must have been between $3 and $4, so I picked it up real fast and had it in my hand. I was planning on running to the sidelines on the next play and giving it to somebody on our bench to keep for me.

"Well, lo and behold, Grayson comes running with the ball toward my end. I had to make a decision. It was the only tackle I made the entire game, but I lost my money in the process."

Howard "Beats" Alabama

Frank Thomas had a new five-year contract, courtesy of that pragmatic old football fan, Dr. Mike Denny. Alabama had a winter, spring, and summer to daydream of the glories of beating Stanford in the Rose Bowl.

The summer would end with the annual breather against Howard, which is now known as Samford. Ho hum. September 28, 1935, was breather day in the Southeastern Conference. Tennessee was playing Southwestern, Georgia was meeting Mercer, Georgia Tech was warming up against Oglethorpe.

Howard was a little school in East Lake in Birmingham. Billy Bancroft, the old baseball hero, was its coach. Its big game was not against Tennessee or Stanford or anybody like that. It was against Birmingham-Southern, and sometimes 15,000 would turn out.

Alabama and Howard played football in two different worlds. One went to Rose Bowls, the other was decidedly minor league. Alabama had lost nine regulars from the great 1934 team, including Howell and Hutson and Lee. Riley Smith (who would make all-American quarterback) was injured and could not play in the 1935 opener. But so what? Howard was still Howard and Alabama was Alabama and nothing could change that.

Howard had made a decent stand the week before in losing to Mississippi State 19-6, but Thomas could not convince his players they had any reason to beware the Bulldogs. Only 4,500 fans were interested enough to come out to Denny Stadium to see the slaughter.

The Bulldogs took it to the Tide immediately. They drove to Bama's six-yard line before linebacker Kay Francis stopped them.

Still, no one worried. And in the second period Joe Riley hit Jimmy Walker for a touchdown. But Paul Bryant was offside, and they called it back. Alabama did not stop, driving from Howard's 46. Jimmy Angelich made 14 in two runs, and Rudy Rhordanz and Joe Kilgrow carried to the four. Angelich scored and Jim Whatley converted, and it was 7-0 at the half.

The third period was scoreless, and a writer in the pressbox joked, "Alabama still hasn't come home from California."

The Tide pushed near Howard's goal in the fourth period, but Norman Cooper and Percy Yeargen covered Riley for a five-yard loss, and the Bulldogs took over at their 16.

Helped by a major roughing penalty against Bama, Howard found itself at the Tide 37. Ewing Harbin gained five but lost a yard on two more tries, and the Bulldogs found themselves with a do-or-die fourth down.

Charley Willcox was sent into the game to substitute for the triple-threat Harbin. But Captain Pat Harrison refused to accept the substitute.

It proved a beneficial disregard of authority. Harbin faded to pass. He spotted Dan Snell in the open near the goal. The ball wobbled but Snell caught it, sidestepped a tackler, and was in the end zone.

Penny Penrod could make history by kicking the point. Cooper snapped it, Pete Allen sat it down, and Penrod sent it on its way. The kick was low. Howard fans froze. It barely cleared the crossbar—but that is all the rules require.

Howard had "beaten" Alabama 7-7. When the game ended Pat Harrison walked to the Tide bench. He had wanted to play at Alabama, but Bama turned him down because of his size. "Am I still too little?" he asked Thomas.

The Bulldogs were going wild in their dressing room when Thomas knocked on the door. He was carrying the game ball. "It's yours," he told the Bulldogs. "You deserve it."

One Little Bone

Alabama slipped to six wins, two losses and a tie in 1935, but the season produced a story that would live in red and white annals.

In the third game, a loss to Mississippi State, Paul Bryant suffered a broken leg in the first period. He returned in the third period and finished the game. No one knew it was broken then, but by the next week Bryant was wearing a cast and was on crutches.

But Bryant made the trip, got the cast off, and started against Tennessee in Knoxville. He played until Bama had the game in hand. The Tide won 25-0.

"It was just one little bone," Bryant would protest later. Red Drew would answer that with, "How many bones do you need to have a broken leg?"

Thomas recognized Bryant's coaching potential and made him an assistant in 1936. Bryant had considered professional football, but he knew he would never be good enough to make the big money, so he accepted the Alabama offer.

Only a scoreless tie with Tennessee spoiled a nine-game 1936 season. Thomas told his men a victory over Vanderbilt in the final game might earn them a bowl bid, for the Sugar and Orange bowls had come into being in 1935, and the Cotton Bowl was preparing to stage its first game.

Alabama won 14-6, but there was no offer. The 1936 team did produce another all-American, though: guard Arthur (Tarzan) White who would garner more fame as a "hero" in pro rasslin'.

In 1937 Thomas molded a 9-0 team that returned to the Rose Bowl. But it would be the only Tide team to be beaten in Pasadena.

That was a good year for Rockne pupils. In addition to Thomas' 9-0, Eddie Anderson of Holy Cross was 8-0, Buck Shaw of Santa Clara 8-0, Clipper Smith of Villanova 8-0, Jim Crowley of Fordham 7-0, Charley Bachman of Michigan State 8-1, Elmer Layden of Notre Dame 6-2, Jack Meagher of Auburn 5-2, and Jim Phelan of Washington 5-2.

Halfback Joe Kilgrow, tackle Jim Ryba, and guard Leroy Monsky, each an all-American, paced the Southeastern Conference champions through their all-winning season that led to the Roses.

Thomas knew the 1937 club was not as strong as some Tides that had represented the South in the Rose Bowl. There had

155

been some close calls during the season. For instance, Sandy Sanford had to kick a fourth-quarter field goal to beat Tulane 9-6. Alabama had been in an illegal formation on the play, but the officials failed to spot the infraction. Bama also required a late field goal by Sanford to trim Vanderbilt 9-7.

Thomas said the 1937 squad had gone further on less material than any he had coached. "We don't have the big guns we had last time we went to the Rose Bowl," he said. "We'll do well to hold down the score."

California was a 3-1 and 2-1 betting favorite. One of its leaders was Jelly Belly Meek, a large individual whose nickname and family name belied his ability as a blocking back.

Stub Allison, the California coach, knew how disparaging articles by coast writers in the past had helped fire up visiting Rose Bowl teams. He detected that pattern developing again and began buttonholing newsmen, asking them to help his

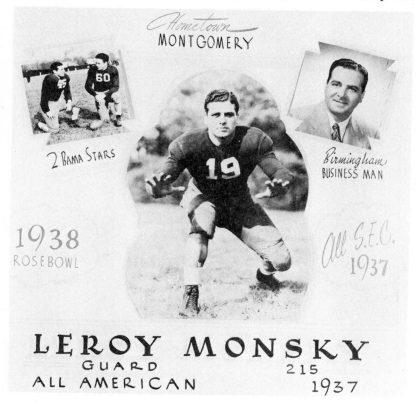

Hometown
MONTGOMERY

2 BAMA STARS

Birmingham
BUSINESS MAN

1938
ROSEBOWL

All S.E.C.
1937

LEROY MONSKY
GUARD   215
ALL AMERICAN   1937

cause.

Prescott Sullivan of the *San Francisco Examiner* poked gentle fun at Allison—and his party-loving fellow newsmen:

"Just in case you're thinking of placing a biscuit or two on California to beat Alabama in the Rose Bowl, I'd advise that you first inquire into the physical fitness and mental attitude of those scriveners who are charged with writing pieces for the papers in advance of the Pasadena opus.

"The warning is suggested by recent conversations I have had with Stub Allison, the California coach, who, addressing me as though I were twins, repeatedly has said, 'You guys can help us a lot.'

"From these words I gather that Allison is counting heavily on the press to assist him over the big hurdle and I, for one, will be only too pleased to cooperate in every way.

"But Allison cannot be sure of the other guys and, indeed,

he is worrying himself into a frazzle this very minute over the possibility that some gentlemen of the Fourth Estate will be sour of mind, or otherwise unsound come New Year's Day.

"Despite almost daily appeals for aid, Allison has received very little assurance that those mugs will keep in training through the next two weeks and he is sick with the fear that they will let him down in his hour of greatest need.

"I wish I could do something to restore Allison's waning faith, but beyond pledging myself to carry on the traditional Sullivan manner, I can do little for him because with my own eyes I have seen the very guys on whom he counts most violating every training rule in the book, and quite recently, too.

"It is practically impossible to believe these renegades will be of any use to the Golden Bears January 1, and in fact it's tough to believe that a few of them will come up for the bell the morning after New Year's Eve."

California did not need any help from newsmen or anyone else. The Bears won 13-0. Vic Bottari, a junior tailback who had skyrocketed from anonymity to stardom, scored both touchdowns on short runs. Alabama lost the ball on fumbles four times and had four passes intercepted.

When the train pulled into Tuscaloosa, most of the 10,000 fans who had been there in 1935 were home listening to the radio or doing whatever people did in 1938. Thomas muttered that nobody loves a loser.

Tide Rose Bowl delegation visited Paramount before 1938 game.

Seven Blocks Of Granite
Get Chipped

Alabama's 1938, 1939, and 1940 teams stayed home on New Year's, though they had records of 7-1-1, 5-3-1, and 7-2. The spate of secondary bowls such as the Liberty and Peach had not occurred then, and teams that today do not claim national headlines were big winners. While Alabama listened to the radio, St. Mary's, Fordham, Georgetown, Carnegie Tech, and Boston College were in New Orleans, Miami, and Dallas.

Wallace Wade, the former Tide coach, was in Pasadena on January 1, 1939, but his Duke team was losing to Southern California 7-3.

The Tide scored major victories, though. The 1938 squad was invited to open against Southern Cal on the Coast because of the tough game it had given California in the Rose Bowl. The Trojans were two-touchdown favorites, but Alabama won 19-7. "That was one of our finest victories," Thomas said years later. "Mind you, when we beat Southern California—a great team— we'd had only 23 days' practice, including three days en route to California." The 1938 team beat a fine Tulane club 3-0 when Vic Bradford kicked a fourth down field goal late in the game.

The 1939 team was Thomas' poorest, but it upset Fordham's famed Seven Blocks of Granite team 7-6 in the Polo Grounds.

Charley Boswell, who in later years would be an international champion blind golfer, was the star, and Jimmy Nelson, a Tide great, scored the touchdown. Sandy Sanford kicked the winning point. Center Carey Cox was a 1939 all-American.

The 1940 team played the first night game in Alabama history, beating Spring Hill 26-0 in the Murphy High School Stadium in Mobile.

Paul Bryant moved to Vanderbilt to serve as an assistant under Red Sanders in 1940. He began traveling a circuitous route that would lead to Maryland, Kentucky, Texas A&M, and finally, back to Tuscaloosa in 1958.

Thomas expected a strong team in 1941—and he got it. That

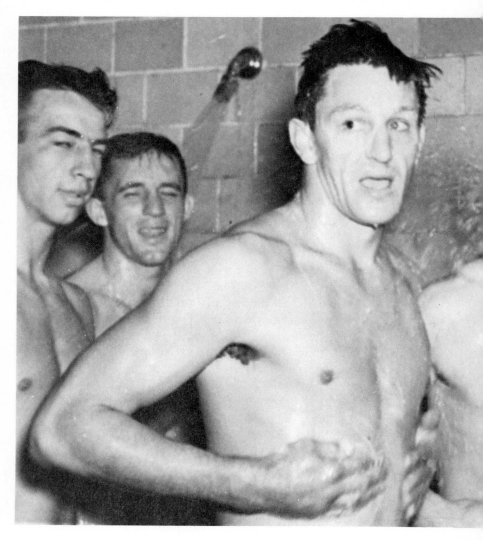

Tide won nine and lost two, including a decision over Texas A&M in the Cotton Bowl. "I've never seen as many great backs on one team," Thomas said early in the year as he watched Jimmy Nelson, William Harrell, Julius Papias, Sumpter Blackman, Paul Spencer, Al Sabo, Vaught Tollett, Carl Mims, Howard Hughes, Bart Avery, Russ Moseley, Lou Scales, Dave Brown,

End of a perfect day. Left to right: Charlie DeShane, Holt Rast, Tom Borders, Cliff Hansen, Tom Maxwell, Fred Davis.

George Gammons, Russ Craft, Don Salls, and Mackey McCoy work out.

Riding the train to Dallas, Thomas confided that he saw no way Texas A&M could stop his backs. Homer Norton, the Aggies' coach, was from Birmingham and had a lot of friends in Alabama. Thomas told his boys they would never hear the last of it if they lost.

There has never been a football game quite like the 1942 Cotton Bowl, before or since. Alabama won 29-21, but. . .

The Tide made only one first down; A&M had 13. Bama gained just 75 yards total offense; the Aggies made 309. The Crimsons completed one pass; the Texans completed 13. The Tide ran 32 plays; A&M ran 79.

But the significant statistics showed Alabama intercepting seven passes and recovering five A&M fumbles.

Nelson scored on a 72-yard punt return and a 21-yard scrim-

Hometown
South Bend, Ind.

Bama Captain '42

ALL S.E.C. '42

Bowl star
1942 Cotton Bowl
1943 Orange Bowl

PRO-BALL
(Dallas "Texans")
BOSTON YANKS

All-Time...
All-Star
ORANGE
BOWL

JOE DOMNANOVICH
CENTER   200 LBS.
ALL AMERICAN   1942

National Football Hall of Fame

Donald B. Whitmire
United States Naval Academy
All America Tackle, 1943-1944

has been granted the highest honors of the National Football Hall of Fame, in recognition of his outstanding playing ability as demonstrated in intercollegiate competition, his sportsmanship, integrity, character, and contribution to the sport of football. this certificate bears witness that his name shall be forever honored in the National Football Hall of Fame

Elected:
January 3, 1956
New Brunswick, N.J.

Bill Cunningham
Chairman, Honors Court

HONOR AND SERVE

mage run to pace Bama to a 23-7 lead. Another TD that did not show in total offense figures was an interception return by all-American end Holt Rast that made it 29-7. The Aggies scored two touchdowns in the fourth quarter to make the score respectable.

Charley Boswell became international champion blind golfer.

"Alabama's brilliant bowl record weighed heavily in the decision of Orange Bowl officials to bring a three-times-beaten team here," the Associated Press ticked over its wires when the 1942 club, which had gone 7-3, was picked to play powerful Boston College.

One of the losses was a 21-10 game against Georgia. Thomas later called it the most shocking reversal of his career. A 47-yard run by Russ Craft and a conversion and a field goal by George Hecht had Alabama ahead 10-0 in the third period. The Tide had stopped the great Frank Sinkwich cold. But Sinkwich began hitting passes, and when the day had ended he had completed

18 of 37 for 231 yards and two touchdowns.

"I believe we are facing the toughest team in the country and I know we will have to play our best to win," Thomas said of Boston College, his Orange Bowl opponent.

"Boston College uses the Chicago Bear T formation and we have never played against this type offense. We have got our work cut out for us."

George Halas, coach of the Bears, said Boston College could whip any pro team in the country.

Halas's opinion appeared justified as the Eagles jumped to a 14-0 lead in the first period. Center Joe Domnanovich, who along with tackle Don Whitmire had represented Alabama on the all-American teams, gathered the team around him. "Don't give up," he said. "We haven't had a chance to go with the ball yet. We're going to receive and we're going to run them into the ground. At halftime Alabama led 22-21. The Tide won 37-21 despite Mike Holovak, who later became a college and pro coach, gaining 154 yards rushing for the Eagles. Johnny August scored a touchdown and passed to Ted Cook for another to pace Bama.

Collegiate football practically went out of business in 1943. Only those schools with Army and Navy programs maintained a schedule. Alabama's team closed up shop that season.

The War Babies

Frank Thomas devoted his time in 1943 to heading War Bond drives, serving as president of the Tuscaloosa Exchange Club, looking after business interests and recruiting.

He was particularly interested in a little tailback at Birmingham's Woodlawn High School. So was everyone else. Of Harry Gilmer, Zipp Newman wrote in the *Birmingham News*: "Harry is as fine a passer as there is in football. This goes for the pros." Naylor Stone of the *Birmingham Post* commented in print: "The kid is just as fine a passer as Sinkwich."

Thomas not only had to contend with other colleges for Gilmer, he was up against the star's general disinterest in attending college at all. "I plan to get me a job and get married," Gilmer said.

Thomas was frustrated. He had to have this fellow who as a sandlotter had developed the jump pass because he was so much smaller than everyone else. Thomas hired Malcolm Laney, Gilmer's prep coach, as an assistant, and soon Harry followed him to the Capstone.

Gilmer brought 155 pounds and an ulcer to the University of Alabama. He was placed on a rigid diet of milk, cream, cereals, and strained vegetables but no meats. The diet did not supply the vitality a football player required, but once Gilmer made up his mind to be a college player his determination never wavered.

Thomas had told the University's athletic committee that he would like to resume the football program in 1944. He said the going would be tough, but he felt he could field a team "that will not disgrace the University." The committee tried to discourage him but finally approved his request.

So many players were in the service that the Southeastern Conference and most others allowed freshmen to play in 1944. The squad that reported to Thomas was mostly frosh and 4-Fs.

Thomas named them his "war babies" and in later years said he loved them more and was prouder of them than any others he coached, this band of teen-agers.

Gilmer was coolness personified. He was lying on his bed in a Baton Rouge hotel before the opener against LSU when someone asked the blond freshman, now down to 150 pounds, if he was excited. "No, it will be just like another high school game," Gilmer said.

The war babies tied LSU but finished the season with a record of five wins, two losses, and a tie. One of the victories was a 19-0 thrashing of previously undefeated Mississippi State and Shorty McWilliams. Thomas was shocked a few days later when his club was invited to meet Duke in the Sugar Bowl.

He told his team Duke was an older, heavier team and said he was not sure it would be fair to the Tide to accept. He left the decision to his players—and they voted to head for New Orleans.

On New Year's Eve, while merrymakers in funny hats yelled on Bourbon Street, Thomas told his wife he was dead tired. It was a condition that had begun to affect him only recently. She told him he was worried about his "babies" and reminded him he was getting older.

Newspapermen criticized Thomas and the University of Alabama for allowing the basically freshman squad to meet Duke and its Navy trainees. But Thomas told his players they were fighters and that he loved each one of them. They whooped it up from the dressing room to the bench.

One of the greatest bowl games in history began. A crowd of 72,000 would watch the lead change four times. The outcome would not be settled in Duke's favor, 29-26, until the last play. In the final analysis, the power and experience of the older Duke players made the difference.

Alabama kicked off and a slaughter appeared imminent. George Clark returned to the 33. On the first scrimmage play he carried for 52 yards. Clark faked a pass and ran for a touch-

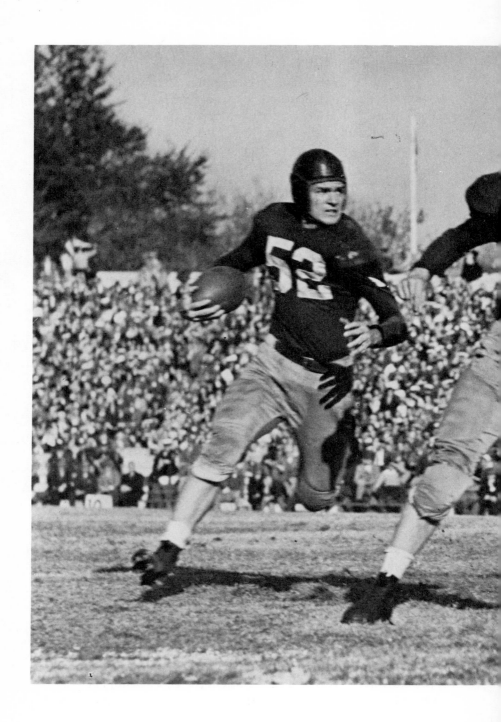

Harry Gilmer runs behind Fred Grant.

down on the next snap. The PAT made it 7-0.

But Gilmer and his cool war babies did not wilt. Duke fumbled, and Ralph Jones recovered on the Blue Devil's 35. Norwood Hodges gained 15, then Hodges and Lowell Tew put it on the eight for a first down. Gilmer flipped a pass to Hal Self who was stopped at the one-foot line. Hodges scored, but Hugh Morrow missed the kick.

Bama held and began a 69-yard touchdown march. Gilmer gained 20 but lost 16 when he fell trying to pass. From the Duke 40 Gilmer threw to Jones who ran to the two before he was stopped. Hodges mowed through center for the touchdown. Again Morrow missed the conversion, but Alabama led 12-7.

Again Alabama's defense did not buckle, and Duke punted dead on the Tide 11. Tew gained 21, and Gilmer and Jones teamed for a 51-yard pass play. Gilmer shot a 10-yard touchdown pass to Jones. Morrow's conversion made it 19-7 in the second period.

But the Blue Devils would not cave in, either. Duke drove 63 yards for a second period touchdown and missed the PAT. Bama led 19-13 at halftime.

Duke's size advantage began to wear down the war babies in the third quarter. The Devils marched 63 yards for a touchdown and kicked the goal, going in front 20-19.

Morrow put Alabama ahead again with an 80-yard touchdown return of a pass interception in the fourth period. He made the placement, and Bama led 26-20.

The husky, experienced Blue Devils pounded on. Alabama stopped Duke at the two on a saving tackle by George Albright. But Thomas did not want his men handling the ball so near their goal, so he gave Duke an intentional safety. Now the Tide's lead was cut to 26-22.

The strategy did not work out. Alabama free-kicked 40 yards, but Duke returned it 20 to the Tide 40. Wingback Jim LaRue gained 20, then Clark scored. The PAT made it 29-26, Duke.

"I'd say that last run by LaRue won the game," Grantland Rice wrote. "He fought his way for 20 yards where he might have been thrown for a loss. He carried two red shirts on his back for the last seven yards and it was this terrific determination to win that saved the day for Duke. I've never seen a more thrilling game.""

With just a smidgen of luck, the war babies still could have won. Gilmer threw a long pass on the final play. Jones caught the ball and eluded all but one tackler. The Duke defender made a desperation dive and caught one foot. Jones nearly wiggled free, but finally he hit the ground as the gun ended the game.

Gilmer had completed eight of eight passes. Rice called him the greatest college passer he had ever seen.

There was a victory celebration for Alabama that night, first at Antoine's and then at the St. Charles Hotel. It finally broke up just before daylight.

Perhaps it was the only time in history a losing team was feted with a victory celebration.

End Of An Era

The war babies were sophomores in 1945. Thomas expected a fine team—but he did not even dream Alabama would catch another train for Pasadena.

The 1945 squad scored a school record 430 points on the way to a 10-0 chart, including a 34-14 win over Southern Cal in the Rose Bowl. Gilmer and center Vaughn Mancha made all-American, but the Helms and Associated Press National championships went to Army's Davis-Blanchard powerhouse.

After only four games, Thomas told his men (or boys, rather) that they had a chance to go all the way—if they could beat Georgia. The game matched Gilmer and Bulldog immortal Charley Trippi. Alabama won 27-14 as Gilmer threw three touchdown passes. At the end of the year, Gilmer was voted most valuable player in the SEC, ahead of Trippi.

Thomas was tired by midseason. He was placed on a strict diet, ordered not to smoke, and told to get plenty of rest. After the season-ending game against Mississippi State, Thomas said he was a worn man and glad football was over.

But he was about to face another month of football. The Rose Bowl called that night and invited the Tide to play Southern California. Thomas gave his club a week's rest—but he needed it worse than the players did.

All sorts of problems plagued the Tide that headed for Pasadena on December 23.

Two snowfalls, rain, and freezing weather had handicapped practice in Tuscaloosa. An outbreak of flu had struck the players. Lowell Tew, a starting back, suffered a broken jaw in the final Tuscaloosa workout. His teeth were wired together. "No football player has been given any more attention than Lowell Tew was given on the trip out," Zipp Newman wrote in the *Birmingham News*. "He was fed on an hourly schedule from early in the morning until tucked in between the blankets at night. In one meal he had the equivalent of 10 pounds of choice beef. Two cases of concentrated foods were put on the train at New Orleans and at every stop new supplies were added for Tew."

The bug even struck assistant coach Happy Campbell who had to remain in his Pullman berth. Campbell deftly turned a phrase: "I'm going to fight this flu germ lying down."

"We won't do as much sightseeing as we did on our previous trips. In the first place, we haven't as much time and in the second place we need to get in a lot of practice," Thomas

Bowl Star
'45 SUGAR
'46 ROSE
'48 SUGAR

1945 Triumvirate

All S.E.C. Honors 1944 - '47

Successful College Coach

VAUGHN MANCHA
CENTER   240 lbs.
ALL AMERICAN   1945

announced. The train had arrived 16 hours late on December 27.

Thomas complained of being tired on the morning of the game and said he was happy the players felt better than he did. He was puzzled that he tired so quickly.

Alabama was favored to win, and a crowd of 93,000 immediately saw why. The Tide was ahead 27-0 in the third period before Southern Cal even made a first down. The Trojans had a net loss of 24 yards in the first half. Gilmer threw only 14 times, but the little tailback gained 116 yards rushing. Hal Self scored twice, sneaking over from the one and catching a 24-yard Gilmer pass. Gilmer tallied from the one, Tew from the two, and Norwood Hodges from the one. Hugh Morrow kicked four extra points.

Alabama, first Southern team to play in the Rose Bowl, in 1926, became the last. The classic closed its doors to all except representatives of the Pacific Coast and Big Ten conferences.

In the spring of 1946 Thomas's doctor told him his blood pressure was very high and ordered him to stop all outside activities.

Thomas had his war babies back as juniors, and several players had left the service to join them, but 1946 would be his most perplexing season. The team won seven and lost four. When Thomas was not directing practice, he was in bed.

He coached the 1946 team from an elevated trailer because he was not able to stand so long on his feet. Thomas used a loud speaker because his voice was weak.

Alabama won its first four games, but before the Tennessee battle Dr. Raymond Paty, president of the University, suggested he resign as head coach for his own good and serve only as athletic director. Thomas replied that he could not quit on his players. In later years he said the decision was "foolish."

After the 1946 season ended, Thomas resigned as head coach but said he would remain as athletic director. He recommended Red Drew as his successor. Drew had been an assistant on Thomas's staff but had become head coach at Ole Miss in 1946. He was happy to return to Tuscaloosa.

Thomas was in and out of hospitals in 1947. He was treated at Duke University Hospital by a world famous high blood pressure expert. Thomas often visited with Wallace Wade and sat on the Duke bench during practice sessions.

In 1952 Thomas resigned as athletic director. Pete Cawthon was appointed as his successor.

In 1953 Thomas was elected to the Football Hall of Fame, along with Don Hutson, his end of two decades before.

Coach Tommy, who had given Alabama its second great era of football, died in Druid City Hospital in Tuscaloosa on May 10, 1954.

Off The Bench,
Into The Headlines

Red Drew was not the winningest coach in Alabama history, but during his eight years as chief his teams played in three of the most historical games.

One was the 1948 Auburn match, which marked renewal of the series with the Plainsmen. Alabama and Auburn had not played each other since 1907. The series had been dropped because of a contract dispute. Several efforts to resume the series had been made over the years without success, but finally, with pressure from the state legislature, they agreed to meet in Birmingham.

On the morning of the game in 1948, Gillis Cammack of Auburn and Willie Johns of Alabama, presidents of their respective student bodies, dug a hole in the ground in Woodrow Wilson Park, tossed a hatchet in, and buried it. It has stayed buried, and the Alabama-Auburn game is the No. 1 sports attraction in the state.

Ed Salem, only man to make all-American under Drew, threw touchdown passes to Clem Welch, Rebel Steiner, and Howard Pierson, ran for one and kicked seven extra points as the Tide buried Auburn, too, 55-0.

Drew's 1952 team killed Syracuse 61-6 in the 1953 Orange Bowl. It was the most lopsided win in bowl history. Alabama led by only 7-6 after one period, but the Tide scored 14 points in the second quarter, 20 in the third, and 20 in the fourth.

Zipp Newman saw history clearly when he wrote in his *Birmingham News* column that day: "Come the years and

Ed Salem led massacre of War Eagles.

Tommy Lewis made football history with one tackle.

Alabama supporters will take their grandchildren on their knees and tell them about the time Alabama beat Syracuse in the 1953 Orange Bowl—smashing 12 records in the most record-breaking bowl game in history."

It was the first New Year's Day on which fans could see on television bowl games in Pasadena, Dallas, New Orleans, and Miami. Many in the crowd of 66,280 at Miami left the stadium in the third period to watch other games.

The game lasted so long that an Orange Bowl committeeman reportedly approached the timekeeper and suggested the game, nearly three hours old at the time, be accelerated because the network was about to cut it off.

Bobby Luna and Tommy Lewis each scored two touchdowns while Corky Tharp, Bobby Marlow, Joe Cummings, Hootie Ingram, and Buster Hill scored one each. Clell Hobson was the regular quarterback, but a freshman sub named Bart Starr would go on to professional football glory.

Marlow, in three seasons, gained 2,560 yards rushing. That was 693 yards more than the next highest total in the conference during the 1950-59 period. Billy Cannon was runnerup. Yet Marlow was not selected on the all-decade team of the SEC.

The third famous game during the Drew years was the 28-6 loss to Rice in the 1954 Cotton Bowl game. Most do not remember the score, many do not even recall who won—but everyone remembers Tommy Lewis' off-the-bench tackle.

Rice was leading 7-6 midway of the second period. The Owls had the ball on their own five. Dick Moegle took a handoff and turned right end. Rice blockers blotted out Tide defenders. Moegle appeared to be home free by the time he reached midfield. But Lewis, bareheaded, charged off the Alabama bench and decked Moegle. The officials awarded Moegle a 95-yard touchdown.

It was one of three he scored. Moegle finished the day with 265 yards rushing in 11 runs.

Lewis was crestfallen. "I'm too emotional," he told a reporter after the game. "I kept telling myself, 'I didn't do it, I didn't do it.' But I knew I had.

"I'm just too full of Alabama. He just ran too close. I know I'll be hearing about it the rest of my life."

At halftime Lewis went to the Rice dressing room to apolo-

Bart Starr as a young Alabama quarterback.

gize. "Don't let it bother you," Coach Jess Neely, a former Tide assistant, said. "My heart went out to him," Neely commented later.

"It happened so quickly I didn't have time to think," Drew said in the dressing room after the game. "I know how Tommy felt and I sent him back in the game when Rice kicked off."

"I felt real sorry for him," Moegle said while he tugged off his uniform in the locker room. "I know how he felt. Yes, I think I could have made it all the way if he hadn't hit me. It was a body block he threw me.

"I saw him when I was about on my 35-yard line. I thought he'd dropped his helmet and it had rolled out on the field, or dropped something. He looked like he was looking for something. But then I had to watch the players chasing me and I just saw Lewis jump at me out of the corner of my eye as I went

180

past. He came up and apologized, said he had just let his emotions carry him away."

It was the closest thing to the Wrong Way Riegels episode in football history. In the 1929 Rose Bowl game against Georgia Tech, California's Roy Riegels recovered a fumble, became confused and ran 64 yards the wrong way. He was downed on his own one-yard line by a teammate. Moments later Tech got a safety and won 8-7.

Riegels, who saw the Lewis boo-boo on television, advised the Alabama back, "Laugh with them. That's all you've got to do."

Moegle thought the incident helped Rice. "They were real nice to me after that. I've never had so much help in getting up after a tackle as they gave me."

The *Dallas Morning News* ran a front-page editorial that concluded:

". . . Tommy Lewis, a genuine competitor even while on the bench, had committed a forgivable error that will live with him forever. He quickly and abjectly apologized to Moegle and the Rice team and he did it three more times, finally, at game's end, walking out of the big stadium with his arm around Moegle.

"Tommy is a very depressed boy, but he has the qualities that will take him far down the road in a country that prospers and survives because of youngsters who compete on or off the bench.

"Texans know competitive spirit. We thrive on it. It might not be a bad idea to drop Tommy a line over at the University of Alabama, Tuscaloosa, Alabama, and let him know he hasn't lost his last friend.

"He's quite a fighter—and we like them that way in Texas."

Red Drew is a native of Maine. He played at Bates College. He coached at Trinity (Connecticut) College, Birmingham-Southern, and Chattanooga before joining Thomas' Alabama staff. He served one season as head coach at Ole Miss before returning to Bama as chief.

Drew's records were 8-3 in 1947, 6-4-1 in 1948, 6-3-1 in 1949, 9-2 in 1950, 5-6 in 1951, 10-2 in 1952, 6-3-3 in 1953, and 4-5-2 in 1954.

Drew inherited Thomas's "war babies" when they were seniors in 1947, and they went to the Sugar Bowl but lost to

181

Texas and Bobby Layne 27-7.

Harry Gilmer experienced the worst day of his career in that game. One the same turf where he had been a hero against Duke three years before, Gilmer completed only three of 11 passes and ran for just five yards. Layne completed 10 of 24 for 183 yards.

Drew's 1953 and 1954 teams lost to Mississippi Southern, and the 1954 squad scored only 14 points in its final six games, closing with a 28-0 loss to Auburn.

Shortly after the end of the season, the University of Alabama announced that J. B. Whitworth was its new head football coach and that Drew would be a professor of physical education and head track coach.

The next day newspapers ran a picture of Drew shaking hands with Whitworth and smiling.

Time Out: Red Drew

Red Drew looked out the window of an alabaster hotel on Miami Beach and sunlight sprinkled the Atlantic Ocean with sequins. Alabama was there to play Oklahoma in the 1963 Orange Bowl, and Drew was there as a fan.

"I had a friend in the real estate business over here on the beach who was doing pretty well," Drew said. "He had quit coaching up in Virginia and came here during the boom with $2,000 or so in savings. Three days later he had $40,000 cold cash. But that wasn't enough. He went for a million.

"Then came that bust.

"He got knocked flat and soon was back to coaching. The bug had him, though, and a couple of years later here he was back again. He made his million this time.

"Before he did, though, he tried to talk me into going with him. I didn't. I went back to coaching.

"I haven't made my million yet."

Drew does not have a million dollars, but he has a million friends. There is no more universally well-liked sports figure than the old Maine Yankee.

At 76 he is a victim of arthritis, and the disease keeps him close to the Tuscaloosa home where he lives with his wife Marian.

"This kind of weather makes it pretty nice," Drew told a springtime caller. "It's a lot better in this kind of weather. But it's a bad thing to have. Don't get it.

"I only went to two football games last year, and no basket-

183

ball games. But I'm hoping I can see some next time."

Drew glanced back over his career and named the 1952 team, the one that beat Syracuse 61-6 in the Orange Bowl, as "probably" his best club. "That team was made up of a lot of good football players."

There was no attempt to embarrass Syracuse, he said. "Our defensive team scored as many points as the offensive team. Everytime they got hold of the ball they scored with it. It was just one of those things that happened. We didn't try to run up the score. Everybody just figured we had a particularly good football team on that particular day.

"Syracuse had to be pretty good to get an invitation. They thought they were, and we did, too. Before the game they thought they were better than we were."

Bobby Marlow was the best back he ever coached, but he will not select a lineman. "I get an awful lot of people asking me who was best, Marlow or Johnny Musso. That's an awfully hard question. Both were awful good. You don't run across their kind every day.

"I had a couple of pretty fair ends when I was with Coach Thomas, in Hutson and Bryant." Drew poo-poos Bryant's stories that he was not an outstanding player. "Bryant was a heck of a football player. That kind of talk was part of Bryant's game."

Drew dismisses Tommy Lewis' off-the-bench tackle in the 1953 Cotton Bowl as "just one of those things that happen. You say it can't happen, but it did. Tommy has taken it pretty well himself over the years."

Drew's wit has never left him. "The first thing I said to Tommy? I don't know. I've heard so many things that were supposed to be the first thing I said that I wouldn't want to say what was."

Alabama had problems before that Cotton Bowl game even started. "Albert Elmore was our first string quarterback. Bart Starr was our second stringer. Elmore was in a car wreck and couldn't play. Bart was just a greenhorn in those days."

Harold Delbert Drew, who would win 55, lose 29, and tie 7 at Alabama, laughs away questions why he never returned to live in his native Maine. "It's too cold up there for me."

Drew was coaching at Trinity (Connecticut) College when he

Bobby Marlow was a ground covering back.

came to Atlanta for a national coach's meeting. He met Dr. Guy Snavely, president of Birmingham-Southern, at the meeting and, first thing you knew, Drew was Southern's head coach.

Drew retired from the university in 1965. He drove away from an A-Day halftime ceremony in a new car.

"I'm not sure that he and Coach Hank still couldn't whip most of the guys they coached," Paul Bryant said that week.

The Dark Years

"We're going after the best boys, boys who want to come to work here and uphold the great tradition that is Alabama football. I'm going to work to keep that tradition, the coaches are going to work and the players are going to work."

J. B. (Ears) Whitworth returned to his alma mater with words full of enthusiasm, but his three-year term as head football coach was a failure.

Whitworth's 1955 team went 0-10, his 1956 and 1957 clubs both 2-7-1. Auburn scored 100 points to Alabama's 7 in beating Whitworth three times.

Whitworth had been a lineman at Alabama under both Wallace Wade and Frank Thomas. He kicked a field goal in the 24-0 licking of Washington State in the 1931 Rose Bowl.

He was an assistant at Alabama, LSU, and Georgia before becoming head coach at Oklahoma A&M. A year remained on his A&M contract, but the school released him from the pact so he could return to his alma mater. Whitworth had had a losing record at A&M and came to the Capstone off a 5-4-1 season.

"I look for Alabama to come back mighty fast," said Whitworth's old Georgia boss, Wally Butts, when he was hired. But it did not happen.

Whitworth produced no all-American, not even an all-Southeastern Conference selection, though end Nick Germanos and guard Billy Rains were second-team all-SEC choices.

Bart Starr played quarterback on Whitworth's 1955 squad, but his college career did not hint at the glory that would come

187

J. B. Whitworth as Bama lineman in 1930.

later with the Green Bay Packers.

On the morning of Whitworth's final game, a 40-0 thrashing that clinched the national championship for Auburn, his players presented him a ring set with a sapphire and two diamonds.

"Coach, I wish I could have played better for you," said one of his players in a quiet dressing room when it was over.

"If I had only coached as hard as you played, that score today would have been reversed," Whitworth replied.

"Coach, I want to thank you for helping me," said another, tears in his voice.

"Aw," Whitworth said, "if you could know the pride I've felt as I watched as a big, old, flabby boy grew into a man, you wouldn't need to do any thanking. . ."

"Coach," the next player said, "thanks for all you've done for me. It's been a honor to play for you."

"Boy, two years from now I'll be reading about you some-place, and I'll be bragging to folks that I knew that little old feller. . . If you keep working, you'll make something of your-self, something big," Whitworth said.

He addressed the entire squad: ". . . The football season is over and my jurisdiction over you is ended. . . Keep your feet on the ground, study hard, work hard and give the new coach as much effort as you have given me, and a year from now I'll be mighty proud of you."

Three days later the University of Alabama announced that its new football coach was Paul Bryant.

In March, 1960, while Bryant was preparing for a spring practice that would lead to a 1961 national championship for Alabama, J. B. Whitworth, who again was a University of Georgia assistant coach, died of a coronary occlusion.

Return Of The Bear

"We have secured, to our way of thinking, the best football coach in the country for the position of head football coach at the University of Alabama," Ernest Williams told the reporters gathered at the Shamrock Hotel in Houston.

Williams, a Tuscaloosa banker, was chairman of a committee named by President-elect Frank Rose to study the Alabama athletic situation. "I never saw anything like it, the feeling back home for Paul," said Fred Sington, a member of the committee. "Not just from Alabama alumni, but from the man in the street, too." Naming of Bryant was hardly a shock. Several newspapers had predicted it.

Bryant signed a 10-year contract as coach and athletic director that day, to the delight of Alabama supporters and to the consternation of Texas A&M men.

Bryant had revived winning football at the bleak Texas school. His first Aggie team in 1954 had won one and lost nine, but then the records had been 7-2-1, 9-0-1, and 8-2 with a Gator Bowl game against Tennessee (a 3-0 loss) still to be played. Bryant was released from his contract at A&M with seven years remaining.

He had left Kentucky (located in a state in which football is the No. 3 sport behind horse racing and basketball) glory years, too. Starting in 1946 Bryant's Kentucky teams had gone 7-3, 8-3, 5-2-2, 9-3, 11-1, 8-4, 5-4-2, 7-2-1. Four Wildcat clubs had visited bowls. Before Bryant, Kentucky folks had hardly known what a bowl was.

Coach Paul Bryant and Mrs. Bryant.

In his one year at Maryland the Terrapins had won six, lost two, and tied one. So it was a 91-39-8 record, achieved under difficult conditions, that Bryant brought to Tuscaloosa.

A contract, he believed, was for the protection of the president of a school. If the coach did not conquer the world in the first year or so, and the alumni hopped on the president's back, the president could point to the coach's contract.

"This is the most difficult thing I ever had to do," Bryant said at that December 3 meeting in Houston. "You don't stay at Texas A&M as long as we did without learning to love it, the traditions, the boys, everything.

"The reason, the only reason, I'm going back is because my school called me."

Mrs. Bryant was pleased to return to Tuscaloosa. Mary Harmon Black had been a University of Alabama co-ed and, of course, had lived in the town when Bryant was an assistant under Frank Thomas. They had enjoyed a nice social life in Lexington, were friends of the governor, and had a new house. She had blanched when she had first seen Texas A&M, an austere institution that has recruiting problems because of its lack of appeal. Don Meredith, who became a star SMU and professional quarterback, told Bryant he would love to play for him—if only he were somewhere else.

"Am I happy to be going home? You KNOW it!" she said at that Shamrock Hotel announcement gathering. The Bryants had two children, Paul, Jr., and Mae Martin.

Kentucky had not been big enough for Bryant and basketball coach Adolph Rupp. Bryant wanted football to be No. 1. Basketball was No. 1, and Rupp intended to preserve its position. They are close now, but co-existence then was a problem.

Bryant asked Hank Crisp, the assistant coach who had begun his Capstone career in 1921 under Xen Scott, to join him in Houston. Crisp had served as athletic director after poor health forced Pete Cawthon out, but he had resigned that post during the season. Bryant would retain his old coach as director of intramurals.

Alabama knew it was getting a coach to whom football had never been just a game. He demanded 100 percent effort at all times. Anyone not willing to give it could buy a train ticket.

It was football that had got Bryant out of Moro Bottom,

Arkansas. It was a vehicle away from driving mules and chopping cotton. Bryant learned that sacrifice could rescue him from a life of poverty. He practiced sacrifice as a player, teaches it as a coach.

Fear of returning to the crushing rural life motivated Bryant. He knew what it was to peddle vegetables off a wagon. When it rained around Moro Creek, his older brothers would hitch up the mules to rescue anyone who got stuck on the rutted roads, anything to make a coin or two. Bryant was one of a dozen children, and his father was a semi-invalid.

Bryant wrestled a bear to earn money.

He had walked in to Fordyce from the farm, and there at the movie theater was a poster offering a dollar a minute to anyone who would wrestle a bear. At the time, Bryant was chopping cotton—for 50 cents a day.

One of his friends egged him on. Bryant went on stage, and they brought the bear out. It was a monster to him, but rather scrawny to his cronies.

Bryant knew enough about wrestling to avoid the bear's clutches and to get a hold of his own. Down they went, and there they stayed. There was no action. The clock ticked away, and Bryant counted his money. The promoter fretted. Finally, the bear worked his muzzle off and took a nice, juicy bite of neck. Bryant fled into the audience.

When he went to collect his money, the promoter and the bear had hit the road. Bryant was as poor as ever, but he had acquired a nickname.

Bryant eventually moved to Fordyce and made the high school football team. He had cleats put on the only pair of shoes he owned and wore them everywhere, to practice, to school, to church.

Arkansas had been a rich vein of recruiting for Alabama over the years, and Bryant was proud to bid adieu to Moro Bottom and Fordyce and chopping cotton and to head for Tuscaloosa.

When his playing days were over, Bryant remained at Alabama as an assistant coach. He and Don Hutson, who had played end opposite him, opened a dry cleaning place. Alabama got new uniforms in 1938, and Bryant sent them to his place for cleaning. They shrank several sizes and could not be used, but Coach Crisp covered for him and ordered new ones.

Bryant moved to Vanderbilt as an assistant in 1940. He served two years but enlisted in the Navy in World War II and attained the rank of lieutenant commander. He returned to civilian life as Maryland's head coach.

Maryland's president fired an assistant coach without consulting Bryant and reinstated a player that Bryant had dismissed from the squad. Bryant resigned and accepted Kentucky's offer. There was a student strike over his leaving College Park. Kentuckians who had complained about the school hiring an unknown coach were quiet now. The student strike had Bryant's name in headlines.

Headlines—not all of them flattering—would be his at Texas A&M immediately, too, because of the "Junction boys." Bryant took two busloads of would-be A&M football players to training camp at Junction, Texas, in September of his first year. Half a load returned. Bryant's total dedication method of football left him with a 27-man squad. All six of his centers quit.

But total dedication football was winning football. It had won at Maryland, Kentucky, and Texas A&M. It would win at Alabama, too.

All They've Got

Paul Bryant munched on a sandwich and talked to Benny Marshall of the *Birmingham News,* who would become his fast friend over the years. Marshall asked him what kind of coach he considered himself.

"I am, I think, just an ordinary coach that works hard," Bryant replied. "Some work a little harder than others. But it's players who make the coaches, my friend. And the mothers and papas have a lot to do with making players, too."

On another occasion Bryant said, "In a situation such as we accepted here, the main thing is getting the material and teaching your kids to forget a losing complex. Teach them to win."

Total-dedication football produced its casualties in 1958. A number of players quit the first three days. Three were denied uniforms when they showed up overweight. But it paid immediate dividends, too. One tackle who had weighed 233 in the spring reported at a trim 215. Many of the players with the most ability quit.

"If a man's a quitter, I want him to quit in practice, not in a game. There has been enough of that," Bryant said. He explained that his demand was for "all they've got. We've got to know now whether we can get it later."

Nobody could complain about being cussed out. Bryant established profanity fines of 25 cents for players, a dollar for assistant coaches, and ten dollars for himself.

Louisiana State would be the first opponent, and Bryant knew his ragged-but-willing bunch needed any edge it could get.

"We won't be talking too much. . ." Bryant told newsmen when practice opened in September, 1957. "We won't be saying too much about who's doing what and where.

"Let 'em guess some at LSU. They can be working on a lot of things. But until that first ball game, we won't be telling them."

LSU had Billy Cannon and would win the national championship. Bryant announced a starting lineup of:

Left end—Jerry Brannen, 186, junior, Anniston.

Left tackle—Carl Valletto, 210, junior, Oakmont, Pennsylvania.

Left guard—Wayne Sims, 190, junior, Columbiana.

Center—Kenneth Roberts, 192, senior, Anniston.

Right guard—Don Cochran, 190, junior, Birmingham.

Right tackle—David Sington, 215, senior, Birmingham.

Right end—Charles Gray, 189, senior, Pell City.

Quarterback—Bobby Jackson, 183, senior, Mobile.

Left halfback—Marlin Dyess, 150, junior, Elba.

Right halfback—Mack Wise, 172, sophomore, Elba.

Fullback—Milton Frank, 184, sophomore, Huntsville.

LSU was figured to be able to name the score. But Paul Dietzel, the head coach, had been an assistant under Bryant, and Dietzel's assistant Charley McClendon had played for Bryant. They knew better.

"Our kids might have taken that game in Mobile lightly," McClendon said years later. "But Paul and I didn't. We knew we were against the master. And we knew what a spot he'd be coming at us from. He loves to attack fat-headed, fat-stomached people. We weren't fat-stomached.

"You'd better believe Paul and I were up for that game. We wanted it so badly we were foaming at the mouth as our kids warmed up.

"And we didn't know a soul else was in the place when here Coach Bryant comes ambling up—you know, with that slow, dignified walk of his, like a big cat.

"He put his arms around us and gave us that slow smile.

"'Boys, boys,' he said, 'you're taking this thing too seriously. After all, it's just a fun game.'

"I don't remember what I said. I remember what I thought. Fun like a monkey's uncle. It's fun if fighting for your life is fun."

Alabama lived by defense in that first game, and for years that would be a Bryant trademark. The Tide held LSU and Cannon scoreless for the first half, but the more talented Tigers finally won it 13-3 in the final two periods.

A Ladd Stadium crowd of 34,000—some of whom were injured when a wooden bleacher collapsed—cheered when Duff Morrison snatched a Cannon fumble out of the air on Alabama's 45 and went to the LSU four before the Tigers caught him. Three runs netted only two yards, and Sington kicked a field goal. Bryant and Alabama led 3-0 in the second quarter.

Louisiana State punctured the defense in the third quarter. The Tigers pushed 67 yards, and Warren Rabb threw to Johnny Robinson for the final nine. Cannon ended the scoring in the fourth quarter on an 11-yard run.

It seems an antique game in the light of today's pass and prayer football. Alabama threw only three passes and did not complete any. LSU passed just 13 times, completed 6 for 73 yards.

And when was the last time you saw a quick kick? Dyess knocked one dead 52 yards on LSU's seven, then quick kicked 55 yards out on the six.

After the game, a reporter asked Bryant, the bitter loser, "Were you satisfied with the overall effort?"

Bryant spat the answer: "I'm never satisfied when I get beat."

Over the years reporters learned not to ask silly questions.

Bryant's first Alabama team won five, lost four, and tied one. Furman fell 29-6, Mississippi State 9-7, Georgia 12-0, Georgia Tech 17-8, and Memphis State 14-0. In addition to the LSU game, Alabama lost to Tennessee 14-7, Tulane 13-7, and Auburn 14-8. There was a scoreless tie with Vanderbilt.

Bryant had won one more game in his first season than Bama had won in its previous 36 games.

Back To The Bowls

Heaven, to an Alabama man, is beating Auburn and going to a bowl game. The Tide had not whipped Auburn since 1953 and had not been bowling since that same club lost to Rice in the Cotton Bowl.

Despite his September frowns ("I'd give everything I've got for just one team") and groans ("Based on what I saw today, I don't think we're as strong in any department as we were last year"), Bryant was about to beat the War Eagles and earn a bowl trip in 1959.

With sophomore Pat Trammell running the offense, Bama beat Houston 3-0, Chattanooga 13-0, Mississippi State 10-0, Tulane 19-7, Georgia Tech 9-7, Memphis State 14-7, and Auburn 10-0. The only defeat—before a 7-0 loss to Penn State in the Liberty Bowl—was a 17-3 licking by Georgia in the opener. Vanderbilt and Tennessee earned 7-7 ties with the Tide.

Trammell, who would die in 1968 in the prime of life, was a running quarterback. He gained more than 500 yards on the ground as a sophomore and led the SEC in total offense.

Trammell was not in the class with Dixie Howell or Harry Gilmer or latter-day stars Joe Namath, Steve Sloan, and Ken (Snake) Stabler as a passer, but he was a cool, no mistakes winner. Often he was compared to scrappy baseballer Eddie Stanky who "couldn't hit, couldn't field, couldn't run—all he could do was beat you."

Alabama came to the final game of the season against Auburn in the familiar role of underdog. "The Tigers appear to have a mite too much again for the Crimson Tide as they go shooting for a sixth straight win over the biggest rival in the biggest game," wrote Benny Marshall of the *Birmingham News.*

Auburn Coach Shug Jordan was apprehensive, though: "We can expect them to shoot the works. Joel Eaves, who has done our scouting job, tells me that in every game Alabama has brought out something new. They're versatile. We've got to be prepared for almost anything."

Nine Tiders were closing their careers (except for the bowl game) and had never beaten Auburn: tackles Fred Sington, Jr., and Chuck Allen, center Jim Blevins, guards Don Cochran, Bill Hannah, and Wayne Sims, end Red Stickney, fullback Gary O'Steen, and halfback Marlin Dyess.

Alabama won 10-0 on a 27-yard field goal by Tommy Brooker and a 39-yard touchdown pass from Bobby Skelton to Dyess. Jordan said Alabama had the best team he had seen all season. Sportswriters voted the 145-pound Dyess the game's most valuable player.

"Before the game we said it'd take a superhuman effort to win, and I think our boys gave it," Bryant said. "If our team played 100 per cent against Georgia Tech, it played 135 per cent to beat Auburn."

The bowls filled up. The Liberty Bowl, a new one, was trying to match Penn State and Navy. "I'm disappointed for our seniors," said Bryant, who thought the football season was over.

Four days later headlines screamed that Alabama would meet Penn State in the Philadelphia Liberty Bowl. The Tide was returning to the scene of the first major victory in Alabama history, the 9-7 whipping of Pennsylvania in 1922. It would be the first of 13 straight bowl appearances for Bryant teams.

Alabama lost 7-0 on a play that Coach Rip Engle put in just two days before the game, a fake field goal. On a cold, windy day, Tommy White got off a punt of only three yards for the Tide. On the final play of the first half, with the ball on Alabama's 18, quarterback Galen Hall knelt to hold for an apparent field goal attempt. But Hall rolled to the right and threw a touchdown pass to Roger Kochman.

The 1960 squad downed Georgia 21-6, Vanderbilt 21-0, Houston 14-0, Mississippi State 7-0, Furman 51-0, Georgia Tech 16-5, Tampa 34-6, and Auburn 3-0. Tennessee beat that Tide

Tommy Brooker was talented all-around end.

Bobby Skelton hit TD against Auburn.

Pat Trammell rarely made mistakes.

20-7, and Tulane got a 6-6 tie. Bama fought Texas to a 3-3 deadlock in the Bluebonnet Bowl.

"Just to look at them, you wouldn't think they belonged on the same field," said pro great Lou Groza who scouted Alabama's little men against Georgia Tech. But Bama won on a last-play field goal by Richard O'Dell, who had never kicked one before and never would again.

Immediately after the victory over Auburn—accomplished by a 22-yard Brooker field goal—Alabama announced it would meet Texas in Houston.

Brooker kicked a 30-yard field goal in the third quarter, and Alabama led 3-0 in the bowl game. Dan Petty booted a 20-yarder for the Longhorns in the fourth quarter.

That would be the last time anybody would strike off even with Alabama for awhile. The Tide was about to win a national football championship.

Best In The Land

A man could have become rich selling ice water at Sanford Stadium in Athens, Georgia, on September 23, 1961. It took courage to even be a fan on that day.

Sanford Stadium is built in a natural valley. It is the loveliest of the Southeastern Conference ballparks, but the wind rarely stirs between the hedges that ring the playing field. It becomes an oven on a sunny, 90-degree day.

On this particular afternoon Alabama opened its 1961 season with a 32-6 rout of Georgia. It was a historical date not only because it marked the first step toward a Tide national championship, but because, for the first time since Noah built the ark, Wally Butts was not Georgia's coach.

Johnny Griffith was Georgia's coach—or at least he was supposed to have been. It was a weird weekend.

Alabama fielded a fine-looking team that September. Names that became synonymous with winning football at the Capstone dotted the roster: Pat Trammell . . . Lee Roy Jordan . . . Darwin Holt . . . Billy Neighbors . . . Mike Fracchia . . . Butch Wilson . . . Bill Battle . . . Tommy Brooker. Alabama was picked to finish high nationally.

Bryant conceded the Tide looked like a winner but hedged, "You can't look at a rabbit and see how fast he can run."

Bryant, who liked to attack from a position of surprise, had a highly touted football team this time. "I can't see how a fellow can sit in New York or Birmingham and tell how good a football team a thousand miles away that he hasn't seen will be.

Top—Billy Neighbors: Mr. Tackle.

Middle—Lee Roy Jordan set a standard for linebackers.

Bottom—Jimmy Sharpe is now a Tide assistant.

No, it doesn't disturb me, us being picked high. I don't do the picking, just the coaching. I hope they know what they're talking about."

Griffith, the new Georgia coach, promoted the widespread praising of the Tide: "Alabama is out of our league. They're sound. They've got a lot of people who have been doing the same thing three years."

Johnny Griffith was doomed to failure at Georgia, and no coach ever got off to a worse start.

On the day before the game, Griffith watched his freshmen scrimmage his B team for a couple of hours, then spent another 45 minutes watching the varsity hustle through its final preparation for the Alabama game.

He was aching inside and when practice ended he went to see his doctor. The doctor told him to go to Athens General Hospital.

Mike Fracchia scores in 1962 Sugar Bowl game.

Griffith called his wife, then left a laconic message at the home of Dan Magill, his public relations man: "I'm going to the hospital to have my appendix out." At the hospital he sent for Charlie Trippi and John Gregory, a couple of assistant coaches, reviewed the game plans, and then went into the operating room.

When the doctors came out, they said, "He's all right, but there wasn't any time to spare. That appendix needed to come out right now." They called it "red hot."

Johnny Griffith began his head coaching career as a radio listener in a hospital bed.

Soon his Georgia team felt as badly as he did. Tim Davis kicked a 41-yard field goal, Mike Fracchia made a couple of short touchdown runs, Pat Trammell threw a 37-yard scoring pass to Wilson, and Mal Moore hit a 10-yard scorer to Red Wilkins. Davis kicked a couple of extra points, and Moore ran for a two-pointer. Holt, Jordan, Neighbors, Brooker, Charley Pell, Jimmy Sharpe, and Bill Rice keyed a defense that held Georgia away.

"I think it was the hottest game we've ever been in," Bryant said. He used 43 of the 44 men who made the trip. Forty played in the first half. A number of spectators had to be removed on stretchers.

The 1961 club allowed only 25 points, lowest Tide total since Frank Thomas's 1933 squad gave up 17. On the way to an 11-0 record, Alabama beat Vanderbilt 35-6, Tulane 9-0, North Carolina State 26-7, Tennessee 34-3, Houston 17-0, Mississippi State 24-0, Richmond 66-0, Georgia Tech 10-0, Auburn 34-0, and Arkansas 10-3 in the Sugar Bowl. The Tide was named national champion after the Auburn game.

Late in the season there had been rumors that the Rose Bowl might end its tie-up with the Big Ten and invite Alabama to return to Pasadena, scene of so many past Crimson glories. But nothing came of it, so the Tide headed for New Orleans.

"I think early in the season that they were the nicest, even the sissiest bunch I'd ever had," Bryant said after the Sugar Bowl game. "I think they read it, because later on they got unfriendly."

Alabama scored in the first period. Fullback Fracchia ran 43 yards to the Arkansas 12. On the next play, Trammell rolled through his left tackle and into the end zone. Davis converted.

Davis kicked a 32-yard field goal in the second period, but Mickey Cissell of Arkansas matched it with a 23-yarder in the third. A touchdown pass trickled off the fingers of Lance Alworth late in the game that could have turned the Sugar Bowl around.

Neighbors, Trammell, and Jordan were named to various all-American teams. They were Bama's first all-Americans since Ed Salem in 1950.

In four years, Bryant had raised Alabama from chump to champ.

Time Out: Charley Pell

Charley Pell sat in the office of the head football coach of Jacksonville State University, his office, and pointed to a picture on the wall, a picture of the 1960 University of Alabama coaching staff.

"Jerry Claiborne, Carney Laslie, Phil Cutchin, Pat James, Gene Stallings, Charlie Bradshaw, Sam Bailey . . . that was a dedicated group of football coaches," he remarked.

Pell's dedication matched theirs. It had to. Otherwise he could not have played college football, certainly not on a national championship team such as the 1961 Alabama club.

"I had never seen the campus before I went there for August practice as a freshman," Pell said. "I saw Coach Bailey and I punched one of the boys who had been recruited real heavily and I asked him if that was Coach Bryant. He said hell, no, and I told him I just didn't know. I didn't know Coach Bryant until he walked into our freshman meeting."

All odds were against Charley Pell being a college player, but he became one of Bryant's "little boys," a tiny tackle who helped win a championship.

Pell never played football until he was a senior at Albertville High School.

"Mamma and Daddy didn't want me to play," he said. "I had a brother who was injured one year and they felt like I'd have the same bad luck.

"Bobby Golden, an Auburn graduate, was the new coach. He walked up to me one day in the hall and asked me why I didn't

Charley Pell was a smiling young Tidesman.

play football. I told him my buddies had come to the house to try to get them to let me play. He asked if Mamma would object to him coming by and I said I wished he would.

"Coach Golden talked to Mamma three-and-one-half hours one day. He was a deacon in the Baptist Church and a Sunday school teacher, so she figured he couldn't be all that bad."

So Pell played the next season—but as a back. He had seen a grand total of one college game when he went to Alabama. He earned a trip to an Auburn-Tennessee game by scoring three touchdowns against Oneonta and being named most valuable back. It was the second time he had ever seen Birmingham.

Alabama wanted Dan Dixon, the captain of the Albertville team. "They offered him a scholarship, but he turned it down because of a bad back and because he wanted to work on his grades," Pell said.

After Dixon said no, Alabama offered Pell a scholarship. "It must have been about the last one left. I didn't think they knew Albertville existed. I would never have had the chance to go to Alabama if it hadn't been for Coach Bryant coming back and rebuilding and getting Alabama players.

"When I got there I found players from a bunch of small towns. Coming to college was an honor, a privilege not many folks in our home towns got.

"I weighed in stripped at 179 that August, and that's the

209

honest truth. The heaviest I ever weighed at Alabama was 188 and that was my last season."

Almost immediately he was switched to the line, despite being a comparative midget.

"I hope I never get to the point that I don't think small kids can play," said the head coach of Jacksonville State University. "But they do have to be blessed with more ability now than they used to."

Pell is glad he missed the recruiting merry-go-round that puts pressure on some prospective players. "I think I was lucky because of that. I had no preconceived notion as to how good I was. Nobody knew me and I only knew one coach, Phil Cutchin. He hadn't even bought me a hot dog. The only time he came, we ate at the house and Mamma fed him like he was a preacher."

The dream of a national championship began as chit-chat in the dorm and was a "dream come true" when it occurred, Pell said. "We like to think we were on the team that got Alabama football back where it ought to be.

"I can't ever remember a problem between the players on that team. I guess every championship team is that way. The people were interested, too. Every night somebody would have a football or a piece of paper at the dorm to get autographs.

"Tommy Brooker, being the businessman he was and being a pretty good artist, drew up a little thing and got our signatures on it and sold them like hotcakes.

"Everybody had a nickname. Billy Richardson was 'Little Bitty Billy with the Big Heart.' That was what he got stuck with around the dormitory.

"Pat Trammell was the top dog of that football team. I'll never forget, we had a big old tackle who would always want to call time out. We were playing both ways then and everybody would want somebody else to call time out. But if he couldn't get anybody else to say it, this tackle would. I remember Pat telling him to shut his damn mouth. Everybody knew he could back it up, too."

Pell feels the principal lesson he learned from Bryant was to "think, then make a plan, then set about making it come true."

The 1961 Tide, with little Charley Pell at tackle, made a dream come true.

The Bomber
From Beaver Falls

Headlines gravitate to Joe Namath like raindrops to the earth. Sometimes they are good headlines. Sometimes they are not. Always they are read.

Touchdown passes . . . a record contract . . . movies . . . suspension . . . bad knees . . . a llama rug . . . a fur coat . . . winning the Super Bowl . . . Raquel Welch . . . saving the AFL . . . Bachelors III—all subjects for Namath headlines.

He broke in with headlines at Alabama, throwing three touchdowns in a 35-0 victory over Georgia. He went out in headlines, signing a contract with the new York Jets for a then-stupendous $400,000.

Since, he has become the most popular player in the biggest town—Broadway Joe, always ready with a quip, and in the center of more than one controversy.

After Namath joined the Jets, a newsman asked him if he majored in basket weaving at Alabama. "Naw, man, I majored in journalism," he replied. "It was easier."

Namath laughed when he read that a veteran pro wondered whether the high-priced Namath would be willing to "pay the price." Namath said anyone who had played for Paul Bryant knew something about paying the price.

He is a free spirit who will ask you how you would like to get up every morning and realize that the world knew every move you were going to make. "I like everybody," Namath said, "even Howard Cosell."

Namath stepped into Pat Trammell's quarterback spot, sur-

Joe Willie attracts the headlines.

rounded by a number of stars from the 1961 national championship team.

Bryant could even joke that September of 1962, "I wish Lee Roy Jordan had come back a little heavier. He's 202, he told

212

me. I'm sure he's in shape anyway. If he's not, I don't want to know about it."

At the end of the season, Jordan was all-American, the greatest linebacker in Alabama history. His team won nine and lost one, including an Orange Bowl victory. Georgia fell 35-0, Tulane 44-6, Vandy 17-7, Houston 14-3, Tennessee 27-7, Tulsa 25-6, Mississippi State 20-2, Miami 36-3, Auburn 36-0, and Oklahoma 17-0 in the bowl. Georgia Tech was the only club to beat this Tide, winning 7-6.

Namath threw a 52-yard touchdown pass to Richard Williamson on the fifth play of the opener against Georgia. Before it ended, the sophomore had pitched TDs of 10 and 12 yards to Cotton Clark.

That game would become more famous as the subject of a 1963 *Saturday Evening Post* article charging that Bryant and Georgia Athletic Director Wally Butts had conspired to "fix" it.

It was an expensive story. Both sued. Bryant earlier had sued over a *Post* article that charged him with brutal coaching methods. After the case went all the way to the Supreme Court, Butts finally was awarded $460,000 plus interest. Bryant received a $300,000 settlement.

By the time Alabama headed for the Orange Bowl, Bryant was rating Namath "potentially the best quarterback I've ever coached." Before Namath's college career ended, Bryant called him the best athlete he had ever seen.

Namath piloted his team 61 yards in 10 plays for a touchdown in the first period against Oklahoma. He flipped a 25-yard pass to Richard Williamson for the points. A sleight-of-hand pitchout to Cotton Clark resulted in a 15-yard touchdown in the second quarter. Tim Davis, who had kicked both extra points, made a 19-yard field goal in the third quarter.

Crisp blocking by Charley Pell, Jimmy Wilson, Jimmy Sharpe, Bill Battle, Butch Wilson, Ed Versprille, Dan Kearley, Frankie McClendon, Lee Roy Jordan, and others had paved the way for the offense.

Fifteen seniors finished the best three years (29-2-2) Alabama had ever known. Capstone football was jetting in this its third great era.

The 1963 team went 9-2, beating Georgia 32-7, Tulane 28-0, Vanderbilt 21-6, Tennessee 35-0, Houston 21-13, Mississippi

Cotton Clark led SEC in scoring.

Top—Dan Kearley was crisp blocker.

Middle—Tim Davis kicked Ole Miss down.

Bottom—Creed Gilmer blocks Texas field goal in 1965 Orange Bowl.

State 20-19, Georgia Tech 27-11, Miami 17-12, and Ole Miss 12-7 in the Sugar Bowl. Losses were to Florida 10-6 and Auburn 10-8. It was Auburn's first win over the Tide since 1958.

The 1963 season was most famous for Namath's suspension. Bryant received a report that his star had been drinking. Namath admitted it.

With two games to go, both on national television, Bryant suspended Namath and told him to move out of the dormitory.

Bryant told his coaches. Every one of them except Gene Stallings wanted, some way, to keep Namath on. Stallings, who had played for Bryant at Texas A&M, said if he had been involved in such a caper he would have been suspended, so Namath should be, too.

Jack Hurlbut did most of the quarterbacking in the final game of the regular season, a 17-12 squeaker over Miami. Gary Martin's 102-yard runback of the opening kickoff got the Tide started properly.

Sophomore Steve Sloan quarterbacked the 12-7 victory over Ole Miss on a Sugar Bowl field surrounded by piled-up snow. But Tim Davis field goals of 31, 46, 22 and 48 yards got all the points. The 48-yarder was the longest in bowl history, and the four field goals were a bowl record.

With Namath and Sloan splitting quarterback time, the 1964 squad went 10-0 in the regular season and won the national championship. Victims were Georgia 31-3; Tulane, 36-6; Vanderbilt, 24-0; North Carolina State, 21-0; Tennessee, 19-8; Florida, 17-14; Mississippi State, 23-6; LSU, 17-9; Georgia Tech, 24-7; Auburn, 21-14.

The championship was voted at the end of the regular season. On New Year's Day, in the Orange Bowl, Texas trimmed the champs 21-17.

"They should have been No. 1 all along," Bryant said after the last regular season victory over Auburn. The Tide had been fourth in the first poll, third in the second, second in the seventh, and finally first in the final poll after Southern Cal had whipped Notre Dame.

"I might have lost confidence several times," Bryant said. "I think I did. But these boys never lost theirs.

"What they did was no accident, either. They didn't win that thing on Thanksgiving Day (against Auburn). They won it in September . . . and maybe on back at their homes in the summer. They won it on a lot of afternoons when maybe they weren't having so much fun, sweating so they could enjoy this kind of fun." Namath, halfback David Ray, tackle Dan Kearley, and guard Wayne Freeman made all-American teams.

It had been a trying season. Namath suffered a knee injury in the fourth game against North Carolina State, and Sloan was the quarterback. Namath was starring by the ninth game, leading a victory over Georgia Tech.

Sloan started the Orange Bowl game after Namath re-injured his knee in practice, but Namath wound up as most valuable player, hitting on 18 of 37 passes for 255 yards and touchdowns of seven yards to Wayne Trimble and 20 yards to Ray Perkins, and playing a game that national televiewers would not forget.

Namath almost won it for the Tide after David Ray kicked a 26-yard field goal to cut Texas' margin to 21-17 in the fourth quarter.

Jimmy Fuller intercepted on the Texas 34. Namath passed for 17 to Ray Ogden and to Steve Bowman for a first down on the six. Bowman gained four. Alabama, which had trailed 14-0 at one time, was only six feet from the goal and had three downs. Bowman gained a foot, then a yard. Namath tried to sneak on fourth down. Many say he made it, but the officials said he did not.

The next morning, while cameras whirred and bright lights beamed in the Harbour Inn on Miami Beach, Joe Namath signed a $400,000 contract with the Jets. The bright lights are still beaming, the cameras still whirring, for Joe Willie.

Time Out: Joe Namath

Joe Namath stopped in the corridor of the University of Alabama's Memorial Coliseum and studied a picture of Harry Gilmer. The camera had stopped Gilmer in midair, his arm drawn behind his head like a whip. Namath stared at the photo on the wall through sunglasses, though the sun could never have reached into these catacombs.

"Last time I threw a jump pass somebody got me right here," Namath said, cuffing himself on the chin with the back of his hand.

Joe Namath, target. Four times doctors' scalpels had opened his knees to repair the parts that could not withstand the unnatural pressures of football. A man's knee was never meant for this game. A cracked collarbone, dislocated finger, fractured wrist and fractured ankle had taken lines on his medical chart, too.

On this summer day, Namath had come to the weight room at the university to strengthen his knee. He had been injured in a preseason game the year before, underwent surgery, missed most of the year, returned for a few late games. It seemed unusual that his team, the New York Jets, would have used him at all in those meaningless games.

"It was unusual for me," Namath said wryly. "Anytime I play it's unusual." Then, seriously, "It wouldn't have been fair to the team for me not to play. I wanted to play. I get tired of sitting around."

The most famous player in Alabama history has done a good

Joe Namath, without the locks.

deal of sitting around. He must have wondered just what he could have accomplished had he not been forced into sitting around so much.

"Only briefly," Namath answered. He would have done Norman Vincent Peale proud with his positive thinking. "If I had never got hurt I might never have played pro football. I would have been in the army."

Bizarre publicity has followed Namath like a puppy after a butterfly. Cynics shook their heads when the army said Namath's knee did not meet its standards. He was damned if he did and damned if he did not. If he said he was glad he did not have to go, he was unpatriotic. If he said he was sorry, he was nuts.

"I didn't say anything," Namath recalled. "I said I'd do what I was supposed to do. The surgeon general even had to issue a report to Congress because it was such a public thing."

Namath pulled on a pair of shorts and rubber-cleated football shoes. He lay down on a bench and lifted 30 pounds on a weight machine with his knee several times.

Then he played pitch with Mike Bite, his lawyer, a little fellow with long black hair like Namath's. Joe burned the football in from six yards away, but Bite did not flinch. Obviously, he had filled this role before. Ray Perkins, a receiver with the Baltimore Colts who had come by to work out, watched.

"In 1965 I went to Florida with him to relax after an operation," Bite said later, holding up his pink swollen hands. "My fingers were stumpy after that trip. You noticed Ray didn't offer to catch any."

It was Bite who negotiated Namath's $400,000 contract after the 1964 season. Neither likes to go into detail about that deal, which at the time was considered incredible.

"It was worth not only that, but more," Bite will say.

"I've never been convinced it should be public knowledge what a man makes," Namath says.

Some newsmen wondered out loud whether Namath, whose gate appeal saved the American Football League and gave it a voice with which to talk merger with the established National Football League, makes enough.

"Nobody knows what I make," Namath said. "I don't think

anybody has ever read or heard me complain about what I made, either, except the usual stuff that you should make more. But everybody says that. It's a two-way street. I think I do a good job and I was fortunate to come to New York."

Namath had weighed an offer by the St. Louis Cardinals against the Jets' offer. He admits more money landed him but says if he had realized the advantages of New York there would have been even more reason for the latter.

Namath's charisma (he made an obscure word popular) raining onto the printing presses of New York's tremendous publicity outlets have helped land him a television talk show, movie roles and business opportunities.

Would he like a full time movie career? "I haven't decided yet."

What kind of actor does he consider himself? "A young one."

At 28 Namath is young. He is handsome, famous, wealthy. His reputation is that of a guy who has, shall we say, seen the elephant and heard the owl. "I'm a normal, healthy American male," Namath answered an obvious question.

Does his private life fit the picture most fans have in their minds? "I don't know what everyone thinks," Namath said, "but I know I'm enjoying my life style. I think I'm doing it right. I could improve on it, but you keep trying to improve on everything."

Namath has no steady girl friend. "I have a few friends, but it's hard to have a steady girl friend when you move about."

Does he figure to get married—some day? "Yeah, but I don't foresee that anytime soon."

Some who knew Namath in college insist he was rather shy. "I didn't go to a lot of parties," he admits. "I didn't party much, I didn't drink much and I didn't belong to a fraternity."

Namath maintains residences in Tuscaloosa, Fort Lauderdale, New York and Beaver Falls, Pennsylvania, his hometown. Tuscaloosa occupies a large spot in the heart of this Yankee.

"I wouldn't be here 11 years if it didn't," Namath said. "I have a condominium apartment in Fort Lauderdale and that's one of the finest places in the world. I sure wouldn't leave it for a place I didn't love."

Namath came to Alabama after failing to pass the entrance exam at Maryland. Alabama landed him because of two facts,

Namath said: his brother Frank was a friend of ex-Alabama assistant coach Howard Schnellenberger, and Bama offered Namath nothing under the table.

"I had some good ones," Namath said of illegal offers from other schools. "But my brother told me, 'You make a deal with these people and you know they don't do anything wrong. What kind of people are you going to be working with?'"

So Namath, a Pennsylvanian, checked in at a Deep South school. "It worked out great. It started off as a strain both for me and the fellows who weren't familiar with Northerners. But one of the greatest thrills I ever got was being elected co-captain with Ray Ogden. It was more of a brotherhood, teammate situation than where you were from or what you were."

Namath did not come from a poor family, as some writers have written. "There were seven of us, counting my mother and father. He worked in a steel mill and made $5,000 a year or whatever. We never went short on anything."

Is Namath irked when he reads the poor boy version? "I stopped getting irked reading things a long time ago."

Namath has had his differences with newsmen. "Any publicity is a two-way street. A lot of times it helps but a lot of times it hurts. Some people say any kind of publicity helps you, but I've known times it didn't help me or my family, when magazines came out and talked about my association with undesirable people. That was all a bunch of bull."

Two college games stick in Namath's mind more than any others: the 7-6 loss to Georgia Tech in 1962 and the 21-17 loss to Texas in the 1965 Orange Bowl after Alabama had won the national championship.

"They were frustrating. We should have won both but we lost." Namath, of course, was called short of the goal line on a crucial quarterback sneak against Texas. He says he was over the goal line. "That was a sick feeling, infuriating."

Namath gained about as much fame for two Alabama games he did not play as for any he did. That was when Coach Paul Bryant dismissed him from the squad in 1963 before the last game of the regular season against Miami and the Sugar Bowl game against Ole Miss. Alabama won both.

Namath is evasive on just what happened. "I broke training regulations," he said. "I think Coach Bryant could explain that better than I could.

"It was a fair decision. I was wrong. It was a trying time. A lot of things went through my mind. It was good experience."

How would Namath compare Bryant and Jets Coach Weeb Ewbank? "Oh, wow. They're different personalities. Bryant is a big, stern-faced, hard-looking guy. Weeb is a little, round-faced, jolly guy. They approach coaching from their own ways of living. One can explain something with a smile on his face and one with a hard look. Both are great leaders, though."

Namath has trotted around the room a few times and is lifting another weight with his foot.

"People don't know what these guys go through," Bite whispers. "See how straight he keeps his leg? He can't let that thing buckle. If he lets it buckle, his knee will puff up. You ought to see the brace he wears when he is playing."

Namath has never considered quitting, despite the long, arduous exercises required to bring a knee back around. The exercises begin immediately after an operation.

"Once I was in the recovery room and the doctor asked me to lift my leg. I said, 'What?' He told me to lift it. I lifted it with the cast on and it felt like the stitches were going to rip out.

"But I've always been lucky in that when I got hurt I always had something ahead of me. I got hurt in college and had a pro football future ahead of me so I had something to shoot for. If I had been hurt earlier and heard some other calling maybe I wouldn't have worked so hard to come back."

"He'll lift up to 65 pounds later with that leg," Bite said. "Didn't you get 65 last time, Joe?"

"I got 90," Namath replied.

How many more years does Namath figure he will play? "I have no idea. There are too many things that come into play. Besides the physical reasons and business reasons, there are my own mental reasons. If I don't feel I can play the game as it should be played, I'll quit.

"The game is still fun. That's the most important thing. But by the same token, it's February or March before I start feeling good for the first time. You take that into consideration, too."

Namath chuckles at suggestions opposing linemen have "let up" on him in the past because of his gate appeal for the league. "There's no tie-in there," he said. "One time Ernie Ladd liked

223

to have ripped my head off. He helped me and said, 'Don't worry, Joe. I'm not going to hit you low.' In the meantime, he had almost ripped my head off and everything else. I was wanting him to hit me low."

"You know what would be a good story?" Bite suggested while Namath showered and dressed. "Somebody ought to interview a guy like Don Maynard and ask him how many yards of tape he has used in 13 years.

"One time when I was the manager here, somebody asked me what was the most important piece of football equipment. Know what I told them?

"Tape."

A Hit And A Miss

They said Paul Bryant was lucky when a jigsaw puzzle of circumstances allowed his 1965 team to go 9-1-1 and win the national championship. But no one could accuse him of being lucky when his undefeated 1966 team lost out to a Notre Dame squad that had an inferior record.

In three and a half months the 1965 club went from the bottom of the SEC to the top of the world.

It was a bizarre game, that opener with Georgia. Alabama lost 18-17 on a play that appeared to be illegal.

Georgia took a 10-0 lead, and led 10-3 at the half, but the Bulldogs were behind 17-10 with just over two minutes to play. With second and eight on the Georgia 27, Kirby Moore passed to Pat Hodgson who lateraled to Bob Taylor who scored. The 72-yard play still left Georgia behind by one point, but Moore passed to Hodgson for a two-pointer and the Bulldogs won, but not until David Ray missed a 42-yard field goal attempt with 10 seconds to go.

"This is not as good as some other Alabama teams I've seen," said Georgia Coach Vince Dooley. "At least not right now. It may be later. Alabama is a good sound football team but it isn't a great team like some of the Alabama teams of the last four or five years. It could be a great team later on."

Dooley said he had borrowed the lateral play that brought Georgia victory. "I got the play from Georgia Tech . . . I don't mind telling you, Tech used it against Auburn four or five years ago when I was there and almost won a game with it. We put it

David Ray was sure-toed placement man.

227

in this week especially for such a desperate situation as we faced today."

Georgia deserved to win, Bryant said in his post-game press conference, but the next day he changed his mind. Bryant saw the game film before he went on his Sunday afternoon television show and decided the lateral play was illegal. He made no comment on his program, but told a reporter, "If I had known then what I know now, though, I'd still be on that field arguing. I would had to be. But it's too late to do anything now. You don't win games in movies on Monday. You win them on the field."

The camera showed Hodgson had both knees on the ground when he lateraled to Taylor. Officials said they ruled Hodgson batted the ball to Taylor, which would have made it legal, but the camera cast doubt that he batted it. One hand appeared to

Ken Stabler and Dennis Homan outstanding battery.

228

Paul Crane was congratulated by Gerald B. Zornow, vice president of Eastman Kodak Company, when he made American Football Coaches All-American team in 1965.

be on top of the football.

That team beat Tulane 27-0, Ole Miss 17-16, Vanderbilt 22-7, Florida State 21-0, Mississippi State 10-7, LSU 31-7, South Carolina 35-14, Auburn 30-3, and Nebraska 39-28 in the Sugar Bowl. Tennessee tied Bama 7-7.

There were some close calls. Steve Sloan had to lead an 89-yard march in the closing minutes against Ole Miss. The sweet-passing quarterback ran nine yards for the touchdown that tied it, and David Ray converted. Sloan completed 12 of 18 passes for 127 yards in that game.

Bama needed a couple of fine defensive plays to beat Mississippi State. After the Tide scored on a 65-yard pass from Sloan to Dennis Homan and a 27-yard Ray field goal and Ray extra point, little Creed Gilmer, a 172-pounder, blocked a 23-yard field goal attempt that would have tied it, and Bobby Johns made a crucial interception at his 17.

Before the bowls the Associated Press poll had Michigan State first, Arkansas second, Nebraska third, and Alabama fourth. All had 10-0 records except Bama which was 8-1-1.

In the afternoon, UCLA beat Michigan State 14-12 in the Rose Bowl and LSU beat Arkansas 14-7 in the Cotton Bowl. The Orange Bowl all of a sudden had a national championship game on its hands that night.

The game was not as close as the 39-28 score indicates. Alabama rolled up 518 yards to Nebraska's 377. Sloan passed to Ray Perkins for two touchdowns, Steve Bowman ran for two, and Les Kelley one. Ray kicked a field goal. Sloan completed 20 passes for 296 yards.

"This is the greatest offensive team I've ever been around," Bryant said after the game. "I was very much concerned about the capabilities of this team at the start of the season. But it came a long way with probably less ability than any team I've ever had."

Sloan and center Paul Crane made all-American teams.

The 1966 Tide, with Ken Stabler at quarterback, surrounded by all-Americans Johns, tackles Cecil Dowdy and Richard Cole, and end Ray Perkins, whipped Louisiana Tech 34-0, Ole Miss 17-7, Clemson 26-0, Tennessee 11-10, Vanderbilt 42-6, Mississippi State 27-14, LSU 21-0, South Carolina 24-0, Southern Mississippi 34-0, Auburn 31-0, and Nebraska 34-7 in the Sugar

Bowl.

This was the season of Notre Dame's "tie one for the Gipper" game with Michigan State.

Notre Dame was ranked No. 1 and Michigan State No. 2 going into their November 19 game. With the score tied 10-10, Notre Dame ran out the clock rather than take a chance on a long pass. With Michigan State players jeering, the Irish refused to try to win.

Later, Notre Dame Coach Ara Parseghian said, "If you say this was wrong, then look at the national polls today."

This particular year, the Associated Press selected its national champion before the bowls. Notre Dame was first in the polls, and Michigan State was second. Their mutual tie was the only blot on either record, but Alabama, the defending champion that had not lost a round, was third.

Parseghian could joke about playing for a tie. "Actually, it was an easy decision to make. When I first became head coach at Notre Dame, I got a telegram from an alumni group saying, 'We're with you, win or tie.'

"But, judging from the mail I got after the MSU tie, I guess that word tie can be dropped."

Alabama took its frustration out on Nebraska in the Sugar Bowl. "This was the greatest college team I've ever seen," Bryant said when it was over.

Stabler completed 12 of 17 passes for 218 yards and ran for 40 more. Les Kelley, Wayne Trimble, Stabler, and Perkins, on a Stabler pass, scored touchdowns. Steve Davis kicked two field goals.

Time Out: Tom Somerville

Alabama's 1965 team acquired confidence like a tree acquires moss, Tom Somerville remembers.

They nicknamed Tom Somerville "Stumpy" because he stood only 5-9. College football teams stayed away from Stumpy Somerville's doorstep when he was a Memphis high schooler. But he was not too little to fit into a national championship Alabama team.

"At the beginning, the feeling was one of doubt. We had had an extremely rough spring practice in 1965, the toughest one we had while I was at Alabama," Somerville related the path to the championship. "After they lost the seniors from 1964, I guess Coach Bryant felt like he had to start all over. We had a lot of sophomores playing in 1965, and a lot of guys who were juniors and seniors who hadn't played much before." Somerville was one of those sophomores, a guard.

"Losing that first game to Georgia didn't help our confidence any. But if something like that has to happen, the first of the year is the best time for it to happen. Then you have nine more games to reclaim whatever you lost.

"Our confidence really came when we beat Ole Miss, especially the way we beat them. We had to come from behind. If we had lost that game we probably would have had a very ordinary team.

"I remember we had to make some first downs on fourth down. I think Jerry Duncan caught two tackle passes on fourth down in that drive near the end. It's a cliche to say that game

232

was the turning point, but it was."

By Orange Bowl time, the squad that was doubtful in September was certain it could beat Nebraska.

"We were pretty sure what we could do," Somerville said. "Coming down the stretch, we had made a lot of progress. After we beat LSU and Auburn as bad as we did, we had a lot of confidence. There was no doubt what we could do to Nebraska.

"Everybody was aware of the combination of things that had to happen for us to get a shot at the championship. I don't know if any of us thought it would happen, though. Probably not. When three teams have to lose, it's out of your hands. You have to wait.

"We watched LSU beat Arkansas on television and we were cheering. We watched the UCLA-Michigan State game up to halftime, then we had to leave. When UCLA won that game, it did wonders for us—but it should have had the same effect on Nebraska."

Alabama's 1966 team, the "uncrowned champion," was better than the 1965 squad, Somerville said. "There's no question about that. A lot of the same guys who played in 1965 had improved by 1966.

"We had essentially the same team. We didn't lose very many, so we were a year older and a year better.

"Everybody was pretty bitter about the way Notre Dame won it, but it was the smart thing for them to do. But I don't think Coach Bryant would have played for a tie like they did. I don't think he would have compromised all the things he has said in the past. I think he would have tried to win.

"The season of 1966 wasn't as satisfying as 1965," Somerville continued. "It was nice to realize where we were in September of 1965, then know that we had won the national championship."

Alabama, Georgia Tech, and Tennessee were the only schools that offered him a scholarship. "Coach Green at Vanderbilt told their recruiter I was too small," he said.

Somerville said his lack of height was more a handicap on offense than defense. "Passing wasn't as important then as it is now, but I did have trouble getting my hands up on a pass rush.

"I remember once when Coach Vaught at Mississippi had said

Passer Steve Sloan could also dive for clutch yardage.

Jerry Duncan caught passes as a tackle.

our program weights couldn't possibly be right, that everybody had to be bigger.

"After an extremely hard Tuesday practice, Coach Bryant had everybody weighed and had the weights notarized—but everybody had lost about 10 pounds. I weighed 179 that day, but I weighed 190 most of the time."

Somerville still plays football—but it is rugby, not American football. He is a South Central Bell employee in Birmingham.

Big End Of The Wishbone

The 1960s ended with Alabama the team of the decade and Paul Bryant the coach of the decade.

The Tide won 90, lost 16, and tied four for the best record in the country. Athletic directors, coaches, and publicity men, in a special NCAA poll, decided Bryant had done the best coaching job.

Twenty times Alabama players were named as all-Americans, 33 times all-SEC. They were on television 23 times, played in 10 consecutive bowl games, won three national championships, and four Southeastern Conference championships.

The 1967 team went 8-2-1 with quarterback Ken Stabler, sideback Bobby Johns, and end Dennis Homan making all-American. Scott Hunter quarterbacked the 1968, 1969, and 1970 squads, often passing with an aching shoulder. Guard Sam Gellerstedt and linebacker Mike Hall were 1968 all-Americans, guard Alvin Samples made it in 1969, and halfback Johnny Musso in 1970. The 1968 squad had an 8-3 record, but the chart slipped to 6-5 in 1969 and 6-5-1 in 1970.

A succession of bowl difficulties set in. Texas A&M beat the 1967 squad 20-16 in the Cotton, Missouri crushed the 1968 Tide 35-10 in the Gator, Colorado downed the 1969 club 47-33 in the Liberty, and the 1970 outfit battled Oklahoma to a 24-24 tie in the Astro-Bluebonnet.

Hunter, the dropback passer, had gone to the pros in 1971. Terry Davis, a tough little fellow but no great passer, was on hand. Musso was perhaps the best runner in Alabama history,

Johnny Musso eludes an Auburn tackler.

Robin Parkhouse led upset of Southern Cal.

and Joe LaBue, Steve Bisceglia, and Ellis Beck were keen ball carriers. John Hannah was a large anchor in the offensive line.

Texas, Houston, and other teams had been successful with a ground offense that featured a triple-option. It took the old split-T option one step further. The quarterback optioned to both the fullback and a trailing halfback. Good running backs and a quick thinking quarterback who could run were indispensable in the offense.

Alabama adopted the wishbone in 1971 and won all 11 of its regular season games before losing to Nebraska in the Orange Bowl's national championship game.

The Tide beat Southern Cal 17-10, Southern Mississippi 42-6, Florida 38-0, Ole Miss 40-6, Vanderbilt 42-0, Tennessee 32-15, Houston 34-20, Mississippi State 41-10, LSU 14-7, Miami 31-3, and Auburn 31-7 before losing to the Cornhuskers 38-6.

Bryant explained his all-or-nothing gamble with the wishbone: "I knew after spring training we couldn't win with dropback passing. We couldn't win last year with it with a pro style passer (Scott Hunter).

"So I flew out to Austin, got with Darrell (Texas Coach Royal), looked at his films, and went home to study the situation.

"About four days before (fall) practice, I just decided we were going to sink or swim with the Texas stuff. And I told the staff and later the players that we weren't going to put it in with any idea we'd leave it after three or four days.

"This was going to be it. A coach is stupid if he doesn't do what the personnel should do best. As I said, we couldn't win with dropback passing.

"Darrell came to Tuscaloosa for the coaches' clinic (in early August). We sat out at my house and talked some more about his stuff.

"We discovered the wishbone complemented what we had been doing well. When practice started, we just went to work."

Southern Cal was the first opponent. The Trojans had embarrassed Alabama 41-21 in Birmingham the season before. Now the Tide had to play on Southern Cal turf in Los Angeles and the home team was an 11-point favorite.

Perhaps Bryant sensed a successful season, though, for he said, "We're playing a great football team. It's a big game for us,

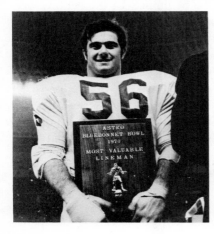

Top—Big John Hannah: back's best friend.

Middle—Terry Davis led change to wishbone.

Bottom—Jeff Rouzie stood out in Astrodome.

the first of 12 big ones for us this year. That's right, I said 12. Alabama teams play 12 games a year."

But Los Angeles sportswriters, professional descendants of those who had knocked Alabama Rose Bowl teams decades before, wrote that the Tide was stepping out of its class. The Trojans were two-touchdown betting favorites.

Musso scored touchdowns on runs of eight and 13 yards, and Bill Davis booted a 37-yard field goal and two extra points. End Robbin Parkhouse led a stingy defense and, first thing you knew, Alabama led 17-0 and won out 17-10.

"I've been around better teams but I've never been prouder of one," Bryant said.

"They took it to us like we did to them last year," Southern Cal Coach John McKay applauded the victors, "and they found us wanting. Alabama outhit us, outran us, outcoached us."

It was Bryant's 200th win, and he called it one of his most satisfying.

The *Los Angeles Herald-Examiner's* story by Bud Furillo began: "Paul (Bear) Bryant, the world's best college coach. . ."

The game gave Alabama confidence, and the wishboning Tide marched all-winningly into the Orange Bowl.

Musso had been tremendous, and he and Hannah, Parkhouse, and linebacker Tom Surlas made various all-American teams.

Auburn Coach Shug Jordan, by season's end, called Davis the nation's most underrated quarterback.

Development of the offensive line had been a key. Buddy Brown had come from nowhere to be named to the sophomore all-American team, and Jim Krapf made a successful switch from defense. David Bailey, who had been a pass-catching end, adapted to the new running offense.

College football, 1971, headed for a titanic Orange Bowl collision, No. 1 Nebraska vs. No. 2 Alabama.

The Tide's dream became a nightmare. The Cornhuskers, led by quarterback Jerry Tagge who ran a team as Pat Trammell used to, flawlessly, won 38-6 and was named national champion.

"This is the biggest win of my career," Nebraska Coach Bob Devaney said.

"This is one of the greatest—if not the greatest—teams I've ever seen," said Paul Bryant, head coach of the bowlingest team

242

Johnny Musso, the Italian Stallion, in gag shot.

in football.

It was a remarkable season, despite the loss. An Alabama team that was not supposed to go anywhere had ridden a radical offense to the SEC championship and to the national finals. Paul Bryant, who had come from Texas A&M in 1958 to answer "mamma's" call to restore greatness, was national Coach of the Year.

That is all part of Alabama tradition, the tradition of Wallace Wade, Frank Thomas, Dixie Howell, Harry Gilmer, Fred Sington, Pat Trammell and the Rose Bowl.

Dr. David Mathews, president of the university, discussed Alabama tradition in a talk to the 1970 football squad. He explained it perfectly:

"No one can help but be aware of the rich tradition that is associated with this team and with this university. There are people too old now to go to the games who still remember wearing a crimson and white jersey, men for whom the University of Alabama has great meaning. There are also some young men who are still too young to be left alone in the stadium now who would like one day to wear a crimson and white jersey and to be a part of the University of Alabama. That is tradition and it's something that is very, very important and very much a part of the University of Alabama.

"Tradition is a burden in many ways. To have a tradition like ours means that you can't quit; to have a tradition like ours means that you can't lose your cool; to have a tradition like ours means that you always have to show class, even when you are not quite up to it; to have a tradition like ours means that you have to do some things that you don't want to do and some you even think you can't do, simply because the tradition demands it of you. On the other hand, tradition is the thing that sustains us. Tradition is that which allows us to prevail in ways that we could not otherwise.

"I'm convinced that greatness in any field has to come out of some kind of tradition. And our job is to make certain that the tradition that is the University of Alabama means as much and stands for as much for those who are yet to come as it has for us and those who have gone before us."

Appendix

ALABAMA'S RECORD AGAINST ALL FOES

Opponent	W	L	T	Pts.	Op.	Opponent	W	L	T	Pts.	Op.
Arkansas	1	0	0	10	3	Mississippi State	43	10	3	1091	373
Auburn	19	16	1	597	549	Missouri	0	1	0	10	35
Birmingham AC	2	3	0	56	19	Montgomery AC	1	0	0	16	0
Birmingham HS	2	0	0	113	0	Nashville U.	1	0	0	19	0
Birmingham Sou.	11	0	0	551	12	Nebraska	2	1	0	79	73
Boston College	1	1	0	44	34	New Orleans AC	0	1	0	0	21
Bryson College	1	0	0	95	0	North Carolina State	3	0	0	64	7
California	0	1	0	0	13	Oglethorpe	2	0	0	75	0
Camp Gordon	0	1	0	6	19	Ohio Am. Corp	1	0	0	7	0
Carlisle	0	1	0	3	20	Oklahoma	1	0	1	41	24
Case College	1	0	0	40	0	Pennsylvania	1	0	0	9	7
Centre	2	1	0	33	17	Penn State	0	1	0	0	7
Chattanooga	8	0	0	284	48	Pensacola AC	1	0	0	10	5
Cincinnati	1	0	0	16	0	Pensacola N.A.B.	2	0	0	82	6
Clemson	10	3	0	300	121	Richmond	1	0	0	66	0
Cumberland	0	1	0	0	44	Rice	0	2	0	13	40
Colorado	0	1	0	33	47	St. Mary's	1	0	0	6	0
Davidson	1	0	0	16	0	Sewanee	17	10	3	495	288
Delta State	1	0	0	89	0	South Carolina	7	0	0	194	20
Duke	0	1	0	26	29	Southern Cal	3	1	0	91	73
Duquesne	3	0	0	122	14	Southern Mil. Inst.	1	0	0	59	0
Florida	11	5	0	412	161	Southern Mississippi	12	2	1	452	130
Florida State	1	0	1	58	37	Sou. Presbyterian	1	0	0	31	0
Fordham	1	1	0	7	8	Southwestern	1	0	0	45	6
Furman	5	0	0	160	19	S. W. Louisiana	3	0	0	155	6
George Washington	3	0	0	86	6	Spring Hill	3	0	0	112	7
Georgia	28	19	4	754	514	Stanford	1	0	1	36	20
Georgia Pre-Flight	0	1	0	19	35	Syracuse	1	1	0	61	29
Georgia Tech	24	19	3	544	493	Tampa	1	0	0	34	6
Haskell	1	0	0	9	8	Taylor School	1	0	0	35	0
Houston	7	0	0	130	57	Tennessee	24	23	7	594	525
Howard	19	0	1	669	34	Texas	0	5	1	37	100
Keesler Field	1	0	0	21	0	Texas A&M	1	1	0	45	41
Kentucky	24	1	1	588	107	Texas Christian	0	3	0	6	72
Louisiana State	21	10	4	588	306	Tulane	23	10	3	532	297
Louisiana Tech	1	0	0	34	0	Tulsa	3	0	0	106	19
Loyola (N. O.)	1	0	0	13	6	Tuscaloosa AC	2	0	0	22	5
Marion Institute	9	0	0	482	0	Union	4	0	0	136	0
Maryland	1	1	0	27	28	Vanderbilt	28	17	4	831	570
Maryville	3	0	0	40	0	Villanova	0	1	0	18	41
Memphis State	2	0	0	28	7	Virginia Tech	6	0	0	151	44
Mercer	2	0	0	40	0	Washington	1	0	0	20	19
Miami (Fla.)	9	2	0	353	115	Washington & Lee	1	0	0	9	0
Millsaps	3	0	0	155	0	Washington State	1	0	0	24	0
Mississippi	23	4	2	797	207	Wetumpka	1	0	0	27	0
Mississippi College	7	0	0	283	10	Wisconsin	0	1	0	0	15

UNIVERSITY OF ALABAMA
ALL-TIME FOOTBALL RECORD
(1892-1971)

1892—WON 2, LOST 2

56	B'ham H. Sch.....	0	Birmingham ..Nov. 11
4	B'ham A. C......	5	Birmingham ..Nov. 12
14	B'ham A. C......	0	Birmingham ..Dec. 10
22	Auburn	32	B'ham....Feb. 22, 1893
96		37	

1893—WON 0, LOST 4

0	B'ham A. C......	4	Tuscaloosa ....Oct. 14
8	B'ham A. C...10		Birmingham ...Nov. 4
0	Sewanee 20		Birmingham ..Nov. 11
16	Auburn 40		Montgomery ..Nov. 30
24		74	

1894—WON 3, LOST 1

0	Mississippi	6	Jackson, Miss..Oct. 27
18	Tulane	6	New Orleans...Nov. 3
24	Sewanee	4	Birmingham ..Nov. 15
18	Auburn	0	Montgomery ..Nov. 29
60		16	

1895—WON 0, LOST 4

6	Georgia	30	Columbus, Ga...Nov. 9
0	Tulane	22	New Orleans...Nov. 6
6	L. S. U.............	12	B. Rouge, La...Nov. 18
0	Auburn	48	Tuscaloosa...Nov. 23
12		112	

1896—WON 2, LOST 1

30	B'ham A. C........	0	Tuscaloosa ....Oct. 3
6	Sewanee 10		Tuscaloosa ......Oct. 31
20	Miss. State	0	Tuscaloosa ....Nov. 4
56		10	

1897—WON 1, LOST 0

6	Tuscaloosa A. C...0		Tuscaloosa

1898—(NO TEAM)

1899—WON 3, LOST 1

16	Tuscaloosa A. C...	5	Tuscaloosa........Oct. 21
16	Montgomery A.C.	0	Tuscaloosa ......Nov. 11
7	Mississippi	5	Jackson, Miss...Nov. 24
0	N. Orleans A.C...21		New Orleans..Nov. 25
39		31	

1900—WON 2, LOST 3

35	Taylor Sch.	0	Tuscaloosa ......Oct. 21
12	Mississippi	6	Tuscaloosa ......Oct. 26
0	Tulane	6	Tuscaloosa ....Nov. 3
5	Auburn	53	Montgomery ..Nov. 17
0	Clemson	35	Birmingham ..Nov. 29
52		100	

1901—WON 2, LOST 1, TIED 2

41	Mississippi	0	Tuscaloosa ......Oct. 19
0	Georgia	0	Montgomery ...Nov. 9
0	Auburn 17		Tuscaloosa ...Nov. 15
45	Miss. State	0	Tuscaloosa .. Nov. 16
6	Tennessee	6	Birmingham ..Nov. 28
92		23	

1902—WON 4, LOST 4

57	B'ham H. S.......	0	Tuscaloosa ......Oct. 10
81	Marion Inst.	0	Tuscaloosa ......Oct. 13
0	Auburn 23		Birmingham ..Oct. 18
0	Georgia	5	Birmingham ...Nov. 1
27	Miss. State	0	Tuscaloosa ......Nov. 8
0	Texas 10		Tuscaloosa ...Nov. 11
26	Ga. Tech	0	Birmingham ..Nov. 27
0	L. S. U.................11		Tuscaloosa........Nov. 29
191		49	

1903—WON 3, LOST 4

0	Vanderbilt	30	Nashville ....Oct. 10
0	Miss. State	11	Colu'bus, Miss. Oct. 16
18	Auburn	6	Montgomery ....Oct. 23
0	Sewanee	23	Birmingham...Nov. 2
18	L. S. U.	0	Tuscaloosa ...Nov. 9
0	Cumberland U...	44	Tuscaloosa ...Nov. 14
24	Tennessee	0	Birmingham ..Nov. 26
60		114	

1904—WON 7, LOST 3

29	Florida State	0	Tuscaloosa ......Oct. 3
0	Clemson 18		Birmingham......Oct. 8
6	Miss. State	0	Colu'bus, Miss. Oct. 15
17	Nashville U........	0	Tuscaloosa ......Oct. 24
16	Georgia	5	Tuscaloosa ....Nov. 5
5	Auburn 29		Birmingham...Nov. 12
0	Tennessee	5	Birmingham ..Nov. 24
11	L. S. U.................	0	B. Rouge ....Dec. 2
6	Tulane	0	N. Orleans ......Dec. 3
10	Pensacola A.C...	5	Pensacola, Fla..Dec. 4
100		62	

1905—WON 6, LOST 4

17	Maryville	0	Tuscaloosa ....Oct. 3
0	Vanderbilt	34	Nashville ....Oct. 7
34	Miss. State	0	Tuscaloosa ......Oct. 14
5	Georgia Tech....	12	Atlanta ....Oct. 21
0	Clemson	25	Columbia, S.C. Oct. 25
36	Georgia	0	Birmingham ...Nov. 4
21	Centre	0	Tuscaloosa ......Nov. 9
30	Auburn	0	Birmingham....Nov. 18
6	Sewanee	42	Birmingham......Nov. 23
29	Tennessee	0	Birmingham......Nov. 30
178		113	

1906—WON 5, LOST 1

6	Maryville	0	Tuscaloosa..........Oct. 6
14	Howard Co.	0	Tuscaloosa..........Oct. 13
0	Vanderbilt	78	Nashville ....Oct. 20
16	Miss. State	4	St'kville, Miss. Nov. 3
10	Auburn	0	Birmingham....Nov. 17
51	Tennessee	0	Birmingham......Nov. 29
97		82	

1907—WON 5, LOST 1, TIED 2

17	Maryville	0	Tuscaloosa ....Oct. 5
20	Mississippi	0	Col'bus, Miss...Oct. 12
4	Sewanee	54	Tuscaloosa ......Oct. 21
0	Georgia	0	Montgomery, ...Oct. 25
12	Centre	0	Birmingham....Nov. 2
6	Auburn	6	Birmingham....Nov. 16
6	L.S.U.	4	Mobile ....Nov. 23
5	Tennessee	0	Birmingham......Nov. 28
70		64	

1908—WON 6, LOST 1, TIED 1

27	Wetumpka	0	Tuscaloosa ....Oct. 3
17	Howard	0	Birmingham ...Oct. 10
16	Cincinnati	0	Birmingham ...Oct. 17
6	Ga. Tech	11	Atlanta ....Oct. 24
23	Chatt'ooga U.	6	Tuscaloosa ......Oct. 31
6	Georgia	6	Birmingham....Nov. 14
9	Haskell Inst.	8	Tuscaloosa .....Nov. 20
4	Tennessee	0	Birmingham....Nov. 26
107		31	

1909—WON 5, LOST 1, TIED 2

16	Union	0	Tuscaloosa ....Oct. 2
14	Howard	0	Tuscaloosa ....Oct. 9
3	Clemson	0	Birmingham ...Oct. 16
0	Mississippi	0	Jackson, Miss. ..Oct. 23
14	Georgia	0	Atlanta ....Oct. 30
10	Tennessee	0	Knoxville ......Nov. 13
5	Tulane	5	N. Orleans ....Nov. 20
6	L. S. U.	12	Birmingham....Nov. 25
68		17	

1910—WON 4, LOST 4

25	B'ham Sou.	0	Tuscaloosa ...... Oct. 1
26	Marion Inst.	0	Tuscaloosa ......Oct. 8
0	Georgia	22	Birmingham ...Oct. 15
0	Ga. Tech	36	Tuscaloosa ......Oct. 22
0	Mississippi	16	Gre'ville, Miss. Nov. 5
0	Sewanee	30	Birmingham....Nov. 12
5	Tulane	3	N. Orleans ....Nov. 19
9	Wash. & Lee	0	Birmingham....Nov. 24
65		107	

1911—WON 5, LOST 2, TIED 2

24	Howard	0	Tuscaloosa .....Sept. 30
47	B'ham Sou.	5	Birmingham ...Oct. 14
3	Georgia	11	Tuscaloosa ...... Oct. 7
6	Miss. State	6	Colu'bus, Miss. Oct. 21
0	Ga. Tech	0	Atlanta ....Oct. 28
35	Marion Inst.	0	Marion, Ala..... Nov. 4
0	Sewanee	3	Tuscaloosa .....Nov. 11
22	Tulane	0	Birmingham....Nov. 18
16	Davidson Col.	6	Birmingham....Nov. 30
153		31	

1912—WON 5, LOST 3, TIED 1

52	Marion Inst.	0	Tuscaloosa .....Sept. 28
62	B'ham Sou.	0	Tuscaloosa .... Oct. 5
3	Ga. Tech	20	Atlanta ....Oct. 12
0	Miss. State	7	Ab'deen, Miss. Oct. 18
9	Georgia	13	Columbus, Ga...Oct. 26
7	Tulane	0	N. Orleans ....Nov. 2
10	Mississippi	9	Tuscaloosa .....Nov. 9
6	Sewanee	6	Birmingham....Nov. 16
7	Tennessee	0	Birmingham....Nov. 28
156		55	

1913—WON 6, LOST 3

27	Howard	0	Tuscaloosa .....Sept. 27
81	B'ham Sou.	0	Tuscaloosa ...... Oct. 4
20	Clemson	0	Tuscaloosa ......Oct. 11
0	Georgia	20	Tuscaloosa ......Oct. 18
26	Tulane	0	N. Orleans ....Oct. 25
21	Miss. Col.	3	Jackson, Miss..Nov. 1
7	Sewanee	10	Birmingham....Nov. 9
6	Tennessee	0	Tuscaloosa .....Nov. 14
0	Miss. State	7	Birmingham....Nov. 27
188		40	

1914—WON 5, LOST 4

13	Howard	0	Tuscaloosa..........Oct. 3
54	B'ham Sou.	0	Tuscaloosa........Oct. 10
13	Ga. Tech	0	Birmingham ...Oct. 17
7	Tennessee	17	Knoxville ......Oct. 24
58	Tulane	0	Tuscaloosa ......Oct. 31
0	Sewanee	18	Birmingham ...Nov. 7
63	Chattanooga	0	Tuscaloosa .....Nov. 13
0	Miss. State	9	Birmingham....Nov. 26
3	Carlisle	20	Birmingham ...Dec. 5
211		64	

*1915—WON 6, LOST 2

44	Howard	0	Tuscaloosa ......Oct. 2
67	B'ham Sou.	0	Tuscaloosa ......Oct. 9
40	Miss. Col.	0	Tuscaloosa ......Oct. 16
16	Tulane	0	Tuscaloosa ......Oct. 23
23	Sewanee	10	Birmingham ...Oct. 30
7	Ga. Tech	21	Atlanta ....Nov. 6
0	Texas	20	Austin, Tex. ...Nov. 13
53	Mississippi	0	Birmingham....Nov. 25
250		51	

1916—WON 6, LOST 3

13	B'ham Sou.	0	Tuscaloosa .....Sept. 30
80	Sou. Univ.	0	Tuscaloosa ......Oct. 7
13	Miss. Col.	7	Tuscaloosa ......Oct. 14
16	Florida	0	Jack'ville, Fla.. Oct. 21
27	Mississippi	0	Tuscaloosa ......Oct. 28
7	Sewanee	6	Birmingham ...Nov. 4
0	Ga. Tech.	13	Atlanta ....Nov. 11
0	Tulane	33	N. Orleans ....Nov. 18
0	Georgia	3	Birmingham....Nov. 30
156		62	

1917—WON 5, LOST 2, TIED 1

7	Ohio Am. Corp.	0	Montgomery ...Oct. 3
13	Marion Inst.	0	Tuscaloosa .....Oct. 12
46	Miss. Col.	0	Tuscaloosa .....Oct. 20
64	Mississippi	0	Tuscaloosa .....Oct. 26
3	Sewanee	3	Birmingham..... Nov. 3
2	Vanderbilt	7	Birmingham....Nov. 10
27	Kentucky	0	Lexington .....Nov. 17
6	Cp. Gordon	9	Birmingham....Nov. 29
169		29	

1918—(NO TEAM)

1919—WON 8, LOST 1

27	B'ham Sou.	0	Tuscaloosa .... Oct. 4
49	Mississippi	0	Tuscaloosa .... Oct. 11
48	Howard	0	Tuscaloosa ......Oct. 18
61	Marion Inst.	0	Tuscaloosa ......Oct. 24
40	Sewanee	0	Birmingham....Nov. 1
12	Vanderbilt	16	Nashville ......Nov. 8
23	L. S. U.	0	Br. Rouge .....Nov. 15
6	Georgia	0	Atlanta ....Nov. 22
14	Miss. State	6	Birmingham....Nov. 27
280		22	

1920—WON 10, LOST 1

59	Sou. Mil. Inst.	0	Tuscaloosa.......Sept. 25
49	Marion Inst.	0	Tuscaloosa.........Oct. 2
45	B'ham Sou.	0	Tuscaloosa.........Oct. 9
57	Miss. Col.	0	Tuscaloosa........Oct. 16
33	Howard	0	Tuscaloosa........Oct. 23
21	Sewanee	0	Birmingham .... Oct. 30
14	Vanderbilt	7	Birmingham..... Nov. 6
21	L. S. U.	0	Tuscaloosa .....Nov. 11
14	Georgia	21	Atlanta ....Nov. 20
24	Miss. State	7	Birmingham ....Nov. 25
40	Case College	0	Cleveland, O....Nov. 27
377		35	

1921—WON 5, LOST 4, TIED 2

34	Howard	14	Tuscaloosa.........Sept. 24
27	Spring Hill	7	Tuscaloosa...........Oct. 1
55	Marion Inst.	0	Tuscaloosa...........Oct. 8
95	Bryson (N.C.)	0	Tuscaloosa..........Oct. 15
0	Sewanee	17	Birmingham ...Oct. 22
7	L. S. U.	7	N. Orleans ....Oct. 29
0	Vanderbilt	14	Birmingham.....Nov. 5
2	Florida	9	Tuscaloosa .....Nov. 11
0	Georgia	22	Atlanta ....Nov. 19
7	Miss. State	7	Birmingham.....Nov. 24
14	Tulane	7	N. Orleans ....Dec. 3
241		104	

1922—WON 6, LOST 3, TIED 1

110	Marion Inst.	0	Tuscaloosa .....Sept. 30
41	Oglethorpe	0	Tuscaloosa ...... Oct. 7
7	Ga. Tech.	33	Atlanta ....Oct. 14
7	Sewanee	7	Birmingham ...Oct. 21
10	Texas	19	Austin, Tex. ...Oct. 28
9	Pennsylvania	7	Philadelphia ...Nov. 4
47	L. S. U.	3	Tuscaloosa .....Nov. 11
0	Kentucky	6	Lexington ....Nov. 18
10	Georgia	6	Montgomery ...Nov. 25
59	Miss. State	0	Birmingham.....Nov. 30
300		81	

1923—WON 7, LOST 2, TIED 1

12	Union	0	Tuscaloosa .....Sept. 29
56	Mississippi	0	Tuscaloosa .... Oct. 6
0	Syracuse	23	Syracuse, N.Y. ..Oct. 13
7	Sewanee	0	Birmingham ...Oct. 20
59	Spring Hill	0	Mobile ....Oct. 27
0	Ga. Tech.	0	Atlanta ....Nov. 3
16	Kentucky	8	Tuscaloosa ....Nov. 10
30	L. S. U.	3	Montgomery ...Nov. 16
36	Georgia	0	Montgomery ...Nov. 24
6	Florida	16	Birmingham ....Nov. 29
222		50	

1924—WON 8, LOST 1

55	Union	0	Tuscaloosa ....Sept. 27
20	Furman Univ.	0	Greenville, S.C. ..Oct. 4
51	Miss. Col.	0	Tuscaloosa ....Oct. 11
14	Sewanee	0	Birmingham .....Oct. 18
14	Ga. Tech.	0	Atlanta ....Oct. 25
61	Mississippi	0	Montgomery.......Nov. 1
42	Kentucky	7	Tuscaloosa ...... Nov. 8
0	Centre Col.	17	Birmingham ....Nov. 15
33	Georgia	0	Birmingham ....Nov. 27
290		24	

1925—WON 10, LOST 0

53	Union Col.	0	Tuscaloosa .....Sept. 26
50	B'ham Sou.	7	Tuscaloosa .....Oct. 3
42	L. S. U.	0	Birmingham ...Oct. 17
27	Sewanee	0	B. Rouge ......Oct. 10
7	Ga. Tech.	0	Atlanta ....Oct. 24
6	Miss. State	0	Tuscaloosa ....Oct. 31
31	Kentucky	0	Birmingham ...Nov. 17
34	Florida	0	Montgomery ...Nov. 14
27	Georgia	0	Birmingham.....Nov. 26
•20	U. of Wash.	19	Rose Bowl...Jan. 1, '26
297		26	

1926—WON 9, LOST 0, TIED 1

54	Millsaps	0	Tuscaloosa .....Sept. 24
19	Vanderbilt	7	Nashville ....Oct. 2
26	Miss. State	7	Meridian, Miss. Oct. 9
21	Ga. Tech.	0	Atlanta ....Oct. 16
2	Sewanee	0	Birmingham ...Oct. 23
24	L. S. U.	0	Tuscaloosa ....Oct. 30
14	Kentucky	0	Birmingham .....Nov. 6
49	Florida	0	Montgomery ...Nov. 13
33	Georgia	6	Birmingham.....Nov. 25
• 7	Stanford	7	Rose Bowl, Jan. 1, '27
249		27	

*Indicates Bowl games.

1927—WON 5, LOST 4, TIED 1

46	Millsaps	0	Tuscaloosa ......Sept. 24
31	So. Pres. U.	0	Tuscaloosa.......Sept. 30
0	L. S. U.	0	Birmingham....Oct. 8
0	Ga. Tech.	13	Atlanta ....Oct. 15
24	Sewanee	0	Birmingham ....Oct. 22
13	Miss. State	7	Tuscaloosa ....Oct. 29
21	Kentucky	6	Birmingham .....Nov. 5
6	Florida	13	Montgomery ...Nov. 12
6	Georgia	20	Birmingham....Nov. 24
7	Vanderbilt	14	Birmingham......Dec. 3
154		73	

1928—WON 6, LOST 3

27	Mississippi	0	Tuscaloosa ....Oct. 6
46	Miss. State	0	St'kville, Miss...Oct. 13
13	Tennessee	15	Tuscaloosa .....Oct. 20
42	Sewanee	12	Birmingham ....Oct. 27
0	Wisconsin	15	Madison, Wis...Nov. 3
14	Kentucky	0	Montgomery ...Nov. 10
13	Ga. Tech.	33	Atlanta ....Nov. 17
19	Georgia	0	Birmingham ...Nov. 29
13	L. S. U.	0	Birmingham ......Dec. 8
187		75	

1929—WON 6, LOST 3

55	Miss. Col.	0	Tuscaloosa.......Sept. 28
22	Mississippi	7	Tuscaloosa ...... Oct. 5
46	Chattanooga	0	Tuscaloosa ....Oct. 12
0	Tennessee	6	Knoxville ....Oct. 19
35	Sewanee	7	Birmingham ....Oct. 26
0	Vanderbilt	13	Nashville ....Nov. 2
24	Kentucky	13	Montgomery .... Nov. 9
14	Ga. Tech.	0	Atlanta ....Nov. 16
0	Georgia	12	Birmingham.....Nov. 28
196		58	

1930—WON 10, LOST 0

43	Howard	0	Tuscaloosa ....Sept. 27
64	Mississippi	0	Tuscaloosa ....Oct. 4
25	Sewanee	0	Birmingham .....Oct. 11
18	Tennessee	6	Tuscaloosa .....Oct. 18
12	Vanderbilt	7	Birmingham ....Oct. 52
19	Kentucky	0	Lexington ....Nov. 1
20	Florida	0	Gainesville .....Nov. 8
33	L. S. U.	0	Montgomery ...Nov. 15
13	Georgia	0	Birmingham ....Nov. 27
•24	Wash. State	0	Rose Bowl, Jan. 1, '31
271		13	

1931—WON 9, LOST 1

42	Howard	6	Tuscaloosa.......Sept. 28
55	Mississippi	6	Tuscaloosa ....Oct. 3
53	Miss. State	0	Meridian, Miss. Oct. 10
0	Tennessee	25	Knoxville ....Oct. 17
33	Sewanee	0	Birmingham ...Oct. 24
9	Kentucky	7	Tuscaloosa .....Oct. 31
41	Florida	0	Birmingham .....No. 7
74	Clemson	7	Montgomery ...Nov. 14
14	Vanderbilt	6	Nashville ....Nov. 26
49	Chattanooga	0	Chattanooga ... Dec. 2
370		57	

1932—WON 8, LOST 2

45	Southwestern	6	Tuscaloosa ......Sept. 24
53	Miss. State	0	Montgomery.......Oct. 1
28	George Wash.	6	Wash. D. C.....Oct. 8
3	Tennessee	7	Birmingham .....Oct. 15
24	Mississippi	13	Tuscaloosa .....Oct. 22
12	Kentucky	7	Lexington .....Oct. 29
9	V. P. I.	6	Tuscaloosa ...... Nov. 5
0	Ga. Tech.	6	Atlanta ....Nov. 12
20	Vanderbilt	0	Birmingham ....Nov. 24
6	St. Mary's	0	San Francisco ...Dec. 5
200		51	

*Indicates Bowl games

248

1933—WON 7, LOST 1, TIED 1
SEC CHAMPIONS

34	Oglethorpe	0	Tuscaloosa	Sept. 30
0	Mississippi	0	Birmingham	Oct. 7
18	Miss. State	0	Tuscaloosa	Oct. 14
12	Tennessee	6	Knoxville	Oct. 21
0	Fordham	2	New York	Oct. 28
20	Kentucky	0	Birmingham	
27	V. P. I.	0	Tuscaloosa	Nov. 11
12	Ga. Tech.	9	Atlanta	Nov. 18
7	Vanderbilt	0	Nashville	Nov. 30
130		**17**		

1934—WON 10, LOST 0
SEC CHAMPIONS

24	Howard	0	Tuscaloosa	Sept. 29
35	Sewanee	6	Montgomery	Oct. 5
41	Miss. State	0	Tuscaloosa	Oct. 13
13	Tennessee	6	Birmingham	Oct. 20
26	Georgia	6	Birmingham	Oct. 27
34	Kentucky	14	Lexington	Nov. 3
40	Clemson	0	Tuscaloosa	Nov. 10
40	Ga. Tech	0	Atlanta	Nov. 17
34	Vanderbilt	0	Birmingham	Nov. 29
*29	Stanford	13	Rose Bowl, Jan. 1, '35	
316		**45**		

1935—WON 6, LOST 2, TIED 1

7	Howard	7	Tuscaloosa	Sept. 28
39	Geo. Wash.	0	Wash. D. C.	Oct. 5
7	Miss. State	20	Tuscaloosa	Oct. 12
25	Tennessee	0	Knoxville	Oct. 19
17	Georgia	7	Athens, Ga.	Oct. 26
13	Kentucky	0	Birmingham	Nov. 2
33	Clemson	0	Tuscaloosa	Nov. 9
38	Ga. Tech.	7	Birmingham	Nov. 16
6	Vanderbilt	14	Nashville	Nov. 28
185		**55**		

1936—WON 8, LOST 0, TIED 1

34	Howard	0	Tuscaloosa	Sept. 26
32	Clemson	0	Tuscaloosa	Oct. 3
7	Miss. State	0	Tuscaloosa	Oct. 10
0	Tennessee	0	Birmingham	Oct. 17
13	Loyola, N. O.	6	N. Orleans	Oct. 24
14	Kentucky	0	Lexington	Oct. 31
34	Tulane	7	Birmingham	Nov. 7
20	Ga. Tech.	16	Atlanta	Nov. 14
14	Vanderbilt	6	Birmingham	Nov. 25
168		**35**		

1937—WON 9, LOST 1*
SEC CHAMPIONS

41	Howard	0	Tuscaloosa	Sept. 25
65	Sewanee	0	Birmingham	Oct. 2
20	S. Carolina	0	Tuscaloosa	Oct. 9
14	Tennessee	7	Knoxville	Oct. 6
19	Geo. Wash.	0	Wash. D. C.	Oct. 23
41	Kentucky	0	Tuscaloosa	Oct. 30
9	Tulane	6	N. Orleans	Nov. 6
7	Ga. Tech.	0	Birmingham	Nov. 13
9	Vanderbilt	7	Nashville	Nov. 25
* 0	California	13	Rose Bowl, Jan. 1, '38	
225		**33**		

1938—WON 7, LOST 1, TIED 1

19	Sou. Calif.	7	Los Angeles	Sept. 24
34	Howard	0	Tuscaloosa	Oct. 1
14	N. Car. State	0	Tuscaloosa	Oct. 8
0	Tennessee	13	Birmingham	Oct. 15
32	Sewanee	0	Tuscaloosa	Oct. 22
26	Kentucky	6	Lexington	Oct. 29
3	Tulane	0	Birmingham	Nov. 5
14	Ga. Tech.	14	Atlanta	Nov. 12
7	Vanderbilt	0	Birmingham	Nov. 24
149		**40**		

*Indicates Bowl games.

1939—WON 5, LOST 3, TIED 1

21	Howard	0	Tuscaloosa	Sept. 30
7	Fordham	6	New York	Oct. 7
20	Mercer	0	Tuscaloosa	Oct. 14
0	Tennessee	21	Knoxville	Oct. 21
7	Miss. State	0	Tuscaloosa	Oct. 28
7	Kentucky	7	Birmingham	Nov. 4
0	Tulane	13	N. Orleans	Nov. 11
0	Ga. Tech.	6	Birmingham	Nov. 18
39	Vanderbilt	0	Nashville	Nov. 30
101		**53**		

1940—WON 7, LOST 2

26	Spring Hill	0	Mobile	Sept. 27
20	Mercer	0	Tuscaloosa	Oct. 5
31	Howard	0	Tuscaloosa	Oct. 12
12	Tennessee	27	Birmingham	Oct. 19
25	Kentucky	0	Lexington	Nov. 2
13	Tulane	6	Birmingham	Nov. 9
14	Ga. Tech.	13	Atlanta	Nov. 16
25	Vanderbilt	21	Birmingham	Nov. 23
0	Miss. State	13	Tuscaloosa	Nov. 30
166		**80**		

1941—WON 9, LOST 2

47	S'wes. La. Inst.	6	Tuscaloosa	Sept. 27
0	Miss. State	14	Tuscaloosa	Oct. 4
61	Howard	0	Birmingham	Oct. 11
9	Tennessee	2	Knoxville	Oct. 18
27	Georgia	14	Birmingham	Oct. 25
30	Kentucky	0	Tuscaloosa	Nov. 1
19	Tulane	14	N. Orleans	Nov. 8
20	Ga. Tech.	0	Birmingham	Nov. 15
0	Vanderbilt	7	Nashville	Nov. 22
21	Miami (Fla.)	7	Miami†	Nov. 28
*29	Texas A.&M.	21	Cotton Bwl, Jan. 1, '42	
263		**85**		

1942—WON 8, LOST 3

54	S'wes. La. Inst.	0	Montgomery	Sept. 25†
21	Miss. State	6	Tuscaloosa	Oct. 3
27	Pen'cola N.A.S.	0	Mobile	Oct. 10
8	Tennessee	0	Birmingham	Oct. 17
14	Kentucky	0	Lexington	Oct. 24
10	Georgia	21	Atlanta	Oct. 31
29	S. Carolina	0	Tuscaloosa	Nov. 7
0	Ga. Tech.	7	Atlanta	Nov. 14
27	Vanderbilt	7	Birmingham	Nov. 21
19	Ga. N. Pre-Flt.	35	Birmingham	Nov. 28
*37	Boston Col.	21	Orange Bwl, Jan. 1, '43	
246		**97**		

1943—(NO TEAM)

1944—WON 5, LOST 2, TIED 2

27	L. S. U.	27	B. Rouge	Sept. 30†
63	Howard	0	Birmingham	Oct. 7
55	Millsaps	0	Tuscaloosa	Oct. 14
0	Tennessee	0	Knoxville	Oct. 21
41	Kentucky	0	Montgomery	Oct. 27†
7	Georgia	14	Birmingham	Nov. 4
34	Mississippi	6	Mobile	Nov. 11
19	Miss. State	0	Tuscaloosa	Nov. 18
*26	Duke	29	Sugar Bowl, Jan. 1, '45	
272		**83**		

1945—WON 10, LOST 0
SEC CHAMPIONS

21	Keesler A.A.F.	0	Biloxi, Miss.	Sept. 29
26	L. S. U.	7	B. Rouge	Oct. 6†
55	S. Carolina	0	Montgomery	Oct. 13
25	Tennessee	7	Birmingham	Oct. 20
28	Georgia	14	Birmingham	Oct. 27
60	Kentucky	19	Louisville	Nov. 3
71	Vanderbilt	0	Nashville	Nov. 17
55	Pen'cola N.A.S.	6	Tuscaloosa	Nov. 24
55	Miss. State	13	Tuscaloosa	Dec. 1
*34	Sou. Calif.	14	Rose Bowl, Jan. 1, '46	
430		**80**		

*Indicates Bowl games.   †—Night

1946—WON 7, LOST 4

26	Furman	7	Birmingham ...Sept. 20
7	Tulane	6	N. Orleans ......Sept. 28
14	S. Carolina	6	Columbia, S.C....Oct. 5
54	S'wes. La. Inst.	0	Tuscaloosa ......Oct. 12
0	Tennessee	12	Knoxville ......Oct. 19
21	Kentucky	7	Montgomery ......Oct. 26
0	Georgia	14	Athens, Ga. ....Nov. 2
21	L. S. U.	31	Baton Rouge .....Nov. 9
12	Vanderbilt	7	Birmingham ....Nov. 16
7	Boston Col.	13	Boston ....Nov. 23
24	Miss. State	7	Tuscaloosa ......Nov. 30
186		**110**	

1947—WON 8, LOST 3

34	Miss. Southern	7	Birmingham...Sept. 20†
20	Tulane	21	New Orleans...Sept. 27
7	Vanderbilt	14	Nashville......Oct. 4
26	Duquesne	0	Tuscaloosa......Oct. 11
10	Tennessee	0	Birmingham......Oct. 18
17	Georgia	7	Athens, Ga......Oct. 25
13	Kentucky	0	Lexington ......Nov. 1
14	Ga. Tech.	7	Birmingham......Nov. 15
41	L. S. U.	12	Tuscaloosa ......Nov. 22
21	Miami (Fla.)	6	Miami ....Nov. 29
• 7	Texas	27	Sugar Bwl., Jan. 1, '48
210		**101**	

1948—WON 6, LOST 4, TIED 1

14	Tulane	21	New Orleans...Sept. 25
14	Vanderbilt	14	Mobile ....Oct. 2
48	Duquesne	6	Tuscaloosa........Oct. 8†
6	Tennessee	21	Knoxville......Oct. 16
10	Miss. State	7	Starkville......Oct. 23
0	Georgia	35	Birmingham......Oct. 30
27	Miss. Southern	0	Tuscaloosa......Nov. 6
14	Georgia Tech.	12	Atlanta ....Nov. 13
6	L. S. U.	26	Baton Rouge......Nov. 20
34	Florida	28	Tuscaloosa......Nov. 27
55	Auburn	0	Birmingham ....Dec. 4
228		**170**	

1949—WON 6, LOST 3, TIED 1

14	Tulane	28	Mobile...........Sept. 24
7	Vanderbilt	14	Nashville ....Oct. 1
48	Duquesne	8	Tuscaloosa......Oct. 7†
7	Tennessee	7	Birmingham......Oct. 15
35	Miss. State	6	Tuscaloosa......Oct. 22
14	Georgia	7	Athens ....Oct. 29
20	Ga. Tech.	7	Birmingham......Nov. 12
34	Miss. Southern	26	Tuscaloosa......Nov. 19
35	Florida	13	Gainesville.......Nov. 26
13	Auburn	14	Birmingham......Dec. 3
227		**130**	

1950—WON 9, LOST 2

27	Chattanooga	0	Birmingham ...Sept. 23
26	Tulane	14	New Orleans...Sept. 30
22	Vanderbilt	27	Mobile............Oct. 7
34	Furman	6	Tuscaloosa.......Oct. 13†
9	Tennessee	14	Knoxville ......Oct. 21
14	Miss. State	7	Tuscaloosa ......Oct. 28
14	Georgia	7	Birmingham......Nov. 4
53	Miss. Southern	0	Tuscaloosa......Nov. 11
54	Ga. Tech.	19	Atlanta ....Nov. 18
41	Florida	13	Jacksonville.....Nov. 25
34	Auburn	0	Birmingham......Dec. 2
328		**107**	

1951—WON 5, LOST 6

89	Delta State	0	Montgomery ...Sept. 21
7	L. S. U.	13	Mobile ....Sept. 29
20	Vanderbilt	22	Nashville ....Oct. 6
18	Villanova	41	Tuscaloosa......Oct. 12
13	Tennessee	27	Birmingham......Oct. 20
7	Miss. State	0	Starkville......Oct. 27
16	Georgia	14	Athens ....Nov. 3
40	Miss. Southern	7	Tuscaloosa......Nov. 10
7	Georgia Tech.	27	Birmingham......Nov. 17
21	Florida	30	Tuscaloosa......Nov. 24
25	Auburn	7	Birmingham......Dec. 1
263		**188**	

1952—WON 10, LOST 2

20	Miss. Southern	6	Montgomery ...Sept. 19
21	L. S. U.	20	Baton Rouge...Sept. 24
21	Miami	7	Miami ....Oct. 3
33	Virginia Tech.	0	Tuscaloosa ......Oct. 11
0	Tennessee	20	Knoxville ......Oct. 18
42	Miss. State	19	Tuscaloosa ......Oct. 25
34	Georgia	19	Birmingham......Nov. 1
42	Chattanooga	28	Tuscaloosa ......Nov. 8
3	Georgia Tech.	7	Atlanta ....Nov. 15
27	Maryland	7	Mobile ....Nov. 22
21	Auburn	0	Birmingham ....Nov. 29
•61	Syracuse	6	Orange Bowl....Jan. 1
325		**139**	

1953—WON 6, LOST 3, TIED 3

19	Miss. Southern	25	Montgomery ...Sept. 18
7	L. S. U.	7	Mobile ....Sept. 26
21	Vanderbilt	12	Nashville ....Oct. 3
41	Tulsa	13	Tuscaloosa ......Oct. 10
0	Tennessee	0	Birmingham ....Oct. 17
7	Miss. State	7	Tuscaloosa ......Oct. 24
33	Georgia	12	Athens ....Oct. 31
21	Chattanooga	14	Tuscaloosa ......Nov. 7
13	Georgia Tech.	6	Birmingham......Nov. 14
0	Maryland	21	College Park...Nov. 21
10	Auburn	7	Birmingham......Nov. 28
• 6	Rice	28	Cotton Bowl.......Jan. 1
178		**152**	

1954—WON 4, LOST 5, TIED 2

2	Miss. Southern	7	Montgomery .. Sept. 11
12	L. S. U.	0	Baton Rouge...Sept. 25
28	Vanderbilt	14	Mobile ....Oct. 2
40	Tulsa	0	Tuscaloosa ......Oct. 9
27	Tennessee	0	Knoxville ......Oct. 16
7	Miss. State	12	Tuscaloosa ......Oct. 23
0	Georgia	0	Birmingham......Oct. 30
0	Tulane	0	New Orleans...Nov. 6
0	Georgia Tech.	20	Atlanta ....Nov. 13
7	Miami	23	Miami ....Nov. 19
0	Auburn	28	Birmingham....Nov. 27
123		**104**	

1955—WON 0, LOST 10, TIED 0

0	Rice	20	Houston ....Sept. 24
6	Vanderbilt	21	Nashville ....Oct. 1
0	T. C. U.	21	Tuscaloosa ......Oct. 8
0	Tennessee	20	Birmingham ....Oct. 15
7	Miss. State	26	Tuscaloosa ......Oct. 22
14	Georgia	35	Athens ....Oct. 29
7	Tulane	27	Mobile ....Nov. 5
2	Georgia Tech.	26	Birmingham ....Nov. 12
12	Miami	34	Miami ....Nov. 18
0	Auburn	26	Birmingham......Nov. 26
48		**255**	

1956—WON 2, LOST 7, TIED 1

13	Rice	20	Houston ....Sept. 22
7	Vanderbilt	32	Mobile ....Oct. 6
6	T. C. U.	23	Tuscaloosa ......Oct. 13
0	Tennessee	24	Knoxville ......Oct. 20
13	Miss. State	12	Tuscaloosa ......Oct. 27
13	Georgia	16	Birmingham ....Nov. 3
13	Tulane	7	New Orleans...Nov. 10
0	Georgia Tech.	27	Atlanta ....Nov. 17
13	Miss. Southern	13	Tuscaloosa ......Nov. 24
7	Auburn	34	Birmingham......Dec. 1
85		**208**	

1957—WON 2, LOST 7, TIED 1

0	L. S. U.	28	Baton Rouge...Sept. 28
6	Vanderbilt	6	Nashville ....Oct. 5
0	T. C. U.	28	Ft. Worth........Oct. 12
0	Tennessee	14	Birmingham......Oct. 19
13	Miss. State	25	Tuscaloosa......Oct. 26
14	Georgia	13	Athens ....Nov. 2
0	Tulane	7	Mobile ....Nov. 9
7	Georgia Tech.	10	Birmingham......Nov. 16
29	Miss. Southern	2	Tuscaloosa ......Nov. 23
0	Auburn	40	Birmingham......Nov. 30
69		**173**	

*Indicates Bowl game.   †—Night game.

1958—WON 5, LOST 4, TIED 1

3	L. S. U.	13	Mobile ....Sept. 27
0	Vanderbilt	0	Birmingham .....Oct. 4
29	Furman	6	Tuscaloosa...... Oct. 11
7	Tennessee	14	Knoxville ....Oct. 18
9	Miss. State	7	Starkville ....Oct. 25
12	Georgia	0	Tuscaloosa......Nov. 1
7	Tulane	13	New Orleans ....Nov. 8
17	Georgia Tech	8	Atlanta ....Nov. 15
14	Memphis State	0	Tuscaloosa......Nov. 22
8	Auburn	14	Birmingham.....Nov. 29
106		75	

1959—WON 7, LOST 2, TIED 2

3	Georgia	17	Athens ....Sept. 19
3	Houston	0	Houston...........Sept. 26
7	Vanderbilt	7	Nashville ....Oct. 3
13	Chattanooga	0	Tuscaloosa ......Oct. 10
7	Tennessee	7	Birmingham......Oct. 17
10	Miss. State	0	Tuscaloosa ......Oct. 24
19	Tulane	7	Mobile ....Nov. 7
9	Ga. Tech	7	Birmingham .....Nov. 14
14	Memphis State	7	Tuscaloosa......Nov. 21
10	Auburn	0	Birmingham......Nov. 28
• 0	Penn State	7	Liberty Bowl....Dec. 19
95		59	

1960—WON 8, LOST 1, TIED 2

21	Georgia	6	Birmingham ....Sept. 17
6	Tulane	6	New Orleans....Sept. 24
21	Vanderbilt	0	Birmingham .... Oct. 1
7	Tennessee	20	Knoxville............Oct. 15
14	Houston	0	Tuscaloosa ......Oct. 22
7	Miss. State	0	Starkville ....Oct. 29
51	Furman	0	Tuscaloosa ....Nov. 5
16	Ga. Tech.	15	Atlanta ....Nov. 12
34	Tampa	6	Tuscaloosa ......Nov. 19
3	Auburn	0	Birmingham .....Nov. 26
• 3	Texas	3	Bl'ebonnet Bwl Dec. 17
183		56	

1961—WON 11, LOST 0
SEC CHAMPIONS

32	Georgia	6	Athens ....Sept. 23
35	Vanderbilt	6	Mobile ....Sept. 30
9	Tulane	0	Nashville ....Oct. 7
26	N. C. State	7	Tuscaloosa ......Oct. 14
34	Tennessee	3	Birmingham......Oct. 21
17	Houston	0	Houston ....Oct. 28
24	Miss. State	0	Tuscaloosa ......Nov. 4
66	Richmond	0	Tuscaloosa......Nov. 11
10	Ga. Tech	0	Birmingham......Nov. 18
34	Auburn	0	Birmingham......Dec. 2
•10	Arkansas	3	Sugar Bowl ......Jan. 1
297		25	

1962—WON 10, LOST 1

35	Georgia	0	Birmingham ....Sept. 22
44	Tulane	6	New Orleans....Sept. 28
17	Vanderbilt	7	Birmingham .... Oct. 6
14	Houston	3	Tuscaloosa ......Oct. 13
27	Tennessee	7	Knoxville ....Oct. 20
25	Tulsa	6	Tuscaloosa ......Oct. 27
20	Miss. State	0	Starkville ....Nov. 3
36	Miami	3	Tuscaloosa.......Nov. 10
6	Georgia Tech.	7	Atlanta ....Nov. 17
36	Auburn	0	Birmingham......Dec. 1
•17	Oklahoma	0	Orange Bowl.....Jan. 1
289		39	

1963—WON 9, LOST 2

32	Georgia	7	Athens ....Sept. 21
28	Tulane	0	Mobile ....Sept. 28
21	Vanderbilt	6	Nashville ....Oct. 5
6	Florida	10	Tuscaloosa ....Oct. 12
35	Tennessee	0	Birmingham ......Oct. 19
21	Houston	13	Tuscaloosa ......Oct. 26
20	Miss. State	19	Tuscaloosa ....Nov. 2
27	Georgia Tech.	11	Birmingham......Nov. 16
8	Auburn	10	Birmingham.....Nov. 30
17	Miami	12	Miami ....Dec. 14
•12	Mississippi	7	Sugar Bowl ......Jan. 1
227		95	

•Indicates Bowl games.

1964—WON 10, LOST 1
SEC CHAMPIONS

31	Georgia	3	Tuscaloosa .....Sept. 19
36	Tulane	6	Mobile ....Sept. 26
24	Vanderbilt	0	Birmingham......Oct. 3
21	N.C. State	0	Tuscaloosa ......Oct. 10
19	Tennessee	8	Knoxville ....Oct. 17
17	Florida	14	Tuscaloosa ......Oct. 24
23	Miss. State	6	Jackson ....Oct. 31
17	L. S. U.	9	Birmingham ....Nov. 7
24	Georgia Tech	7	Atlanta ....Nov. 14
21	Auburn	14	Birmingham.....Nov. 26
•17	Texas	21	Orange Bowl.....Jan. 1
240		88	

1965—WON 9, LOST 1, TIED 1
SEC CHAMPIONS

17	Georgia	18	Athens .... Sept. 18
27	Tulane	0	Mobile ....Sept. 25
17	Mississippi	16	Birmingham .... Oct. 2
22	Vanderbilt	7	Nashville ....Oct. 9
7	Tennessee	7	Birmingham ....Oct. 16
21	Florida State	0	Tuscaloosa ......Oct. 23
10	Miss. State	7	Jackson ....Oct. 30
31	L. S. U.	7	Baton Rouge ...Nov. 6
35	So. Carolina	14	Tuscaloosa ..... Nov. 13
30	Auburn	3	Birmingham ....Nov. 27
•39	Nebraska	28	Orange Bowl ...Jan. 1
256		107	

1966—WON 11, LOST 0, TIED 0
SEC CHAMPIONS

34	La. Tech	0	Birmingham ...Sept. 24
17	Mississippi	7	Jackson ....Oct. 1
26	Clemson	0	Tuscaloosa ......Oct. 8
11	Tennessee	10	Knoxville ....Oct. 15
42	Vanderbilt	6	Birmingham ....Oct. 22
27	Miss. State	14	Tuscaloosa......Oct. 29
21	L. S. U.	0	Birmingham .....Nov. 5
24	South Carolina	0	Tuscaloosa ..... Nov. 12
34	Sou. Miss.	0	Mobile ....Nov. 26
31	Auburn	0	Birmingham .....Dec. 3
•34	Nebraska	7	Sugar Bowl ......Jan. 2
301		44	

1967—WON 8, LOST 2, TIED 1

37	Florida State	37	Birmingham......Sept. 23
25	Sou. Miss.	3	Mobile ....Sept. 30
21	Mississippi	7	Birmingham.......Oct. 7
35	Vanderbilt	21	Nashville ....Oct. 14
13	Tennessee	24	Birmingham ....Oct. 21
13	Clemson	10	Clemson ....Oct. 28
13	Miss. State	0	Tuscaloosa......Nov. 4
7	L. S. U.	6	Baton Rouge...Nov. 11
17	So. Carolina	0	Tuscaloosa ..... Nov. 18
7	Auburn	3	Birmingham......Dec. 2
•16	Texas A&M	20	Cotton Bowl....Jan. 1
204		131	

1968—WON 8, LOST 3

14	Va. Tech	7	Birmingham.....Sept. 21
17	Sou. Miss.	14	Mobile ....Sept. 28
8	Mississippi	10	Jackson ....Oct 5
31	Vanderbilt	7	Tuscaloosa......Oct. 12
9	Tennessee	10	Knoxville ....Oct. 19
21	Clemson	14	Tuscaloosa......Oct. 26
20	Miss. State	13	Tuscaloosa......Nov. 2
16	L.S.U.	7	Birmingham.....Nov. 9
14	Miami	6	Miami ....Nov. 16
24	Auburn	16	Birmingham......Nov. 30
•10	Missouri	35	Gator Bowl ....Dec. 28
184		139	

1969—WON 6, LOST 5

17	Va. Tech	13	Blacksburg .....Sept. 20
63	So. Miss	14	Tuscaloosa .....Sept. 27
33	Mississippi	32	Birmingham ..... Oct. 4
10	Vanderbilt	14	Nashville ...... Oct. 11
14	Tennessee	41	Birmingham......Oct. 18
38	Clemson	13	Clemson ....Oct. 25
23	Miss. State	19	Jackson ....Nov. 1
15	L.S.U.	20	Baton Rouge...Nov. 8
42	Miami	6	Tuscaloosa ..... Nov. 15
26	Auburn	49	Birmingham......Nov. 29
•33	Colorado	47	Liberty Bowl....Dec. 13
314		268	

1970—WON 6, LOST 5, TIED 1	
21 Southern Cal. ...42	Birmingham ....Sept. 12
51 Virginia Tech. 18	Birmingham ....Sept. 19
46 Florida 15	Tuscaloosa .....Sept. 26
23 Mississippi 48	Jackson ....Oct. 3
35 Vanderbilt 11	Tuscaloosa .....Oct. 10
0 Tennessee 24	Knoxville ....Oct. 17
30 Houston 21	Houston ....Oct. 24
35 Miss. State 6	Tuscaloosa .....Oct. 31
9 L. S. U. 14	Birmingham ....Nov. 7
32 Miami 8	Miami ....Nov. 14
28 Auburn 33	Birmingham ....Nov. 28
24 Oklahoma 24	Bluebonnet
	Bowl.............Dec. 31
334 264	

1971—WON 11, LOST 1	
17 Southern Cal. 10	Los Angeles ...Sept. 10
42 Southern Miss.... 6	Tuscaloosa ......Sept. 18
38 Florida 0	Gainesville ...Sept. 25
40 Mississippi 6	Birmingham ......Oct. 2
42 Vanderbilt 0	Nashville ....Oct. 9
32 Tennessee 15	Birmingham ...Oct. 16
34 Houston 20	Tuscaloosa ......Oct. 23
41 Miss. State 10	Jackson ....Oct. 30
14 L. S. U. 7	Baton Rouge ...Nov. 6
31 Miami 3	Tuscaloosa .....Nov. 13
31 Auburn 7	Birmingham ...Nov. 27
6 Nebraska 38	Orange Bowl ....Jan. 1
368 122	

ALABAMA'S FOOTBALL HISTORY

Year	Coach	Captain	Record	Pts.	Opp.
1892	E. B. Beaumont (Penn)	W. G. Little	2-2-0	96	37
1893	Eli Abbott (Penn)	G. H. Kyzer	0-4-0	24	74
1894	Eli Abbott	S. B. Slone	3-1-0	60	16
1895	Eli Abbott	H. M. Bankhead	0-4-0	12	112
1896	Otto Wagonhurst (Penn)	S. B. Sloan	2-1-0	56	10
1897	Allen McCants (Alabama)	Frank S. White, Jr.	1-0-0	6	0
1898	No Team	T. G. Burk—Elected	No Team		
1899	W. A. Hartin (Virginia)	T. W. Wert	3-1-0	39	31
1900	M. Griffin	W. E. Drennen	2-3-0	52	100
1901	M. H. Harvey (Auburn)	W. E. Drennen	2-1-2	92	23
1902	Eli Abbott, J. O. Heyworth	J. R. Forman	4-4-0	191	49
1903	W. B. Blount (Yale)	W. S. Wyatt	3-4-0	60	114
1904	W. B. Blount	W. S. Wyatt	7-3-0	100	62
1905	Jack Leavenworth (Yale)	B. A. Burks	6-4-0	178	113
1906	J. W. H. Pollard (Dartmouth)	Washington Moody	5-1-0	97	82
1907	J. W. H. Pollard	Emile Hannon	5-1-2	70	64
1908	J. W. H. Pollard	Henry Burks	6-1-1	107	31
1909	J. W. H. Pollard	Derrill Pratt	5-1-2	68	17
1910	Guy S. Lowman (Springfield)	O. G. Gresham	4-4-0	65	107
1911	D. V. Graves (Missouri)	R. H. Bumgardner	5-2-2	153	31
1912	D. V. Graves	Farley W. Moody	5-3-1	156	55
1913	D. V. Graves	C. H. Van de Graaff	5-3-0	188	40
1914	D. V. Graves	C. A. "Tubby" Long	5-4-0	211	64
1915	Thomas Kelly (Chicago)	William L. Harsh	6-2-0	250	51
1916	Thomas Kelly	Lowndes Morton	6-3-0	156	62
1917	Thomas Kelly	Jack Hovater	5-2-1	169	29
1918	No Team	Dan Boone—Elected	No Team		
1919	Xen C. Scott (Western Reserve)	Isaac J. Rogers	8-1-0	280	22
1920	Xen C. Scott	Sid Johnston	10-1-0	377	35
1921	Xen C. Scott	Al Clemens	5-4-2	241	104
1922	Xen C. Scott	Ernest E. Cooper	6-3-1	300	81
1923	Wallace Wade (Brown)	Al Clemens	7-2-1	222	50
1924	Wallace Wade	A. T. S. Hubert	8-1-0	290	24
1925	Wallace Wade	Bruce Jones	10-0-0	297	26
1926	Wallace Wade	Emile "Red" Barnes	9-0-1	249	27
1927	Wallace Wade,	Freddie Pickhard	5-4-1	154	73
1928	Wallace Wade	Earle Smith	6-3-0	187	75
1929	Wallace Wade	Billy Hicks	6-3-0	196	58
1930	Wallace Wade	Charles B. Clement	10-0-0	271	13
1931	Frank W. Thomas (Notre Dame)	Joe Sharpe	9-1-0	370	57
1932	Frank W. Thomas	John Cain	8-2-0	200	51
1933	Frank W. Thomas	Foy Leach	7-1-1	130	17
1934	Frank W. Thomas	Bill Lee	10-0-0	316	45
1935	Frank W. Thomas	James Walker	6-2-1	185	55
1936	Frank W. Thomas	Jas. "Bubber" Nisbet	8-0-1	168	35
1937	Frank W. Thomas	Leroy Monsky	9-1-0	225	33
1938	Frank W. Thomas	Lew Bostick	7-1-1	149	40
1939	Frank W. Thomas	Carey Cox	5-3-1	101	53
1940	Frank W. Thomas	Harold Newman	7-2-0	166	80
1941	Frank W. Thomas	John Wyhonic	9-2-0	263	85
1942	Frank W. Thomas	Joe Domnanovich	8-3-0	246	97

Year	Coach	Captains	Record	Pts	Opp
1943	No Team	No Team	No Team		
1944	Frank W. Thomas	Game Captains	5-2-2	272	83
1945	Frank W. Thomas	Game Captains	10-0-0	430	80
1946	Frank W. Thomas	Game Captains	7-4-0	186	110
1947	H. D. Drew (Bates)	John Wozniak	8-3-0	210	101
1948	H. D. Drew	Ray Richeson	6-4-1	228	170
1949	H. D. Drew	Doug Lockridge	6-3-1	227	130
1950	H. D. Drew	Mike Mizerany	9-2-0	328	107
1951	H. D. Drew	Jack Brown	5-6-0	263	188
1952	H. D. Drew	Bobby Wilson	10-2-0	325	139
1953	H. D. Drew	Bud Willis	6-3-3	178	152
1954	H. D. Drew	Sid Youngleman	4-5-2	123	104
1955	J. B. Whitworth (Alabama)	Nick Germanos	0-10-0	48	255
1956	J. B. Whitworth	Jim Cunningham-Wes Thompson	2-7-1	85	208
1957	J. B. Whitworth	Jim Loftis-Clay Walls	2-7-1	69	173
1958	Paul W. Bryant (Alabama)	Dave Sington-Bobby Smith	5-4-1	106	75
1959	Paul W. Bryant	Marlin Dyess-Jim Blevins	7-2-2	95	59
1960	Paul W. Bryant	Leon Fuller-Bobby Boylston	8-1-2	183	56
1961	Paul W. Bryant	Pat Trammell-Billy Neighbors	11-0-0	297	25
1962	Paul W. Bryant	LeeRoy Jordan-Jimmy Sharpe	10-1-0	289	39
1963	Paul W. Bryant	Benny Nelson-Steve Allen	9-2-0	227	105
1964	Paul W. Bryant	Joe Namath-Ray Ogden	10-1-0	250	88
1965	Paul W. Bryant	Steve Sloan Paul Crane	9-1-1	256	107
1966	Paul W. Bryant	Ray Perkins-Richard Cole	11-0-0	301	44
1967	Paul W. Bryant	Ken Stabler-Bobby Johns	8-2-1	198	131
1968	Paul W. Bryant	Mike Hall-Donnie Sutton	8-3-0	184	139
1969	Paul W. Bryant	Danny Ford-Alvin Samples	6-5-0	314	268
1970	Paul W. Bryant	Danny Gilbert-Dave Brungard	6-5-1	334	264
1971	Paul W. Bryant	Johnny Musso-Robin Parkhouse	11-1-0	368	122

SOUTHEASTERN CONFERENCE FOOTBALL CHAMPIONS

1933 ALABAMA (5-0-1)	1945 ALABAMA (6-0-0)	1958 L. S. U. (6-0-0)
1934 ALABAMA (7-0-0)	1946 Georgia (5-0-0)	1959 Georgia (7-0-0)
Tulane (8-0-0)	Tennessee (5-0-0)	1960 Mississippi (5-0-1)
1935 L. S. U (5-0-0)	1947 Mississippi (6-1-0)	1961 ALABAMA (7-0-0)
1936 L. S. U. (6-0-0)	1948 Georgia (6-0-0)	L. S. U. (6-0-0)
1937 ALABAMA (6-0-0)	1949 Tulane (5-1-0)	1962 Mississippi (6-0-0)
1938 Tennessee (7-0-0)	1950 Kentucky (5-1-0)	1963 Mississippi (5-0-1)
1939 Tennessee (6-0-0)	1951 Georgia Tech (7-0-0)	1964 ALABAMA (8-0-0)
Georgia Tech (6-0-0)	Tennessee (5-0-0)	1965 ALABAMA (6-1-1)
Tulane (5-0-0)	1952 Georgia Tech (6-0-0)	1966 ALABAMA (6-0-0)
1940 Tennessee (5-0-0)	1953 ALABAMA (4-0-3)	Georgia (6-0-0)
1941 Miss. State (4-0-1)	1954 Mississippi (5-0-0)	1967 Tennessee (6-0-0)
1942 Georgia (6-1-0)	1955 Mississippi (5-1-0)	1968 Georgia (5-0-1)
1943 Georgia Tech (3-0-0)	1956 Tennessee (6-0-0)	1969 Tennessee (5-1-0)
1944 Georgia Tech (4-0-0)	1957 Auburn (7-0-0)	1970 L. S. U. (5-0-0)
		1971 ALABAMA (7-0-0)

CRIMSON TIDE FOOTBALL LETTERMEN

(NOTE: The University of Alabama Athletic Publicity Department has listed all known lettermen from 1892 through 1971. Naturally there are errors in the years of some of the earlier lettermen.)

"A"

Abbott, Eli '92 '93
Abbruzzese, Raymond '60 '61
Abston, Bill '48 '49
Adams, George '35
Adkinson, Wayne '70 '71
Aland, Jack '42
Albright, George '44
Almon, William Lewis '21 (Mgr.)
Allen, Charles G. '57 '58 '59
Allen, Steve '61 '62 '63
Andrews, Mickey '63 '64
Angelich, James Dykes '33 '34 '35
Arthur, Paul '49
Ashford, Leon (Mgr.) '69
August, Johnny '42 '46 '47
Austill, Huriecsco '04
Austill, Jere '08
Averitte, Warren '38 '39 '40
Avinger, Clarence (Butch) '48 '49 '50

"B"

Bailey, David A. '69 '70 '71
Bailey, Harle Grady '33 (Mgr.)
Ballard, Clarence Bingham '01 '02
Bankhead, William Brockman '92 '93
Bannister, Gary '70 (Mgr.)
Barnes, Emile '25 '26
Barker, Troy '31 '32 '33
Barron, Marvin '70 '71
Barron, Randy '66 '67 '68
Barry, Dick '51
Bartlett, Charles '20 '21
Baswell, Ben '35
Bates, C. F. '14
Bates, Tim '64 '65
Battle, William (Bill) '60 '61 '62
Baty, William C., Jr. '21 '22
Baughman, Bill '46
Baughman, Jim '42
Bealle, Sherman '29
Bean, Dickie '66
Beard, Jeff '69 '70 '71
Beard, Jeff '69 '70
Beard, Ken '63
Beck, Ellis '71
Beck, Willie '56 '57
Beddingfield, David '69

Bedwell, David '65 '66 '67
Bell, Stanley '59
Bentley, Edward K., Jr. '70
Bite, Mike '52 (Mgr.)
Bird, Ron '63
Bires, Andy '42
Bisceglia, Steve '71
Blackmon, Sumpter '41
Blackwell, Gene '37 '38 '39
Blackwood, J. E. '21
Blair, Bill '68 '69 '70
Blalock, Ralph '56 '57
Blevins, James Allen '57 '58 '59
Boler, Clark '62 '63
Boman, T. D. '14 '15
Bone, George '68
Bookmeier, Robert L. '56
Boone, Alfred Morgan '17
Boone, Ike '19
Booth, Baxter '56 '57 '58
Boozer, Young '34 '35' '36
Borders, Tom '39
Boschung, Paul '67, '68 '69
Bostick, Lewis '37 '38
Boswell, Charlie '38 '39
Bowdoin, James L. '27 '28
Bowdoin, Jimmy '54 '55 '56
Bowman, Jim (Mgr.) '69
Bowman, Steve '63 '64 '65
Box, Jimmy '60
Boykin, Gideon Frierson '94
Boykin, Dave '28 '29
Boylston, Robert W. (Bobby) '59 '60
Bradford, Vic '37 '38
Brannan, Troy Crampton '14
Brannen, Jerre Lamar '57 '58
Brasfield, Davis '27
Brewer, Richard, '65 '66 '67
Brooker, William T. (Tommy) '59 '60 '61
Brooks, William S. '54 '55 '56
Bross, Joe '66 (Mgr.)
Brown, Billy '28
Brown, Carl Abercrombie '98 '99
Brown, Dave '40 '41 '42
Brown, Halver (Buddy) '71
Brown, Jack '48 '49 '50 '51
Brown, John Mack '23 '24 '25
Brown, Marshall '55 '56 '57

254

Brown, Randy '68
Brown, Robert C. '16 '17
Brown, Tolbert '26 '27
Brown, T. L. '19 '20
Browne, Randall R. '08 '09
Bruce, Ed '25 (Mgr.)
Brungard, David A. '70
Bryant, Paul W. '33 '34 '35
Buck, Oran '69
Buckler, William E. '23 '24 '25
Bumgardner, Robert H. '09 '10
Burkart, C. T. '20
Burkett, Jim '49 '50
Burks, Auxford '03 '04 '05
Burks, Basil Manly '13 '14
Burks, Henry Thomas '06 '07
Burnett, Hunter Tennille '14 '15
Burr, Borden '93 '94
Busbee, Kent '67
Bush, Jeff '29 '33 '34
Bush, Jim '45 '46
Butler, Clyde '70

"C"

Cadenhead, Billy '46 '47 '48 '49
Cain, Jim '45 '46 '47 '48
Cain, Johnny '30 '31 '32
Caldwell, Blackie '36
Caldwell, Herschel '25 '26
Calvert, John '65 '66
Calvin, Tom '48 '49 '50
Chamberlain, B. B. '04 '05
Camp, Joseph S. (Pete) '23 '24 '25
Campbell, John '28 '29 '30
Campbell, Tilden (Happy) '34 '35
Canterbury, Frank '64 '65 '66
Cargille, C. J. '14
Carrigan, Ralph B. '51 '52 '53
Carroll, Jimmy '65 '66
Cash, Jeraull Wayne '70 '71
Cashio, Gri '47
Cassidy, Francis '44 '45 '46 '47
Causey, Joe '31
Chaffin, Phil '68 '69 '70
Chambers, Jimmy '67
Chapman, Herb '47
Chappell, Howard '31 '32 '33
Chatwood, David '65 '66 '67
Childers, Morris '60
Childs, Bob '66 '67 '68
Chiodetti, Larry '50 '51
Christian, Knute Rockne '54 '55
Ciemny, Richard Lee '69 '70
Clark, Cotton '61 '62

Clark, Frank Barnard '03 '04
Clark, Phil '56
Clay, Hugh Stephen '69
Clemens, Al '21 '22
Clement, C. B. (Foots) '28 '29 '30
Coats, ick (Mgr.) '71
Cochran, Bob '47 '48 '49
Cochran, Donald G. '57 '58 '59
Cochran, Henry '37
Cochran, Ralph '49
Cochrane, David '31
Cohen, Andy '23 '24
Cokely, onald '70 '71
Cole, Richard '64 '65
Compton, Ben E. '23 '24 '25
Compton, Charley '42 '46 '47
Compton, Joe '49 '50 '51
Comstock, Charles Dexter '95 '96
Comstock, Donald '56
Connor, Don '55
Conway, Bob '50 '51 '52
Conway, William '44
Cook, Elbert '60 '61 '62
Cook, Ted '42 '46
Cook, Thomas '31 (Mgr.)
Cook, Wayne '64 '65 '66
Cope, Robert '92 '93
Corbitt, James (Corky) '45 '46
Couch, L. B. '49 '50
Cox, Carey '37 '38 '39
Coyle, Dan Joseph Jr. '54 '55
Craddock, French Hood '09 (Mgr.)
Craft, Russ '40 '41 '42
Crane, Paul '63 '64 '65
Crenshaw, Curtis '61
Creen, Cecil L. '16
Crowson, Roger '68
Croyle, John '71
Culpepper, Ed '51 '52 '53 '54
Culwell, Ingram '61 '62
Cummings, Joe '52 '53
Cunningham, E. A. '55 '56
Curtis, Joe '50 '51 '52
Curtis, Nathan Stephenson '06

"D"

Davis, Alvin (Pig) '37 '38
Davis, Bill '71
Davis, Charley '48 '49
Davis, Fred '38 '39 '40
Davis, Fred, Jr. '64
Davis, Jim '51 '52 '53
Davis, Steve '65 '66 '67
Davis, Terry Ashley '70 '71
Davis, Terry Lane '70

255

Davis, Tim '61 '62 '63
Davis, William (Junior) '67 '68
Davidson, James LaFayette '00
Dean, Mike '67 '68 '69
DeLaurentis, Vincent '52 '53
Dempsey, Benny '56 '57
Demyanovich, Joseph '32 '33 '34
DeShane, Charley '40
Dildy, Jim '31 '32 '33
Dildy, Joe '34
Dill, Jimmy '62 '63
Dixon, Dennis '67 '68
Dobbs, Edgar '28 '30
Dobbs, Floyd T. '27 '28
Domnanovich, Joe '40 '41 '42
Donald, Joseph Glenn '05 '06
Donaldson, Paul '54
Doran, Stephen Curtis '69 '70
Dotherow, Autrey '30 '31
Dowdy, Cecil '64 '65 '66
Dowling, Hugh R. '26 (Mgr.)
Downey, James A., Jr. '17 '18
Drinkard, Ried '68 '69 '70
Duncan, Jerry '65 '66
Drennen, Earle '00 '01
Duke, Jim '67 '68 '69
Durby, Ron '63 '64
Dye, George '27
Dyess, Marlin '57 '58 '59

"E"

Eberdt, Jess '29 '30
Eckerly, Charles '52 '53 '54
Edward, Allen '70 (Mgr.)
Edwards, Marion '44
Ellett, Alvie '55
Ellis, Raiford '34
Ellis, Billy '28
Elmore, Albert Sr. '29 '30
Elmore, Albert Jr. '53 '54 '55
Elmore, Grady '62 '63 '64
Emerson, Kenneth '69 '70
Emmett, J. H. '19 '20 '21 '22
Emmons, James Thomas '54
Enis, Ben '26
Erdreich, M. K. '30 (Mgr.)

"F"

Fedak, Frank '45
Feld, Phillip '32 (Mgr.)
Ferguson, Burr '91 '92
Ferguson, Charles M. '68 '69
Ferguson, Hill '95 '96
Ferguson, Richard '69
Fichman, Leon '42
Fields, William H. '44

Filippini, Bruno '44 '45 '46 '47
Finlay, Louis Malone '09 '10
Finnell, Edward Judson '11
Fiorette, Anthony Raymond '20
Fletcher, Maurice '37
Flowers, Dick '46 '47 '48
Flowers, Lee '45
Forbus, Roy '56
Ford, Danny '67 '68 '69
Ford, Mike '66 '67 '68
Fortunato, Steve '46 '47 '48
Foshee, Jess '37 '38
Fowler, Conrad '66 '67 '68
Fracchia, Mike '60 '61 '63
Francis, Kavanaugh (Kay) '34 '35
Frank, Milton '58 '59
Frank, Morris '62
Franko, Jim '47 '48 '49
Frazer, Thomas Sydney '93
Freeman, Wayne '62 '63 '64
French, Buddy '63 '64
Frey, Calvin '31 '32 '33
Fuller, Jimmy '64 '65
Fuller, Leon '59 '60

"G"

Gage, Fred Harrison '16
Gambrell, D. J. '45 '46
Gammon, George '41 '42
Gandy, Joseph Maury '12 '13
Gandy, Ralph '32 '33 '34 '35
Gantt, Greg '71
Garrett, Broox Cleveland '09
Garrett, Coma, Jr. '05 '06
Gaston, Finus (Mgr.) '71
Gellerstedt, Sam '68
Gerber, Elwood '40
Germanos, Nicholas (Nick) '54 '55
Gibbons, James Booth '14
Gibson, Richard '45
Gilbert, Danny '68 '69 '70
Gillis, Grant '24 '25
Gilmer, Cred '64
Gilmer, Harry '44 '45 '46 '47
Glasgow, Harold '48 (Mgr.)
Glover, Jerry '64 (Mgr.)
Godfree, Newton '30 '31 '32
Gornto, Red '38
Gosa, R. E. '11 '12
Gossett, Don Lee '69
Graham, Glen W. '55 '56
Grammar, James W. '69 '71
Grammer, Richard '67 '68 '69
Granade, James Napoleon '98 '99
Granade, Joe C. '99 '00

Grant, Fred '45 '46
Grantham, Jim '45 '46
Graves, Bibb '92 '93
Gray, Charlie '56 '57 '58
Grayson, David Allison '92 '93
Green, Jack '45
Greenhill, N. F. '13
Greer, Charles West '10 '11
Gresham, Owen Garside '08 '09
Griffith, Tom W. '11 (Mgr.)
Gwin, James C. B. '03

"H"

Hagler, Ellis '27 '28
Hall, Mike '66 '67 '68
Hall, Wayne '71
Hamer, Norris '67, '68
Hamner, Robert Lee '25 '26 '27
Hand, Mike '68 '69 '70
Hannah, Herb '48 '49 '50
Hannah, William C. '57 '58 '59
Hannah, John '70 '71
Hannah, John '70
Hansen, Cliff '40 '41
Hanson, John '40
Harkins, Grover '37 '38
Harpole, Allen (Bunk) '65 '66 '67
Harrell, Billy '40
Harris, Charles '65 '66 '67
Harris, Don '68 '69 '70
Harris, Hudson '62 '63 '64
Harsh, G. R., Jr. '13 '14
Harsh, W. L. '15
Hayden, Neb '69 '70
Heard, Victor John '10
Heard Virgil Willis '11
Heath, Donnie '60
Hecht, George '40 '41 '42
Helms, Sandy '49 '50
Henry, Butch '61 '62 '63
Hewes, William '31 '32
Hickerson, Ed '38 '40
Hicks, Billy '28 '29
Hicks, Jack (Mgr.) '63
Hicks, J. W. '12 '13
Higginbotham, George Stephen '69 '70
    '71
Higginbotham, Robert '67 '68
Hill, Buster '52
Hill, Marvin '54
Hilman, R. G. '95
Hines, Edward T. '70
Hinton, Robert Poole '22 '23
Hite, John H. '44
Hobbs, Sam '07

Hobson, Clell '50 '51 '52
Hodges, Norwood '44 '45 '46 '47
Holcomb, Don '56
Holder, Harry '27
Holdnak, Ed '48 '49
Holley, Hilmon D. '30 '31 '32
Hollis, William C. '54 '55
Holm Bernard '27 '28 '29
Holm, Charlie '37 '38
Holm, Tony '28 '29
Holmes, Gordon '26
Holsomback, Roy '59 '60
Holt, Darwin '60 '61
Homan, Dennis, '65 '66 '67
Hood, Bob '46 '47 '48
Hood, E. P. '20
Hopper, Mike '61 '62 '64
Horton, Jimmy '71
Houston, Ellis (Red) '30 '31 '32
Hovater, Dexter Louis '14 '15
Hovater, Jack '19 '20 '21
Hovater, Walter E. '17 '18 '19
Howard, Frank '28 '29 '30
Howell, Millard (Dixie) '32 '33 '34
Hubert, A. T. S. (Pooley) '23 '24 '25
Hudson, Ben A. '23 '24 '25
Hudson, H. Clayton '21 '22
Huey, Dennis '62 (Trainer)
Hughes, Hal '37 '38
Hughes, Howard '41
Hughes, Larry '31 '32 '33
Hundermark, John '33
Hunt, Ben '21 '22
Hunt, Travis '50 '51 '52
Hunter, Scott '68 '69 '70
Hupke, Tom '31 '32 '33
Hurd, Clarence S. '08 '09
Hurlbut, Jack '62 '63
Hurt, Cecil A. '27 '28
Husband, Hunter '67 '68 '69
Husband, Woodward August '69 '70
Hutson, Don '32 '33 '34

"I"

Inglis, Clifford T. '23 (Mgr.)
Ingram, Cecil (Hooty) '52 '53 '54
Israel, Jimmy Kent '66
Israel, Thomas Murray '69
Ivy, Hryle Jr. '51 '52

"J"

Jackson, Bobby '57 '58
Jackson, Max '30 '31
Jackson, Wilbur '71

Jacobs, Parks '66 (Mgr.)
James, Kenneth Morris '69 '70
Jenkins, John Felix '94 '95
Jenkins, Jug '49 '50 '51
Jenkins, Tom '42
Jilleba, Pete '67 '68 '69
Johns, Bobby '65 '66 '67
Johnson, Billy '65 '66 '67
Johnson, Cornell '59 '60
Johnson, Harold '51
Johnson, James '25
Johnson, Roy M. Jr. '41
Johnston, Donny '66 '69
Johnston, J. Goree '15 '16
Johnston, Sidney '19 '20
Johnston, Wm. McDow '14
Jones, Albert D. '57
Jones, Bruce '23 '24 '25
Jones, Brice Sidney '06 '07
Jones, Howard Criner '14
Jones, H. H. '01
Jones, Ralph '44
Jones, Ralph Lee '17 '18
Jordan, Lee Roy '60 '61 '62
Jordan, Lint '50 '51
Joyce, Thomas (Mgr.) '26

"K"

Kearley, Dan '62 '63 '64
Kelley, Joe '66 '67 '68
Kelley, Max '54 '55 '56
Kelley, Leslie '64 '65 '66
Kelly, William Milner '20 '21
Kennedy, President John F.
   (Honorary) '61
Kerr, Dudley '66 '67
Kilgrow, Joe '36 '37
Killgore, Terry '65 '66 '67
Kilroy, William '52
Kimball, Morton '41
Kinderknecht, Donald H. '55 '56
King, Billy (Mgr.) '38
Kirby, Lelias E. '20 '21
Kirkland, B'Ho '31 '32 '33
Kling, Billy '38 (Mgr.)
Knapp, David '70 '71
Knight, William '57
Kohn, Julian H. '36 (Mgr.)
Krapf, James Paul '70 '71

"L"

LaBue, Joseph II '70 '71
Lambert, Jerry '52 '56
Langhorne, Jack '21 '22 '23
Langdale, Noah '40 '41

Langhorne, Jack '25
Langston, Griff '68 '69 '70
Lanier, M. B. '05
Lary, Al '48 '49 '50
Lary, Ed '49 '50 '51
Laslie, Carney '30 '31 '32
Lauer, Larry '48 '49 '50
Law, Phil '71
Lawley, Benjamin Lane '70
Layton, Dale '62
Leach, Foy '31 '32 '33
Lee, Bill '32 '33 '34
Lee, Harry C. '51 '52 '53 '54
Lee, Mickey '68 '69
Leeth, Wheeler '42
Lenoir, Edward Bertram '18 '19
Leon, Tony '42
Letcher, Marion '93 '94
Lett, Frank Montague '01 '02
Little, W. G. '93
Lewis, Al '61 '62 '63
Lewis, Tommy '51 '52 '53
Lockridge, Doug '48 '49
Loftin, James '56 '57
Long, Charles Allen '13 '14
Long, Jess '25 (Mgr.)
Long, Leon '29 '30 '31
Lowman, Joseph Allen '16 '17
Lumpkin, Billy Neal '55
Luna, Robert K. (Bobby) '51 '52 '53 '54
Lusk, Thomas Joseph III '70
Lutz, Harold (Red) '49 '50 '51
Lyda, Henry '66 (Mgr.)
Lynch, Curtis R. '53 '54 '55
Lyon, Charles '33 '34 '35
Lyon, Samuel Hamilton '34 '35

"M"

Machtolff, Jack '37
Malcolm, Charles '52
Mancha, Vaughn '44, '45 '46 '47
Manley, Harold '50 '51
Mann, Frank '68 '69 '70
Manning, Thomas '10 '11
Marcus, Van J. '50 '51 '52
Marlow, Bobby '50 '51 '52
Marr, Charles '34
Marshall, Fred H. '70 '71
Martin, Gary '61 '62 '63
Martin, Kenny '66 '67
Marx, Nathan '37 (Mgr.)
Mason, George L. '52 '53 '54
May, Walter '49
Mayfield, Dave '49 '50

Melton, Bimbo '49 '50 '51
Merrill, Walter '37 '38 '39
Miller, Floyd '48 '49
Miller, Hugh '29 '30
Miller, John '28 '29 '30
Miller, Murray '14
Mims, Fred '51 '52
Mitchell, John '71
Mitchell, Ken '64
Mizerany, Mike '48 '49 '50
Montgomery, Robert M. '70
Montgomery, Wm. Gabriel '20 '21
Monsky, LeRoy '36 '37
Mooneyham, Marlin '62
Moore, Harold '65 '66
Moore, Jimmy '28 '29 '30
Moore, John '62
Moore, Mal '62
Moore, Pete '68 '69
Moore, Randall Hugh '70
Moore, Robert W. '58 '59 '60
Moorer, Jefferson '53 '54
Morgan, Ed '66 '67 '68
Morrison, Duff '58 '59 '60
Morrison, William '26
Morrow, Bob Ed '34
Morrow, Hugh '44 '45 '46 '47
Morrow, Hugh '93
Morton, Farris '62
Moseley, Elliott '60
Moseley, Frank (Chesty) '31 '32 '33
Mosley, Hershel (Herky) '37 '38 '39
Mosley, John '64 '65 '66
Mosley, Norman '42 '46 '47
Mosley, Russ '42
Moss, Stan '65 '66 '67
Moye, Lamar '34 '35 '36
Mudd, Joseph Paul '08 '09
Musso, Johnny '69 '70 '71

"Mc"

MacAfee, Ken '51
McBee, Jerry '55
McCain, George '50 '51
MacCartee, Allen Graham '22 '23
McClendon, Frank '62 '63 '64
McClintock, P. G. '25 '27
McCollough, Gaylon '62 '63 '64
McConville, John '44
McCorquodale, John C. '02
McCorvey, Gessner T. '00 '01
McDonald, James T. '27
McDowell, Holt Andrews '11 '12
McGahey, T. A. '34 '35
McGee, Sam (Mgr.) '52

McGill, Larry '62 '63
McGuire, Jack '28 (Mgr.)
McKewen, Jack '41 '42
McKewen, Jack II '68
McKinney, Robert B. Jr. '70 '71
McKosky, Ted '42
McLeod, Ben '65
McMakin, David '71
McLeod, Ben W. '34 '35 '36
McMillian, Thomas E. '33
McQueen, Billy '29 (Mgr.)
McQueen, John Douglas '01 '02
McRight, Ralph '28 '29 '30
McWhorter, Jim '42

"N"

Namath, Joe '62 '63 '64
Nathan, R. L. '12 '13
Neighbors, Billy '59 '60 '61
Neighbors, Sidney '56 '57
Nelson, Benny '61 '62 '63
Nelson, Charles '56
Nelson, Jimmy '39 '40 '41
Newman, Hal '38 '40
Newton, Tom '23
Nisbet, James '36
Noland, John Phillip '17 '18
Noojin, Augustus Young '08
Noonan, L. W. (Red) '46 '47 '48 '49
Norris, Lanny S. '70 '71
Northington, M. P. '93

"O"

Oates, W. C. '06
O'Dell, Richard '59 '60 '62
O'Connor, J. T. '19 '20
Ogden, Ray '62 '63 '64
Olenski, Mitchell '42
O'Linger, John '59 '60 '61
Oliver, William '52 '53
Oliver, William '60 '61
Oliver, W. S. '25
O'Steen, Robert (Gary) '57 '58 '59
O'Sullivan, Pat '47 '48 '49 '50
Owens, Donald E. '56 '57
Owen, Wayne '66 '67 '68

"P"

Palmer, Thomas W. '08 '09
Papias, Julius '41
Parkhouse, Robin '69 '70 '71
Parsons, Don '58
Partlow, W. D. '29 (Mgr.)
Patterson, Jim '71
Patton, David Dare '98 '99 '00
Patton, James A. '59. '61

Patton, Walter P. '01 '02
Patton, William P. '06
Payne, Leslie '27
Pearce, Clarke '26 '27 '28
Pearl, James H. '44
Peavy, John Roberts '02 '03 '04
Peebles, Emory Bush '10
Pell, Charles R. '60 '61 '62
Pepper, Raymond W. '26 '27
Perkins, Ray '64 '65' '66
Perry, Claude '25
Perry, Wm. Berney '22 (Mgr.)
Peter, G. F. '94 '95
Peters, William E. '36 '37
Pettee, Robert A. (Bob) '60 '61 '62
Pettus, Gordon '45 '46 '48
Pharo, Edward '52 '56
Phillips, Gary '58 '59 '60
Phillips, O. E. '50 '51 '52
Pickens, W. C. '96 (Mgr.)
Pickhard, Frederick '26 '27
Pierson, Marion '54 (Mgr.)
Piper, William (Billy) '60 '62 '63
Pittman, Alec Noel '70
Poole, John Paul '55 '58
Pope, Jesse D. '03
Posey, Fred '46 (Mgr.)
Potts, Douglas '54 '55 '56
Powe, Frank Houston '99 '00 '01
Powell, Harold Mustin '10 '11
Pratt, Derrill B. '08 '09
Pratt, G. W. '07 '08
Pratt, Henry Merrill '92 '93 '94
Propst, Clyde '22 '23
Propst, Eddie '66 '67
Pritchett, James P. '55
Prom, John '51

"Q"

Quick, Cecil Van '70

"R"

Raburn, Gene '65 '66
Radford, James Solomon '35 '36
Raines, Billy '56 '57
Raines, James Patrick '70 '71
Ranager, George '68 '69 '70
Randman, David '40 (Mgr.)
Rankin, Carlton, '62
Rast, Holt '39 '40 '41
Ray, David '64 '65
Reaves, Pete '58
Redden, Guy '04 '05
Redden, Jake '37 '38
Reilly, Mike '66 '67 '68

Reitz, John David '65 '66 '67
Reese, Kenny '42
Rhoads, Wayne R. '69 '70
Rice, William Jr. (Bill) '59 '60 '61
Rich, Jerry '59
Richardson, Jesse '50 '51 '52
Richardson, Ron '71
Richardson, W. E. '59 '60 '61
Richeson, G. W. '41
Richeson, Ray '46 '47 '48
Riddle, Charles D. '12 '13
Riley, Joe '36
Rippetoe, Benny '71
Rives, Al '26 (Mgr.)
Roberts, Babs '40 '42
Roberts, Johnny '37
Roberts, Kenneth '56 '57 '58
Robertson, James '45 '46
Roddam, J. D. '49
Roddam, Ronnie '68 '69
Rogers, Eddie Bo '66 '67
Rogers, Leo O. '35
Rogers, O'Neal '27
Rohrdanz, Clarence '35
Ronsonet, Norbie '58 '59 '60
Root, Steve '71
Rosenfeld, David, '25 '26
Rosenfeld, Max '20 '21
Rosser, Jimmy Lynn '69 '70 '71
Rouzie, Jefferson Carr '70 '71
Rowe, Harry '19
Rowell, Terry '69 '70 '71
Rustin, Nathan '66 '67
Rutledge, Jack '59 '60 '61
Ryba, Jim '37

"S"

Sabo, Al '40 '42
Salem, Ed '48 '49 '50
Salem, George '56
Salls, Don '40 '41 '42
Salmon, Farley R. '23 '24
Samples, Alvin '67 '68 '69
Sanford, Donald '30 '31 '32
Sanford, Heyward (Sandy) '36 '37
Sansing, Walter '58
Sartain, Harvey '04
Sasser, Mike '66 '69
Savage, Frank '92 '93
Sawyer, Bubba '69 '71
Scales, Lou '42 '45
Scott, Arthur '57
Scroggins, Billy '67 '68
Seay, Buddy '69 '70
Self, Hal '45 '46

Selman, Tom '50
Sessions, Tram '17 '19 '20
Sewell, J. Luke '19 '20
Sewell, Joe '17 '18 '19
Sewell, Toxey '13 '14
Shankles, Don '67
Sharpe, Jimmy '60 '61 '62
Sharpe, Joe '29 '30 '31
Sharpe, Sam '40 '41 '42
Shepherd, Joe Rufus '35 '36
Sherrill, Jackie '63 '64 '65
Sherrill, Wm. Swift '01 '02 '03
Shevinsky, J. Harold '38 (Mgr.)
Shipp, Billy '49 '52 '53
Shoemaker, Perron '37 '38 '39
Sides, John (Brownie) '66 '67
Simmons, James R. Jr. '69 '70 '71
Simmons, Jim '62 '63 '64
Sims, Wayne '58 '59
Sims, T. S. '05 '06
Sims, William Comer '31
Sington, Dave '56 '57 '58
Sington, Fred Sr. '28 '29 '30
Sington, Fred Jr. '58 '59
Sisia, Joseph '60
Skelton, Joseph '60
Skelton, Robert (Bobby) '57 '59 '60
Skidmore, Jim '28
Slemons, Billy '37 '38
Sloan, Steve '63 '64 '65
Slone, Samuel Byron '94 '95
Smalley, Jack '51 '52 '53
Smith, D. H. '93
Smalley, Roy '50
Smith, Ben '29 '30 '31
Smith, Bobby '56 '57 '58
Smith, Earl '26 '27 '28
Smith, Jack '49
Smith, Molton '28 '29
Smith, Riley H. '34 '35
Smith, Sammy Wayne '57
Smith, Truman A. '03 '04
Smith, William Earle '26 '27 '28
Snoderly, John M. '52 '56
Somerville, Tom '65 '66 '67
Speed, Elliott '48 '49 '50
Spencer, Paul '40
Spruiell, Jerry '60
Stabler, Ken (Snake) '65 '66 '67
Stanford, Robert F. '69
Stapp, Charlie '35
Stapp, Laurien '58 '59 '60
Starling, Hugh '28 '29
Starr, Bryan Bartlett (Bart) '52 '53
    '54 '55

Staples, John '42 '46
Steakley, Rod '71
Steiner, Rebel '45 '47 '48 '49
Stephens, Bruce '65 '66 '67
Stephens, Charles '62 '63 '64
Stephens, Gerald '62
Stephenson, Riggs '17 '18 '19
Stephenson, Lovick Leonidas '15
Stewart, Arthur Walter '01
Stewart, Vaughn '41
Stevens, Wayne '66
Stickney, Enoch Morgan '12
Stickney, Frederick Grist '01 '02
Stickney, Ravis (Red) '57 '59
Stone, G. E. '94
Stone, Rocky '69
Stone, William Joseph (Bill) '53 '54 '55
Stowers, Max Frederick '16 '17
Strickland, Chuck '71
Strickland, Lynwood '65
Strickland, William Ross '70
Strum, Richard '57
Stuedeman, Vince (Mgr.) '69
Sturdivant, Raymond '06 '07
Sugg, Joseph Cullen '38 '39
Sullivan, Johnny '64 '65 '66
Surlas, Thomas John '70 '71
Suther, John '28 '29 '30
Sutton, Donnie '66 '67 '68
Swafford, Bobby '67 '68
Swaim, M. M. '31 '32

"T"

Taylor, Archie '26 '27
Taylor, J. K. '14 '15
Taylor, Paul '48
Terlizzi, Nicholas '45
Tew, Lowell '44 '45 '46 '47
Tharp, Thomas A. (Corky) '51 '52 '53 '54
Theris, Bill '48
Thomas, Daniel Martin '70
Thomas, Lester '21
Thomason, Frank Boyd '19
Thompson, Louis '65 '66
Thompson, Richard (Dickey) '65 '66 '67
Thompson, Wesley '51 '55 '56
Tidwell, Robert Earl '03 '04
Tillman, Thomas (Tommy) '52 '53 '54
Tipton, Jim '36 '37
Tolleson, Tommy '63 '64 '65
Trammell, Pat '59 '60 '61
Trimble, Wayne '64 '65 '66
Tuck, Floyd '27

261

Tucker, John '30 '31
Tutwiler, Edward McGruder '98
Tyson, A. P., Jr. '02

"V"

Vagotis, Christ '66
Valletto, Carl '57 '58
Van de Graaff, Adrian V. '12
Van de Graaff, Hargrove '13
Van de Graaff, W. T. '12 '13 '14 '15
Varnado, Carey Reid '70
Veazy, Louis '55
Verner, Edward E. '16 (Mgr.)
Versprille, Eddie '61 '62 '63
Vickery, Roy Leon '56
Vines, Melvin '26 '28 '29

"W"

Wade, Steve '71
Wade, Tommy '67 '68 '70
Waites, W. L. '38
Walker, Bland Jr. '57
Walker, Erskine (Bud) '31 '32 '33
Walker, Hillman '36
Walker, James E. '35
Walker, Noojin '55
Walker, William Mudd '92
Walker, Wayne D. '44
Wall, Larry '61 '62 '64
Walls, Clay '55 '56 '57
Watkins, David '71
Ward, Wm. LaFayette '04 '05
Warren, Erwin T. (Tut) '37 '38 '39
Watford, Jerry '50 '51 '52
Weaver, Sam '28 '29
Weeks, George '40 '41 '42
Weigand, Tommy '68
Wellborn, Arthur '99 (Mgr.)
Wert, Thomas William '99
Welsh, Clem '48
Wesley, William Earl (Buddy) '58 '59 '60
Wesley, L. O. '22 '23
Whaley, Frank '65 '66
Whatley, James W. '33 '34 '35
Whatly, Seaborn Thornton '06
Wheeler, Wayne '71
White, Arthur P. (Tarzan) '34 '35 '36

White, Ed '47 '48 '49
White, Gary '59 '60 '61 (Mgr.)
White, Jack '71
White, Tommy '58 '59 '60
Whitley, Tom '44 '45 '46' 47
Whitmire, Don '41 '42
Whittaker, Hulet '25
Whittlelsey, C. S. '16 '17
Whitworth, J. B. (Ears) '30 '31
Wicke, Dallas '38 '39
Wieseman, Bill '62 '63
Wilbanks, Danny '57
Wilcox, George Spigener '03 '04
Wilder, Ken '68 '69
Wilga, Bob '51 '52 '53
Wilhite, Al '49 '50 '51
Wilkins, Red '61
Williams, Billy '51 '52
Williams, John (Byrd) '65 '66
Williams, Steven Edward '69 '70
Williamson, Richard '61 '62
Williamson, Temple '35
Willis, Perry '67
Willis, Virgil (Bud) '51 '52
Wilson, Bobby '50 '51 '52
Wilson, George (Butch) '60 '61 '62
Wilson, Jimmy '61 '62
Windham, Edward Price '97
Winslett, Hoyt '24 '25 '26
Wise, Mack '58
Wood, Bobby '37 '38
Wood, William B. '57
Wood, William Dexter '70
Woodruff, Glenn '71
Wozniak, John '44 '45 '46 '47
Wright, Steve '62 '63
Wyatt, Ferral '70 (Mgr.)
Wyhonic, John '40 '41

"Y"

Yates, Ollie Porter '54
Yessick, Tommy (Mgr.) '71
Yolles, Sam '33 (Mgr.)
Young, Cecil Hugh '02 '03
Young, William A. '36
Youngleman, Sidney '52 '53 '54

"Z"

Zivich, George '37 '38 '39

★★★

Scoring Streak Reached 115 Games

When Alabama lost to Tennessee, 24-0, in 1970 it ended the Crimson Tide's string of having scored in 115 consecutive games, dating back to the 1959 Liberty Bowl game against Penn State, when the Tide lost 7-0. The national record of consecutive scoring games is 123 by Oklahoma from 1946 to 1957. Alabama's 115 games is the second longest in collegiate history.

ALABAMA'S ALL-AMERICAS

1971—Johnny Musso, halfback (O)
    John Hannah, guard (O)
    Tom Surlas, linebacker (D)
    Robin Parkhouse, end (D)
1970—Johnny Musso, tailback (O)
1969—Alvin Samples, guard (O)
1968—Mike Hall, linebacker (D)
    Sam Gellerstedt, guard (O)
1967—Dennis Homan, split end (O)
    Bobby Johns, halfback (D)
    Kenny Stabler, q'back (D)
1966—Richard Cole, tackle (O)
    Ray Perkins, end (O)
    Cecil Dowdy, tackle (O)
    Bobby Johns, halfback (D)
1965—Paul Crane, center
    Steve Sloan, quarterback

1964—Wayne Freeman, guard
    Dan Kearley, tackle
    David Ray, halfback
    Joe Namath, quarterback
1962—Lee Roy Jordan, center
1961—Billy Neighbors, tackle
    Pat Trammell, quarterback
    Lee Roy Jordan, center
1950—Ed Salem, halfback
1945—Harry Gilmer, halfback
    Vaughn Mancha, center
1942—Don Whitmire, tackle
    Joe Domnanovich, center
1941—Holt Rast, end
1939—Carey Cox, center

1937—James Ryba, tackle
    Leroy Monsky, guard
    Joe Kilgrow, halfback
1936—Arthur "Tarzan" White g'd
1935—Riley Smith, quarterback
1934—Millard "Dixie" Howell, hb
    Don Hutson, end
    Bill Lee, tackle
1933—Tom Hupke, guard
1931—Johnny Cain, fullback
1930—Fred Sington, tackle
1930—John Suther, halfback
1929—Tony Holm, fullback
1926—Hoyt "Wu" Winslett, end
1925—A.T.S. "Pooley" Hubert, qb
1915—W.T. "Bully" Van de Graaff, t

ALL-SOUTHEASTERN CONFERENCE FIRST TEAM

1933—Tom Hupke, guard
1933—Millard "Dixie" Howell, hb
1934—Don Hutson, end
1934—Charlie Marr, guard
1934—Bill Lee, tackle
1934—Millard "Dixie" Howell, hb
1935—Riley Smith, quarterback
1935—James Whatley, tackle
1936—Arthur "Tarzan" White, g'd
1936—Riley Smith, quarterback
1937—Leroy Monsky, guard
1937—Erwin "Tut" Warren, end
1937—Joe Kilgrow, back
1938—Charles Holm, back
1940—Fred Davis, tackle
1940—Holt Rast, end
1940—Jimmy Nelson, back
1941—Holt Rast, end
1941—John Wyhonic, guard
1941—Jimmy Nelson, back
1942—Joe Domnanovich, center
1942—Don Whitmire, tackle
1945—Rebel Steiner, end
1945—Tom Whitley, tackle
1945—Harry Gilmer, back
1946—Harry Gilmer, back
1947—John Wozniak, guard

1945—Vaughn Mancha, center
1947—Harry Gilmer, back
1949—Ed Holdnak, guard
1950—Mike Mizerany, guard
1950—Pat O'Sullivan, center
1950—Ed Salem, back
1951—Bobby Marlow, back (D)
1952—Jerry Watford, guard (O)
1952—Bobby Marlow, back (O)
1952—Cecil Ingram, back (D)
1953—Corky Tharp, back
1954—Corky Tharp, back
1961—Pat Trammel, back
1961—Billy Neighbors, guard
1961—Lee Roy Jordan, center
1961—Mike Fracchia, back
1962—Lee Roy Jordan, center
1963—Benny Nelson, back
1964—Steve Bowman, back (O)
1964—Joe Namath, back (O)
1964—David Ray, back (O)
1964—Dan Kearley, tackle (D)
1965—Tommy Tolleson, end (O)
1965—Paul Crane, center (O)
1965—Steve Bowman, fullback (O)
1965—Creed Gilmer, end (D)
1965—Bobby Johns, halfback (D)

1964—Wayne Freeman, guard (O)
1966—Cecil Dowdy, tackle (O)
1966—Bobby Johns, halfback (D)
1966—Ray Perkins, end (O)
1966—John Calvert, guard (O)
1966—Dicky Thompson, back (D)
1967—Mike Ford, end (O)
1967—Kenny Stabler, q'back (O)
1967—Dennis Homan, end (O)
1967—Mike Hall, linebacker (D)
1967—Bruce Stephens, guard (O)
1967—Bobby Johns, halfback (D)
1968—Mike Hall, linebacker (D)
1968—Sam Gellerstedt, guard (D)
1968—Mike Ford, end (D)
1968—Alvin Samples, guard (O)
1969—Alvin Samples, guard (O)
1969—Danny Ford, tackle (O)
1970—Johnny Musso, Tailback (O)
1971—Johnny Musso, halfback (O)
1971—John Hannah, guard (O)
1971—Tom Surlas, linebacker (O)
1971—Jimmy Grammer, center (O)
1971—Steve Higginbotham, b (O)
1971—Robin Parkhouse, end (D)
1971—Jim Krapf, tackle (O)
1971—David Bailey, end (O)

SECOND TEAM

1933—Bill Lee, tackle
1934—Paul Bryant, end
1934—Joe Demyanovich, center
1935—Kavanaugh Francis, center
1936—Perron Shoemaker, end
1936—Joe Kilgrow, back
1937—Perron Shoemaker, end
1937—Charles Holm, back
1938—Vic Bradford, back
1939—Fred Davis, tackle
1940—Ed Hickerson, guard
1942—Mitchell Olenski, tackle
1942—George Hecht, guard
1942—Russ Craft, back
1944—Ralph Jones, end
1944—Vaughn Mancha, center
1944—Harry Gilmer, back
1945—Jack Green, guard
1945—Lowell Tew, back

1946—Vaughn Mancha, center
1947—Vaughn Mancha, center
1947—Lowell Tew, back
1951—Ralph Carrigan, center (D)
1951—Jess Richardson, guard (D)
1951—Red Lutz, end (D)
1952—Travis Hunt, tackle (O)
1952—Corky Tharp, back (O)
1952—Ed Culpepper, tackle (D)
1952—Ralph Carrigan, center (O)
1953—Ralph Carrigan, center
1955—Nick Germanos, end
1957—Billy Rains, guard
1958—Don Cochran, guard
1959—Don Cochran, guard
1962—Cotton Clark, back
1963—Joe Namath, back
1964—Steve Sloan, back (D)
1964—Gaylon McCollough, c. (O)

1964—Tommy Tolleson, end (O)
1964—Paul Crane, center (D)
1965—Steve Sloan, quarterback (O)
1965—Tim Bates, linebacker (D)
1966—Wayne Cook, end (O)
1966—Jerry Duncan, tackle (O)
1966—Richard Cole, tackle (O)
1967—Steve Davis, kicker (O)
1968—Donnie Sutton, back (O)
1968—Randy Barron, tackle (O)
1969—Johnny Musso, back (O)
1970—David Bailey, End (O)
1970—Jonh Hannah, Tackle (O)
1970—Frank Mann, Punter (O)
1970—David Bailey, tackle (O)
1970—John Hannah, tackle (O)
1970—Frank Mann, punter (O)
1971—Jeff Rouzie, linebacker (D)
1971—Greg Gantt, punter (O)

THIRD TEAM

1933—Don Hutson, end
1934—Riley Smith, back
1935—Paul Bryant, end
1935—Arthur "Tarzan" White, g'd
1937—Joe Ryba, tackle
1938—Perron Shoemaker, end
1938—Walter Merrill, tackle
1939—Harold Newman, end
1939—Walter Merrill, tackle
1940—Warren Averitte, center

1940—Harold Newman, end
1941—George Hecht, guard
1942—Sam Sharp, end
1944—Tom Whitley, tackle
1946—Ted Cook, end
1947—Rebel Steiner, end
1947—Charles Compton, tackle
1948—Bill Cadenhead, back
1949—Mike Mizerany, guard
1949—Butch Avinger, back

1950—Butch Avinger, back
1951—Bobby Wilson, back (D)
1951—Jerry Watford, guard (O)
1954—Sid Youngleman, tackle
1954—George Mason, tackle
1960—Billy Neighbors, guard
1960—Leon Fuller, fullback
1961—Tommy Brooker, end
1962—Richard Williamson, end

263

ALL-SOUTHERN CONFERENCE

1908—C. C. Countess, center	1924—Johnny Mack Brown, back	1926—Emile Barnes, back
1914—W. T. Van de Graaff, tackle	1925—Bill Buckler, guard	1927—Fred Pickhard, tackle
1915—W. T. Van de Graaff, fullb'k	1925—A. T. S. Hubert, back	1929—Fred Sington, tackle
1920—Riggs Stephenson, fullback	1925—Johnny Mack Brown, back	1929—Tony Holm, back
1923—Al Clemens, end	1926—Hoyt Winslett, end	1930—Fred Sington, tackle
1923—Grant Gillis, quarterback	1926—Gordon Holmes, center	1930—John Henry Suther, back
1924—Bill Buckler, guard	1926—Fred Pickhard, tackle	1931—Johnny Cain, back
1924—A. T. S. Hubert, back	1926—Hershel Caldwell, back	1932—Tom Hupke, guard
		1932—Johnny Cain, back

OTHER PLAYER HONORS

NATIONAL FOOTBALL HALL OF FAME:
1953—Coach Frank Thomas
1953—End Don Hutson
1955—Coach Wallace Wade
1955—Tackle Fred Sington
1956—Guard Don Whitmire
1957—Back Johnny Mack Brown
1964—A. T. S. (Pooley) Hubert
1970—Millard "Dixie" Howell

BIRMINGHAM MONDAY MORNING QUARTERBACK CLUB:
Outstanding Back
Halfback Bobby Marlow, 1952
Quarterback Pat Trammell, 1961
Quarterback Steve Sloan, 1965
Quarterback Ken Stabler, 1967
Halfback Johnny Musso, 1971
Outstanding Lineman
Tackle Billy Neighbors, 1961
Center Lee Roy Jordan, 1962
Center Paul Crane, 1965
End Ray Perkins, 1966

ATLANTA TOUCHDOWN CLUB:
(Originated in 1939. Beginning in 1946, a back and a lineman were chosen as co-recipients)
1945—Halfback Harry Gilmer
1961—Quarterback Pat Trammell
1962—Center Lee Roy Jordan
1965—Quarterback Steve Sloan
1966—End Ray Perkins
1967—Quarterback Ken Stabler
1971—Halfback Johnny Musso

NASHVILLE BANNER AWARD: (Originated in 1933)
Most Valuable Player
1934—Halfback Millard "Dixie" Howell
1945—Halfback Harry Gilmer
1961—Quarterback Pat Trammell
1965—Quarterback Steve Sloan
1971—Halfback Johnny Musso
Coach-of-the-Year
1945—Frank Thomas
1952—Harold "Red" Drew
1961—Paul W. Bryant
1964—Paul W. Bryant
1971—Paul W. Bryant

HELMS FOUNDATION HALL OF FAME AWARD:
Coach Wallace Wade
End Don Hutson
Coach Henry G. Crisp
Coach Frank Thomas
Back Johnny Mack Brown
Guard Don Whitmire

ROSE BOWL OUTSTANDING PLAYER AWARDS:
1926—Back Johnny Mack Brown
1927—Tackle Fred Pickhard
1931—Back John Campbell
1935—Back Millard "Dixie" Howell
1946—Back Harry Gilmer

ASTRO-BLUEBONNET BOWL OUTSTANDING PLAYER AWARD:
1970—Linebacker Jeff Rouzie
(Outstanding Defensive Player)

SUGAR BOWL OUTSTANDING PLAYER AWARDS:
1962—Fullback Mike Fracchia
1964—Field Goal Kicker Tim Davis
1967—Quarterback Ken Stabler

ORANGE BOWL OUTSTANDING PLAYER AWARDS:
1963—Linebacker Lee Roy Jordan
1965—Quarterback Joe Namath
1966—Quarterback Steve Sloan

ALABAMA PLAYERS ON ALL-TIME BOWL TEAMS:
Rose Bowl
HB Johnny Mack Brown, 1926
HB Millard "Dixie" Howell, 1935

Sugar Bowl
Center Vaughn Mancha, 1945
Tackle Tom Whitley, 1948
HB Harry Gilmer, 1945
Guard Ray Richeson, 1948

Cotton Bowl
End Holt Rast, 1942
Tackle Don Whitmire, 1942
HB Jimmy Nelson, 1942

Orange Bowl
Center Joe Domnanovich, 1943
Tackle Don Whitmire, 1943

NATIONAL FOOTBALL FOUNDATION SCHOLAR-ATHLETE AWARD:
1971—Johnny Musso, halfback

MIAMI TOUCHDOWN CLUB OUTSTANDING SEC PLAYER AWARD:
1971—Johnny Musso

JACOBS AWARD: (This award has been given annually since 1935 by Dr. W. J. Jacobs of Clinton, S.C., based on a poll of SEC coaches as a recognition for outstanding blocking ability)

1935—Quarterback Riley Smith	1949—Quarterback Butch Avinger	1962—Back Butch Wilson
1937—Guard Leroy Monsky	1950—Quarterback Butch Avinger	1966—Tackle Cecil Dowdy
1946—Quarterback Hal Self	1961—Tackle Billy Neighbors	

MODERN UNIVERSITY OF ALABAMA FOOTBALL RECORDS
(1933-1971)

The year of the formation of the Southeastern Conference is taken as a convenient breaking point as almost no records were kept prior to that time.

Bowl Games Not Included

TEAM DEFENSE—Season

Net Yards Allowed (Rushing-Passing)	701	1938	(9 games)
Net Yards Averaged (Rushing-Passing)	77.9	1938	(9 games)
Net Yards Averaged Rushing	33.9	1945	(9 games)
Net Yards Allowed Rushing	305	1938	(9 games)
	410	1945	(9 games)
Net Yards Allowed Passing	291	1938	(9 games)
Net Yards Averaged Passing	32.5	1938	(9 games)
Lowest Yardage Per Rush	0.95	1945	(9 games)
Fewest First Downs Allowed	35	1938	(9 games)
Most Fumbles	47	1952	(11 games)
Most Fumbles Lost	27	1952	(11 games)
Fewest Fumbles	9	1945	(9 games)
Fewest Fumbles Lost	1	1938	(9 games)
Most Yards Allowed (Rushing-Passing)	3956	1969	(10 games)
Most Yards Averaged (Rushing-Passing)	395.6	1969	(10 games)
Most Times Penalized	70	1961	(10 games)
Most Yards Penalized	667	1961	(10 games)
Fewest Times Penalized	31	1949	(10 games)
Fewest Yards Penalized	263	1967	(10 games)

TEAM SCORING—Season

Most Points	396	1945	(9 games)
Most Touchdowns	58	1945	(9 games)
Most Points After Touchdown	46	1945	(9 games)
Most Field Goals	14	.1971	(11 games)
Most Safeties	2	Several Times	
Most Games Held Scoreless	5	1957	(10 games)
Most Consecutive Games Held Scoreless	3	1954	(11 games)
Fewest Points	48	1955	(10 games)

TEAM TOTAL OFFENSE—Season

Most First Downs	249	1970	(11 games)
Most Net Yards (3007 rushing, 1571 passing)	4578	1950	(11 games)
Most Yards Averaged	416.1	1950	(11 games)
Most Plays from Scrimmage (506 runs, 322 passes)	828	1970	(11 games)

TEAM RUSHING—Season

Most Yards Gained	3565	1950	(11 games)
	2679	1945	(9 games)
	2737	1952	(11 games)
Most Rushing Plays	705	1971	(11 games)

TEAM PASSING—Season

Most Yards Gained Passing	2707	1969	(10 games)
Most Passes Attempted	328	1969	(10 games)
Most Passes Completed	195	1969	(10 games)
Fewest Had Intercepted (171 attempts)	3	1965	(10 games)
Most Passes Had Intercepted	25	1970	(11 games)
Most Passes Intercepted By	24	1952	(11 games)
		1966	(10 games)
		1968	(10 games)
Most Yards Interceptions Returned	336	1952	(11 games)
Most Scoring Passes	18	1950	(11 games)
	17	1966	(10 games)
Best Completion Average (100 minimum)	62.7	1964	(10 games)

TEAM PUNTING—Season

Most Times Punted	92	1941-46	
Most Yards Punted	3497	1946	
Best Punting Average	41.9	1971	
Most Punts Returned	71	1946	
Most Yards Punts Returned	783	1946	
Most Punts Blocked By	5	1940	(9 games)
	4	1947	(10 games)

TEAM OFFENSE—One Game

Most First Downs	31	1970 vs. Auburn
	31	1969 vs. So. Miss
Most Yards Gained Rushing	572	1945 vs. Kentucky
Most Yards Gained Passing	484	1969 vs. Auburn
Most Yards Gained Rushing-Passing	616	1961 vs. Richmond
Most Passes Attempted	55	1969 vs. Auburn
Most Passes Completed	32	1969 vs. Tennessee
Most Passes by Opponent	52	1969 by Mississippi
Most Passes Completed by Opponent	33	1969 by Mississippi
Most Passes Intercepted by Alabama	7	1965 vs. Auburn
Most Yards Interceptions Returned by Alabama	114	1940 vs. Howard
Most Touchdown Passes	7	1950 vs. Miss. Sou.
Most Points Scored	89	1951 vs. Delta State
Most Touchdowns	13	1951 vs. Delta State
Most Points After Touchdown	11	1951 vs. Delta State
Most Punts Both Teams	40	1932 19, vs. Tenn. 21
Most Yards Penalized	133	1957 vs. Vanderbilt
Fewest Yards Penalized Both Teams	5	1940 0 vs. Spg. Hill 5;
		1965 5 vs. Tenn. 0
Most Fumbles	12	1952 vs. Miss. Sou.
Most Fumbles Lost	7	1952 vs. Miss. Sou.
Most Fumbles Both Teams	16	1952 vs. Miss. Sou.
	15	1949 vs. Tennessee
Most Points in Tie Game	74	1967 vs. Fla. State
Fewest Yards Allowed Rushing	—36	1938 vs. Sewanee
Most Yards Allowed Passing	436	1969 vs. Mississippi
Most Passes Intercepted by Opponent	8	1970 by Tennessee
Most Yards Interceptions Returned by Opponent	133	1970 by Tennessee

INDIVIDUAL PUNTING—Season

Most Punts	81	Dixie Howell	1933
Best Punting Average (Min. 25)	43.2	Charley Boswell	1942
	42.4	Buddy French	1964
	42.1	Dixie Howell	1934
	41.9	Gregg Gantt	1971
	41.9	Bobby Wilson	1951
	41.7	Steve Davis	1965
	41.4	Bart Starr	1953
	41.3	Laurien Stapp	1960
	41.1	Butch Avinger	1949
	41.1	Hershel Mosley	1938
	41	Jimmy Nelson	1940
Most Yards Punted	3,216	Dixie Howell	1933
Most Punts Returned	37	Harry Gilmer	1946
Most Yards Punts Returned	436	Harry Gilmer	1946

KICKOFF RETURNS—Season

Most Returned	22	Buddy Seay	1970
Most Yards Returned	471	Buddy Seay	1970

INDIVIDUAL PASSING—One Game

Most Attempted	55	Scott Hunter (Auburn, 1969)
	35	Scott Hunter (Tennessee, 1969)
	35	Scott Hunter (La. State, 1969)
	32	Harry Gilmer (Tennessee, 1946)
	32	Ken Stabler (Tennessee, 1967)
Most Completed	30	Scott Hunter (Auburn, 1969)
	23	Scott Hunter (Tennessee, 1969)
	22	Scott Hunter (Mississippi, 1969)
	19	Scott Hunter (Tennessee, 1968)
	19	Ken Stabler (So. Miss, 1967)
Most Yards Passing	484	Scott Hunter (Auburn, 1969)
	300	Scott Hunter (Mississippi, 1969)
	284	Scott Hunter (La. State, 1969)
Most Passes Caught	12	David Bailey (Tennessee, 1970)
	12	David Bailey (Tennessee, 1969)
	11	Dennis Homan (So. Miss, 1967)
Most Yards By Receiver	187	David Bailey (Auburn, 1969)
	162	Ken MacAfee (Villanova, 1951)
Most Scoring Passes Thrown	3	Neb Hayden (Ole Miss 1970)
	3	Jimmy Nelson (Vanderbilt 1940)
	3	Bart Starr (Georgia 1953)
	3	Wayne Trimble (Miss. State 1966
	3	Ken Stabler (Sou. Miss. 1967)
	3	Steve Sloan (Auburn 1965)
	3	Albert Elmore (Tennessee 1954)
	3	Joe Namath (Georgia 1962)
	3	Ken Stabler (Sou. Miss. 1966)
	3	Joe Namath (Houston 1963)
Most Passes Had Intercepted	5	Scott Hunter (by Tennessee 1970)
	5	Ken Stabler (by Tennessee 1967)

INDIVIDUAL RUSHING—One Game

Most Rushes	42	Johnny Musso (Auburn 1970)
	33	Johnny Musso (Houston 1970)
	33	Johnny Musso (Auburn 1971)
	28	Pete Moore (Miss. State, 1968)
	28	Bobby Marlow (Auburn 1952)
	28	Joe Riley (Kentucky 1936)
	28	Steve Bowman (Miss. State, 1965)
Most Net Yards	233	Bobby Marlow (Auburn 1951)
	221	Johnny Musso (Auburn 1970)

INDIVIDUAL PUNTING—One Game

Longest Punt	89	Dixie Howell (Tennessee 1933)
	86	Dixie Howell (Ga. Tech 1933)
	85	Gregg Gantt (Miss. St. 1971)
	83	Dixie Howell (Kentucky 1933)
	81	Tommy White(Memphis St. 1959)
	78	Russ Mosley (Georgia 1942)
	76	Joe Riley (Vanderbilt 1946)

INDIVIDUAL OFFENSE AND SCORING—One Game

Most Plays	59	Scott Hunter (Auburn, 1969)
	55	Scott Hunter (Tennessee, 1968)
	50	Ken Stabler (Tennessee 1967)
Most Points	24	Bobby Marlow (Ga. Tech 1950)
	24	Johnny Musso (Florida 1971)
Most Touchdowns	4	Bobby Marlow (Ga. Tech 1950)
	4	Johnny Musso (Florida 1971)
Most Points After Touchdown	11	Red Lutz (Delta State 1951)
		(10 kicks, 1 run)
	9	Hugh Morrow (Howard 1944)
		(Without missing)
	9	Hugh Morrow (Vanderbilt 1945)
Most Yardage	457	Scott Hunter (Auburn, 1969)
		(Minus 27 rush, 484 pass—59 plays)

INDIVIDUAL SCORING—One Season

Most Points	100	Johnny Musso	1971
	92	Cotton Clark	1962
	78	Johnny Musso	1969
	72	Bobby Marlow	1951
	72	Bobby Luna	1952
	71	David Ray	1964
	66	Fred Grant	1945
Most Touchdowns (10 games)	16	Johnny Musso	1971
(10 games)	14	Cotton Clark	1962
(10 games)	13	Johnny Musso	1969
(11 games)	12	Bobby Marlow	1951
Most Touchdowns Accounted For (Rushed for 9, passed for 13)	22	Harry Gilmer	1945
Most Points After Touchdown	46	Hugh Morrow	1945
Most Consecutive Points After Touchdown	18	Steve Davis	1967
Best P.A.T. Average	100.0	Steve Davis (18 of 18)	1967
	92.0	David Ray (23 of 25)	1964
	91.3	David Ray (21 of 23)	1965
	90.0	Bill Davis (36 of 40)	1971
	89.7	Richard Ciemny (26 of 29)	1970
	89.3	Steve Davis (25 of 28)	1966

Most Field Goals	13	Bill Davis (16 att'pts)	1971
	12	David Ray (17 att'pts)	1964
	10	Richard Ciemny (17 att'pts)	1970

INDIVIDUAL TOTAL OFFENSE—Season

| Most Plays (Rushes, Passes) | 301 | Scott Hunter | 1969 |
| | 293 | Harry Gilmer | 1946 |

Most Net Yards (160 Passes, 104 Rushes)	2157	Scott Hunter	1969
	1499	Steve Sloan	1965
	1457	Harry Gilmer	1945
	1437	Dixie Howell	1934
	1428	Scott Hunter	1968
	1427	Harry Gilmer	1946
	1421	Joe Namath	1962
	1327	Ken Stabler	1967
	1314	Pat Trammell	1961
	1252	Ed Salem	1950
	1200	Scott Hunter	1970
	1166	Johnny Musso	1970
	1157	Dixie Howell	1934

| Most Yards Averaged (10 games) | 215.7 | Scott Hunter | 1969 |

| Best Average Gain (167 plays) | 8.72 | Harry Gilmer | 1945 |

INDIVIDUAL RUSHING—Season

| Most Rushes | 226 | Johnny Musso | 1970 |

| Most Net Yards (11 games) | 1137 | Johnny Musso | 1970 |

| Best Average Gain (88 rushes) | 8.13 | Lowell Tew | 1945 |
| (118 rushes) | 7.47 | Bobby Marlow | 1950 |

Most Yards Averaged Per Game (10 games)	108.8	Johnny Musso	1971
Most Yards Averaged Per Game (11 games)	103.4	Johnny Musso	1970
(11 games)	85.36	Bobby Marlow	1952
(9 games)	79.44	Lowell Tew	1945

INDIVIDUAL PASSING—Season

| Most Attempted | 266 | Scott Hunter | 1969 |
| | 227 | Scott Hunter | 1968 |

Most Completed	157	Scott Hunter	1969
	122	Scott Hunter	1968
	103	Ken Stabler	1967
	103	Scott Hunter	1970
	97	Steve Sloan	1965

Most Yards Gained (10 games)	2188	Scott Hunter	1969
	1471	Scott Hunter	1968
	1453	Steve Sloan	1965
	1240	Scott Hunter	1970
	1214	Ken Stabler	1967
	1192	Joe Namath	1962

Best Completion Average (75 Min.)	64.8	Harry Gilmer	1945
(110 Min.)	64.9	Ken Stabler	1966
(96 Min.)	57.3	Bart Starr	1955

| Most Had Intercepted (11 games) | 15 | Scott Hunter | 1970 |

Fewest Had Intercepted (160 Min.)	3	Steve Sloan	1965
(125 Min.)	2	Pat Trammell	1961
(75 Min.)	3	Harry Gilmer	1945

| Most Consecutive Att'pted Without Interception | 91 | Steve Sloan | 1965 |

| Most Yards Per Completion | 20.0 | Ed Salem | 1950 |
| | 15.9 | Harry Gilmer | 1945 |

Most Touchdown Passes (10 games)	13	Joe Namath	1962
(9 games)	13	Harry Gilmer	1945
	10	Steve Sloan	1965
	10	Ed Salem	1950
	10	Scott Hunter	1968

Most Passes Caught	56	David Bailey	1969
	55	David Bailey	1970
	54	Dennis Homan	1967
	35	Al Lary	1950
	33	Ray Perkins	1966

| Most Yards by Receiver | 820 | Dennis Homan | 1967 |
| | 790 | David Bailey | 1970 |

| Most Yards Averaged by Receiver (25 Min.) | 21.6 | Al Lary | 1950 |

| Most Touchdowns by Receiver | 10 | Al Lary | 1950 |

| Most Passes Intercepted | 10 | Cecil "Hooty" Ingram | 1952 |
| | 8 | Harry Gilmer | 1946 |

| Most Yards Interceptions Runback | 163 | Cecil "Hooty" Ingram | 1952 |

ALL-TIME SEC STANDINGS

(Includes 1971 Season)

Team	Years	Games	Won	Lost	Tied	Pct.
ALABAMA	38	262	167	76	19	.674
Tennessee	38	228	144	69	15	.665
Mississippi	38	219	129	76	14	.621
Louisiana State	39	233	128	89	16	.588
Georgia	39	226	115	100	11	.533
Auburn	38	246	119	114	13	.514
Florida	38	217	87	117	13	.431
Mississippi State	38	231	78	142	11	.362
Vanderbilt	37	235	75	145	16	.353
Kentucky	37	225	68	145	12	.329

SEC TITLES BY TEAMS

	Won	Tied
ALABAMA—1933—34*—37—45—53—61**—64—65—66#—71	7	3
Tennessee—1938—39‡—40—46†—51§—56—67—69	5	3
Ole Miss—1947—54—55—60—62—63	6	0
Georgia—1942—46†—48—49—66#—68	4	2
L. S. U.—1935—36—58—61**—70	4	1
Kentucky—1950	1	0
Mississippi State—1941	1	0
Auburn—1957	1	0
Florida	0	0
Vanderbilt	0	0

*Alabama and Tulane tied (1934).   ‡Tennessee, Georgia Tech and Tulane tied (1939).
†Georgia and Tennessee tied (1946). §Georgia Tech and Tennessee tied (1951).
**Alabama and L.S.U. tied (1961).   #Alabama and Georgia tied (1966)

CAREERS OF ALABAMA COACHES

Coach	Coaching Years	Total Years	Games	Won	Lost	Tied	Percent.
E. B. Beaumont	1892	1	4	2	2	0	.500
Eli Abbott	1893-1895, 1902	4	19	7	12	0	.368
Otto Wagonhurst	1896	1	3	2	1	0	.667
Allen McCants	1897	1	1	1	0	0	1.000
W. A. Martin	1899	1	4	3	1	0	.750
M. Griffin	1900	1	5	2	3	0	.400
H. M. Harvey	1901	1	5	2	1	2	.600
W. B. Blount	1903-1904	2	17	10	7	0	.588
Jack Leavenworth	1905	1	10	6	4	0	.600
J. W. H. Pollard	1906-1909	4	29	20	4	5	.776
Guy Lowman	1910	1	8	4	4	0	.500
D. G. Graves	1911-1914	4	36	21	12	3	.625
Thomas Kelly	1915-1917	3	25	17	7	1	.700
Xen C. Scott	1919-1922	4	41	29	9	3	.744
Wallace Wade	1923-1930	8	77	61	13	3	.812
Frank Thomas	1931-1946*	15	146	115	24	7	.812
H. D. Drew	1947-1954	8	91	55	29	7	.643
J. B. Whitworth	1955-1957	3	30	4	24	2	.167
Paul W. Bryant	1958-Present	14	153	119	28	8	.804
TOTALS		77	705	480	185	41	.710

*No team 1943

No team 1898 and 1918

ALABAMA CAREER RECORDS (1933-71)

Most Yards Rushing: 2,741 by Johnny Musso .... 3 years (1969-71)
Most Passes Attempted: 672 by Scott Hunter .... 3 years (1968-70)
Most Passes Completed: 382 by Scott Hunter .... 3 years (1968-70)
Most Passes Had Intercepted: 32 by Scott Hunter .... 3 years (1968-70)
Most Yards Passing: 4,899 by Scott Hunter .... 3 years (1968-70)
Most Touchdown Passes: 28 by Joe Namath .... 3 years (1962-64)
Most Total offense Plays: 806 by Harry Gilmer .... 4 years (1944-47)
Most Total Offense Yards: 4,785 by Scott Hunter .... 3 years (1968-70)
Most Passes Caught: 132 by David Bailey .... 3 years (1969-71)
Most TD Passes Caught: 18 by Dennis Homan .... 3 years (1965-67)
Highest Punting Average: 40.4 by Butch Avinger .... 3 years (1948-50)
Most Points Scored: 232 by Johnny Musso .... 3 years (1969-71)
Most Field Goals: 22 by Tim Davis .... 3 years (1961-63)
Points By Kicking: 128 by Hugh Morrow .... 4 years (1944-47)
Most Rushing Attempts: 574 by Johnny Musso .... 3 years (1969-71)
Most Touchdowns Scored: 38 by Johnny Musso .... 3 years (1969-71)
Most Touchdowns Scored Rushing: 34 by Johnny Musso ...... 3 years (1969-71)
Most Yardage Pass Receiving: 1,857 by David Bailey .... 3 years (1969-71)

WINNING STREAKS

(Consecutive Victories)

20 . . . Last game of 1924 thru ninth game of 1926. Wallace Wade coach.

19 . . . Full 1961 season thru eighth game of 1962. Paul Bryant coach.

17 . . . Final six games of 1965 thru 1966 season and bowl. Paul Bryant coach.

14 . . . Final four games of 1933 thru 1934 season. Frank Thomas coach.

14 . . . Final five games of 1936 thru regular season of 1937. Frank Thomas coach.

14 . . . Final 1945 season thru first four games of 1946. Frank Thomas coach.

13 . . . Full 1930 season and first three games of 1931. Wallace Wade coach in 1930 and Frank Thomas in 1931.

12 . . . Last two 1963 games and thru regular season of 1967. Paul Bryant coach.

11 . . . Final three games of 1919 season thru eighth game of 1920. Xen C. Scott coach.

11 . . . Full 1971 season. Paul Bryant coach

THEY WEREN'T EVEN CLOSE

Alabama has had some one-sided games on its schedule during its football history, both winning and losing by large margins.

VICTORIES			DEFEATS		
Year	Opponent	Score	Year	Opponent	Score
1922	Marion Institute	110-0	1906	Vanderbilt	0-78
1921	Bryson (Tenn.)	95-0	1907	Sewanee	4-54
1951	Delta State	89-0	1900	Auburn	5-53
1913	B'ham-Southern	81-0	1895	Auburn	0-48
1902	Marion Institute	81-0	1903	Cumberland	0-44
1916	B'ham-Southern	80-0	1957	Auburn	0-40
1945	Vanderbilt	71-0	1905	Sewanee	6-42
1931	Clemson	74-7	1910	Georgia Tech	0-36
1915	B'ham-Southern	67-0	1900	Clemson	0-35
1961	Richmond	66-0	1948	Georgia	0-35

CRIMSON TIDE IN ALL-STAR ACTION

COLLEGE ALL STAR GAME (Chicago)

Thomas, Frank, Coach, 1935.

Cain, James, End '49
Cook, Ted, End, '45
Craft, Russ, Halfback, '45
Hecht, George, Guard, '44
Homan, Dennis, End, '68
Hupke, Tom, Guard, '34
Hutson, Don, End, '35
Jackson, Bobby, Quarterback, '59
Jordan, Lee Roy, Center-Linebacker, '63
Kilgrow, Joe, Halfback, '38
Lee, Bill, Tackle, '35
Merrill, Walter, Tackle, '40
Monsky, Leroy, Guard, '38
Olenski, Mitchell, Guard, '46
Rast, Holt, End, '42
Riley, Joe, Halfback, '37
Ryba, Jim, Tackle, '38
Sloan, Steve, Quarterback, '66
Smith, Riley, Quarterback, '36
Wilson, Bobby, Quarterback, '53
Wozniak, John, Guard, '48

COACHES ALL-AMERICA GAME
(Buffalo-Atlanta-Lubbock)

Bryant, Paul, Coach, 1972

Bailey, David, End, '72
Brungard, Dave, Fullback, '71
Crane, Paul, Center-Linebacker, '66
Dowdy, Cecil, Tackle, '67
Hall, Mike, Linebacker, '69
Homan, Dennis, End, '68
Hunter, Scott, Quarterback, '71
Johns, Bobby, Defensive Halfback, '68
Jordan, Lee Roy, Center-Linebacker, '63
Musso, Johnny, Back, '72
Neighbors, Billy, Tackle, '62
Ranklin, Carlton, Halfback, '62
Sloan, Steve, Quarterback, '66
Tolleson, Tommy, End, '66

SOUTHWEST CHALLENGE BOWL (San Antonio)

Clark, Cotton, Back, '62
Williamson, Richard, End, '62

BLUE-GRAY (Montgomery)

Avinger, Clarence, Back, '50
Blevins, Jim, Center, '59
Bostick, Lew, Guard, '39
Bowdoin, Jim, Back, '56
Boylston, Bobby, Tackle, '60
Cadenhead, Bill, Back, '49
Cochran, Don, Guard, '59
Cook, Ted, End, '44 & '45
Cox, Cary, Center, '39
Davis, Alvin, Back, '39
Dyess, Marlin, Back, '59
Eckerly, Charles, Guard, '54
Foshee, Jesse, Guard, '39
Ford, Danny, Tackle, '69
Germanos, Nick, End, '55
Gilmer, Harry, Back, '46
Harkins, Grover, Guard, '39
Jackson, Bobby, Quarterback, '58
Jilleba, Pete, Back, '69
Lary, Al, End, '50
Lauer, Larry, Center, '50
Loftin, Jim, Back, '57
Lynch, Curtis, Tackle, '55
McCoy, Jack, Back, '45
Mancha, Vaughn, Center, '46
Melton, Jimbo, Back, '51
Moore, Pete, Back, '69
Nelson, Jimmy, Back, '44
Newman, Hal, End, '40
Samples, Alvin, Guard, '69
Sanford, Hayward, End, '39
Starr, Bart, Quarterback, '55
Steiner, Rebel, End, '49
Tew, Lowell, Back, '46
Tharp, Corky, Back, '54
Wozniak, John, Guard, '46
Youngleman, Sid, Tackle, '54

U. S. BOWL GAME (Washington, D. C.)

Abruzzese, Ray, Halfback, '62
Brooker, Tommy, End, '62
O'Linger, John, Center, '62
Rutledge, Jack, Guard, '62

CRUSADE BOWL GAME (Baltimore)

Pell, Charlie, Tackle, '62
Rankin, Carlton, Back, '62

EAST-WEST (San Francisco)

Davis, Fred, Tackle, '41
Francis, Kavanaugh (Kay), Center, '36
Holm, Tony, Back, '30
Hupke, Tom, Guard, '34
Merrill, Walter, Tackle, '40
Nelson, Jimmy, Back, '44
Smith, Riley, Back, '36

NORTH-SOUTH GAME (Miami)

Bryant, Paul, Coach, '60
Booth, Baxter, End, '58
Cain, Jim, End, '48
Culpepper, Ed, Tackle, '54
Fulleon, Leon, Halfback, '60
Hannah, Herb, Tackle, '50
Hood, Bob, End, '48
Lutz, Harold (Red), End, '51
Mason, George, Tackle, '54
Mizerany, Mike, Guard, '50
Noonan, L. W., Back, '49
Richeson, Ray, Tackle, '48
Skelton, Bobby, Quarterback, '60
Stapp, Laurien, Fullback, '60

SENIOR BOWL GAME (Mobile)

Avinger, Clarence, Back, '51
Bailey, David, End, '71
Battle, Bill, End, '63
Bowman, Steve, Fullback, '66
Carrigan, Ralph, Center, '54
Ciemny, Richard, Kicker, '70
Cochran, Don, Guard, '60
Cook, Wayne, End, '67
Crane, Paul, Center-Linebacker, '66
Dill, Jimmy, End, '64
Dowdy, Cecil, Tackle, '67
Dyess, Marlin, Back, '60
Germanos, Nick, End, '56
Hall, Mike, Linebacker, '69
Hannah, Herb, Guard, '51
Homan, Dennis, End, '68
Hunter, Scott, Quarterback, '70
Jackson, Bobby, Quarterback, '59
Johns, Bobby, Defensive Halfback, '67
Jordan, Lee Roy, Center-Linebacker, '63
Kearley, Dan, Tackle, '65
Lauer, Larry, Center, '51
Lewis, Tommy, Back, '54
Loftin, Jim, Back, '57
McClendon, Frankie, Tackle, '65
Melton, Bimbo, Back, '52
Musso, Johnny, Back, '71
Namath, Joe, Quarterback, '65
Neighbors, Billy, Tackle, '62
Nelson, Benny, Halfback, '64
Ogden, Ray, Back, '65
Parkhouse, Robin, End, '71
Perkins, Ray, End, '67
Ray, David, Back, '66
Rice, Bill, Tackle, '62
Richardson, Billy, Halfback, '62
Salem, Ed, Back, '51
Samples, Alvin, Guard, '69
Shipp, Billy, Tackle, '54
Sloan, Steve, Quarterback, '66
Sutton, Donnie, Back, '69
Tharp, Corky, Back, '55
Trimble, Wayne, Back, '67
Wade, Tommy, Defensive Back, '70
Willis, Bud, End, '54
Wilson, Butch, End, '63

AMERICA BOWL (Tampa)

Bryant, Paul, Coach, '69
Brungard, Dave, Back '70
Hall, Mike, Linebacker, '69

HULA BOWL (Honolulu)

Blair, Bill, Def. Back, '70
Higginbotham, Steve, Def. Back, '71

LONG TOUCHDOWN PLAYS

Passing

Yards	Passer and Receiver	Team and Opponent	Year
87	Albert Elmore to Bobby Luna (58 yds. in air)	Alabama vs. Tulsa	1954
79	Ken Stabler to Dennis Homan	Alabama vs. Louisiana Tech	1966
77	Ed Salem to Bill Abston	Alabama vs. Tulane	1949
75	Clell Hobson to Ken MacAfee	Alabama vs. Villanova	1951
73	Scott Hunter to Donnie Sutton	Alabama vs. Miami	1968
68	Bobby Smith to Marshall Brown	Alabama vs. Georgia	1957
68	Bobby Jackson to Marlin Dyess	Alabama vs. Memphis State	1958
65	Steve Sloan to Dennis Homan	Alabama vs. Miss. State	1965

Rushing

95	Harry Gilmer	Alabama vs. Kentucky	1945
92	Bobby Marlow	Alabama vs. Georgia Tech	1950
84	Dave Brown	Alabama vs. South Carolina	1942
83	Lowell Tew - Bill Cadenhead	Alabama vs. Georgia	1947
83	Corky Tharp	Alabama vs. V.P.I.	1952
81	Joe Kilgrow	Alabama vs. Miss. State	1936
80	Herschel Mosley	Alabama vs. Vanderbilt	1939
80	Benny Nelson	Alabama vs. Auburn	1963
78	Gordon Pettus	Alabama vs. Kentucky	1945
76	J. D. Roddam	Alabama vs. Duquesne	1949
76	Young Boozer	Alabama vs. Miss. State	1934

Kickoff Returns

100	George Ranager	Alabama vs. Auburn	1969
100	Ray Ogden	Alabama vs. Auburn	1964
100	Gary Martin	Alabama vs. Miami	1963
100	Jim Burkett	Alabama vs. Duquesne	1949
97	Benny Nelson	Alabama vs. Vanderbilt	1963
95	Harry Gilmer	Alabama vs. L.S.U.	1944
95	Jimmy Nelson	Alabama vs. Howard	1941
95	Bob Conway	Alabama vs. L.S.U.	1952
93	Buddy Seay	Alabama vs. Vanderbilt	1970
93	Jimmy Nelson	Alabama vs. Georgia Tech	1940
92	Butch Wilson	Alabama vs. Auburn	1962
88	Tom Calvin	Alabama vs. Florida	1949
85	Lowell Tew	Alabama vs. Miss. State	1945
80	Young Boozer	Alabama vs. Miss. State	1934

Intercepted Passes

96	Corky Tharp	Alabama vs. Tennessee	1954
88	Jimmy Nelson	Alabama vs. Howard	1940
87	Joe Grambrell	Alabama vs. Southwest La.	1946
87	Fred Grant	Alabama vs. Miss. State	1944
80	Steve Higginbotham	Alabama vs. Houston	1970
76	Don Salls	Alabama vs. Kentucky	1940
74	Jimmy Nelson	Alabama vs. Georgia	1941
72	Elliott Speed	Alabama vs. Georgia Tech	1948
70	James Angelich	Alabama vs. Vanderbilt	1934
69	Mike Dean	Alabama vs. Miami	1968

Punt Returns

92	Herschel Mosley	Alabama vs. Howard	1937
92	Harry Gilmer	Alabama vs. L.S.U.	1947
91	Cotton Clark	Alabama vs. Tulsa	1962
86	Corky Tharp	Alabama vs. Georgia	1953
85	Jimmy Nelson	Alabama vs. Miami	1941
80	Harry Gilmer	Alabama vs. Georgia	1947
72	Gordon Pettus	Alabama vs. Duquesne	1948
71	Tommy Wade	Alabama vs. Virginia Tech	1970